T0358448

ROUTLEDGE LIBRARY EDITIONS:
DEVELOPMENT

URBANISATION, HOUSING AND THE DEVELOPMENT PROCESS

URBANISATION, HOUSING AND THE DEVELOPMENT PROCESS

DAVID DRAKAKIS-SMITH

Volume 67

Routledge
Taylor & Francis Group

LONDON AND NEW YORK

First published in 1981

This edition first published in 2011
by Routledge
2 Park Square, Milton Park, Abingdon, Oxon, OX14 4RN

Simultaneously published in the USA and Canada
by Routledge
270 Madison Avenue, New York, NY 10016

Routledge is an imprint of the Taylor & Francis Group, an informa business

© 1981 David Drakakis-Smith

British Library Cataloguing in Publication Data
A catalogue record for this book is available from the British Library

ISBN 13: 978-0-415-58414-2 (Set)
eISBN 13: 978-0-203-84035-1 (Set)
ISBN 13: 978-0-415-59499-8 (Volume 67)
eISBN 13: 978-0-203-83682-8 (Volume 67)

Publisher's Note
The publisher has gone to great lengths to ensure the quality of this reprint but
points out that some imperfections in the original copies may be apparent.

Disclaimer
The publisher has made every effort to trace copyright holders and welcomes
correspondence from those they have been unable to contact.

Urbanisation, Housing and the Development Process

DAVID DRAKAKIS-SMITH

CROOM HELM LONDON

© 1981 David Drakakis-Smith
Croom Helm Ltd, 2-10 St John's Road, London SW11

British Library Cataloguing in Publication Data

Drakakis-Smith, David William
  Urbanisation, housing and the development
  process.
  1. Undeveloped areas - Housing
  2. Undeveloped areas - Cities and Towns
  3. Undeveloped areas - Poor
  I. Title
  301.5'4   HD7391

  ISBN 0-7099-0464-9

CONTENTS

TABLES

FIGURES

PLATES

FOR
ANGELA, CHLOE
AND EMMANUEL

PREFACE

This book examines the problem of housing provision for the urban poor in the Third World. Shelter cannot be isolated from other aspects of urban life and both its production and consumption are closely linked to other difficulties experienced by low-income groups. For this reason the question of housing provision is examined here within the development process as a whole and is related in the early chapters to current ideas on this subject. However, as this book is intended to be a course text, these concepts are reviewed rather than discussed in detail. Further clarification and investigation of particular issues can be followed through in the reference bibliography.

Four main types of accommodation, government, private, squatter and slum, are examined in terms of their current and potential roles in meeting low-cost housing needs. The crucial question asked is whether the present system in any particular country meets the real needs of the urban poor or is intended to satisfy other goals set by the established elites of the society, whether government or private. This is examined in a series of detailed case studies drawn from a deliberately restricted number of Asian countries. It is obvious from these profiles that economic and political, rather than welfare, objectives predominate and that the range of implemented programmes is both disturbingly narrow and ineffectual. Whilst there is a clear need for more flexibility to meet the changing circumstances of both supply and demand, it is also apparent that adjustments to the programmes themselves will not meet the real housing needs of the urban poor unless policy motivation is changed.

This book is essentially based on my own experiences in the Third World but I owe a considerable debt of gratitude to Denis Dwyer and Terry McGee for both the initial stimulation they provided and later guidance in the development of conceptual approaches. Needless to say, any inadequacies are my own. In the cities where I undertook field-work the people who have helped me are too numerous to mention individually but I would like to single out Rusen Keles, Frank King and Ted Pryor for particular thanks.

The preparation of the book would have been a time-consuming task without the considerable and much appreciated assistance of Christine McMurray and Jane Hurst. Pauline Falconer and Rowena Barker typed the original manuscript, Keith Mitchell drew all the maps and diagrams, and Ken Lockwood prepared many of the prints. To all of these people I owe many thanks. Finally, I would like to acknowledge the support given to me by my wife Angela in both a practical and spiritual sense.

1 THE URBANISATION PROCESS IN DEVELOPING COUNTRIES

Although it is axiomatic to state that houses comprise the greater part of any city, this sheer physical dominance does not mean that housing provision is important enough to be discussed in isolation from other aspects of urban life. Housing as a commodity has many different characteristics so that its importance and nature vary from producer to consumer. Castells (1977) has argued that the 'housing crisis' does not derive from exploitation but from the mechanistic relation between supply and demand. However, in the Third World, where massive short-ages of conventional houses exist, the socio-economic characteristics of the production process determine the nature of this 'crisis' and these almost inevitably involve exploitation. As such, housing provision is a function of the national and international structural relationships which have given rise to Third World cities; it is not unique and shares many features with other important and diverse components of urban life, such as the distribution of political power, or the availability of employment.

In this opening chapter it will be useful to examine the general characteristics of the urbanisation process in the Third World in order to identify some of the broader forces involved. Later chapters will focus on more specific issues, such as housing provision *per se* and its individual components, illustrating the main arguments with reference to case studies. It is important to remember, however, that the struc-tural relationships discussed in this initial overview are omnipresent throughout the spatial hierarchy.

The Statistical Dimensions of Urbanisation

Most statistical information on an international scale is assembled by multinational organisations such as the United Nations or the World Bank. The national data collated in such summaries often exhibit con-siderable differences in both working definitions and reliability, and where possible some form of standardisation is employed to enable more useful international comparisons to be made. Thus 'urban' data cover settlements of at least 20,000 inhabitants, whilst 'cities' are taken

1

to be urban agglomerations of more than 10,000 people. These figures are essentially population counts for official administrative districts and may not correlate either with the actual metropolitan area or with the socio-economic functions of the settlement.

The general scarcity of uniform and reliable data in the Third World also means that aggregate tables may vary widely in the accuracy of their individual components. This is particularly true for intra-urban social phenomena, such as health indicators or housing quality. The latter is usually poorly defined and gives rise to very misleading comparative figures; for example, most tabulations which purport to summarise both slum and squatter populations invariably cover only squatter settlements simply because they are visually more distinctive and appear easier to record. There are relatively few criticisms of such international aggregations and their data are too readily accepted by eager quantifiers. Admittedly, neither the United Nations nor the World Bank claim complete accuracy for their statistical compilations but the prestige of such information sources often lends a credibility which far exceeds reality. Criticisms and data peculiarities may be found in almost every country in the Third World and it would serve no useful purpose to itemise them all at this point. Suffice it to say that basic caveats do exist and should be borne in mind when national or international statistics are utilised. Where possible in the broad overview which follows, such data will be supplemented by information from detailed subnational surveys.

Basic Characteristics

It is advisable when analysing urban growth to distinguish at the outset between the absolute numbers and the relative rates or proportions which are involved. The rise in the urban proportion of total population in the Third World does not appear to be unduly remarkable if comparisons are made between the developing countries and industrial nations during their initial growth period. Over the last two decades the average annual rate of population growth in the Third World was 2.5 per cent (World Bank 1979); the comparable figure for developed countries during their most rapid growth periods was 3.1 per cent. However, the averaged figure for the Third World covers a much wider range of demographic and urban circumstances than that for developed nations, making excessive generalisation on this scale of somewhat dubious value. The individual statistics in Table 1.1 are more indicative of the real situation and illustrate several important characteristics.

First, contemporary urban growth in developing countries has such large absolute dimensions as to distinguish it clearly from nineteenth-century trends in Europe and America. Between 1800 and 1900 the total city population of Europe (including Russia) increased by some 4.3 million, whereas in the less developed countries of Asia the urban population has risen by 160 million in just the last twenty-five years. Moreover, rural populations have also been increasing at unprecedented rates throughout the Third World: at equivalent growth periods in the developed countries few rural populations showed comparable expansion. The overall scale of urban development is therefore more massive than ever before and is likely to continue to accelerate throughout the present century since many Asian and African countries have yet to reach their forecasted maximum rates of urban growth. In general terms the expansion in urban populations can be correlated with economic growth (Figure 1.1), although it would be unwise to infer a causal relationship either way. The precise nature of the connection between the two elements has generated strong discussion around contrasting arguments which will be considered later in this chapter.

Table 1.1: Growth in Total, Urban and Principal City Populations Between 1960 and 1975 in Selected Developing Countries

COUNTRY	Total Population 1977 (millions)	Percentage Annual Growth Rate 1970-77	Urban Population 1975 (millions)	Percentage Annual Growth Rate 1970-75	Percentage Urban Population 1960	1970	1975	Principal City	Population 1975¹ (millions)	Percentage Annual Growth Rate¹ 1960-75	Principal City Population as of Urban Population 1975
CAMEROON	7.9	2.2	2.0	8.0	8.0	21.4	27	Douala	0.4	6.4	21
ETHIOPIA	30.2	2.6	3.6	7.0	6.0	8.6	12	Addis Ababa	1.3	5.9	35
GHANA	10.6	3.0	3.2	5.1	23.1	33.4	32	Accra	1.1	5.8	33
IVORY COAST	7.5	5.9	2.2	9.3	16.0	29.0	33	Abidjan	0.7	9.1	32
KENYA	14.6	3.8	1.6	7.0	7.6	9.9	12	Nairobi	0.8	7.4	53
MALAGASY	8.1	2.5	1.4	4.3	11.0	16.6	16	Tananarive	0.5	6.6	38
MALAWI	5.6	3.1	1.0	18.4	3.0	6.7	20	Blantyre	0.2	9.3	23
NIGERIA	79.0	2.6	13.5	4.6	17.0	24.2	18	Lagos	2.3	8.6	17
SENEGAL	5.2	2.6	1.2	2.9	23.7	25.1	24	Dakar	0.8	5.1	64
SOMALIA	3.7	2.3	0.9	5.0	20.0	21.1	27	Mogadishu	0.3	5.3	29
SUDAN	16.9	2.6	3.1	6.9	8.3	8.5	20	Khartoum	0.9	7.5	30
TANZANIA	16.4	3.0	1.3	8.5	5.0	7.0	9	Dar es Salaam	0.6	10.1	47
UGANDA	12.0	3.0	1.2	8.5	2.4	6.3	10	Kampala	0.6	10.2	50
UPPER VOLTA	5.5	1.6	0.5	3.6	4.0	3.0	8	Ougadougou	0.2	8.6	36
ZAIRE	25.7	2.7	8.6	5.4	15.0	29.2	35	Kinshasa	2.2	5.7	25
ZAMBIA	5.1	3.1	1.7	5.4	19.0	25.7	34	Lusaka	0.5	3.0	3C
EGYPT	37.8	2.2	16.4	2.7	38.0	44.2	44	Cairo	6.0	3.6	39
IRAQ	11.8	3.4	7.3	5.6	39.2	44.4	66	Baghdad	3.9	7.5	53
JORDAN	2.9	3.3	1.8	4.5	47.4	46.2	53	Amman	0.5	3.5	36
MOROCCO	18.3	2.8	6.2	4.1	29.3	30.0	37	Casablanca	1.7	4.0	28
TURKEY	41.9	2.5	17.3	4.7	27.0	30.4	43	Istanbul	4.0	7.4	23
AFGHANISTAN	14.3	2.2	1.8	5.5	6.0	7.9	13	Kabul	0.4	0.0	22
INDIA	631.7	2.1	127.7	3.1	18.0	25.5	21	Calcutta	7.7	1.9	6
INDONESIA	133.5	1.8	23.8	3.3	28.9	16.0	18	Djakarta	5.5	5.0	23
IRAN	34.8	3.0	15.0	5.0	31.4	39.1	45	Teheran	4.4	6.0	29
KHMER REPUBLIC	8.4	2.5	1.0	n.a.	12.0	12.4	13	Phnom Penh	0.3	n.a.	26
KOREA, SOUTH	36.0	2.0	17.3	5.4	28.0	45.4	49	Seoul	7.1	6.2	41
MALAYSIA	13.0	2.7	3.7	4.8	42.7	47.5	30	Kuala Lumpur	1.0	5.4	26
NEPAL	13.3	2.2	0.5	4.4	2.8	4.9	4	Katmandu	0.2	-1.2	30
PAKISTAN	74.9	3.1	18.0	4.1	13.1	22.7	26	Karachi	3.9	4.4	21
PHILIPPINES	44.5	2.7	14.3	3.5	35.3	24.3	34	Manila	4.3	3.0	30
SRI LANKA	14.1	1.7	3.3	3.7	15.0	16.6	24	Colombo	0.6	-3.1	17
THAILAND	43.8	2.9	5.9	3.5	11.8	16.2	14	Bangkok/Thonburi	4.1	7.4	69
BRAZIL	116.1	2.9	65.3	4.5	45.1	53.4	61	Sao Paulo	10.4	5.7	16
CHILE	10.6	1.7	8.1	2.5	67.2	75.7	79	Santiago	3.5	4.0	43
COLOMBIA	24.6	2.1	15.6	3.9	46.0	61.4	66	Bogota	3.7	7.8	24
GUATEMALA	6.4	2.9	2.3	3.6	31.0	33.1	37	Guatemala City	0.9	4.2	38
HONDURAS	3.3	3.3	0.9	5.3	30.5	26.4	32	Tegucigalpa	0.3	5.8	33
MEXICO	63.3	3.3	37.8	4.6	51.0	58.2	63	Mexico City	12.1	12.6	32
PANAMA	1.8	2.7	0.9	8.1	41.5	47.0	51	Panama City	0.6	5.2	65
PERU	16.4	2.8	9.7	4.5	47.1	50.4	63	Lima	3.8	5.3	39
URUGUAY	2.9	0.3	2.3	0.4	72.0	84.2	83	Montevideo	1.2	1.6	53
VENEZUELA	13.5	3.4	9.6	4.4	62.0	68.8	80	Caracas	2.6	5.3	27
FIJI²	0.6	1.7	0.2	5.4	23.4	33.4	37.2	Suva	0.06	2.5	20
NEW HEBRIDES²	0.1	2.5	0.02	0.02	9.2	17.5	20.7	Vila	0.02	16.4	77
PAPUA NEW GUINEA	2.9	2.4	0.4	8.0	6.1	11.1	13	Port Moresby	0.09	17.5	25

Sources: United Nations Demographic Yearbook 1976, World Bank 1972a, Grimes 1976, World Bank 1979.

1 Extrapolated from principal city and urban population estimates.
2 Urban data to 1976.

Figure 1.1: Urbanisation and Economic Growth, 1974

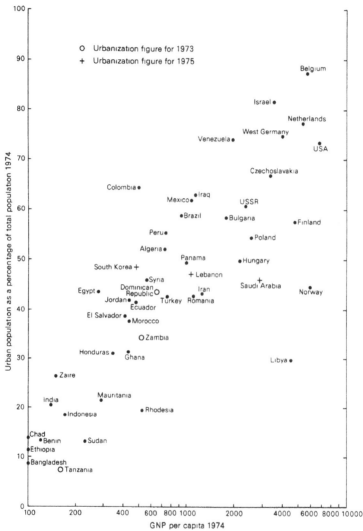

One less controversial characteristic which can be identified in most developing countries is the allometric nature of urban growth, i.e. the way in which the largest cities have experienced the most rapid increase. In most regions the development of cities with populations in excess of 100,000 has been virtually double that of overall urban expansion (Figure 1.2). This is not to say, however, that definite correlations may be drawn up between size, economic functions and urban growth rates. Considerable variation again exists from country to country in relation to different economic and political situations.

Figure 1.2: Regional Growth Rates of Total, Urban and City Populations

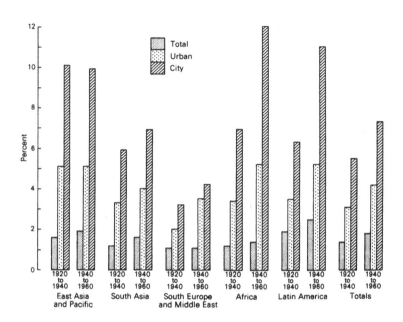

This general comment can also be extended to the phenomenon of primacy in which one city is seen to dominate the urban hierarchy within a particular country. Linsky (1969) has argued that high urban primacy occurs most frequently in small, populous, poor countries with colonial histories, but here again variations exist. A considerable degree of primacy also exists in countries such as Hungary, Denmark and Britain; on the other hand, Thailand, where the capital Bangkok is almost 30 times larger than the second city of Chieng Mai, has never been a *de facto* colony. Many developing countries do not, in fact, exhibit any marked urban primacy at all, a characteristic which tends to undermine the mathematical generalisations on urban primacy attributed to the Third World.

Such conclusions call into question the validity and utility of related concepts, such as the rank-size rule and urban hierarchy, as well as the notion of primacy itself. As Janet Abu-Lughod (1973a) has pointed out, most of the standard measures which have characterised such analyses have been derived from a period of European urban-industrial growth which was distinctly abnormal compared to that which preceded or followed it. She has consequently illustrated that the urban primacy and imbalance, which supposedly characterises the various Middle

Eastern countries, disappears when the artificiality of recent political boundaries is ignored and the region is examined as a whole. Unfortunately, having criticised Western notions of primacy and hierarchies, Abu-Lughod goes on to describe a regional urban hierarchy in the Middle East, ranking downwards from Cairo, through the subregional centres of Baghdad, Beirut and Damascus to the subnational cities such as Homs, Kirkuk and Basra. Not only does this hierarchy contain all the traits previously criticised but it also ignores the Israeli cities in the region.

Santos (1977a:16) has been even more critical of contemporary geographical theory on urban growth and urbanisation, taking the stochastic models related to innovation diffusion severely to task. Contrary to prevailing thought on this subject, Santos claims that the direction and nature of development diffusion is a function of external influences and laws based on the interest of the sender in order to maximise results (profits). Quantitative models may also be criticised for their failure to take social structures and relationships into consideration, as well as their neglect of historical information. In the context of the Third World, these factors are of crucial importance in attempting to understand the nature of the development process. Santos (1977a:18) again summarises the situation succinctly: 'an essentially dynamic phenomenon is reduced to a morphological piece of data. Process is reduced to a form. Reality is deformed into bastardized mathematical models fit [sic] into a Procrustean bed.'

The variation which characterised and has affected the urbanisation process in the Third World argues against excessive generalisation, particularly along Western lines. So many criticisms can be made of the facile typologies produced to date that the value of such work must be seriously questioned. The remainder of this chapter will accordingly concentrate on offering an explanatory framework within which the urban growth characteristics of any one city or nation may be usefully placed.

Causes of Urban Population Growth

Natural Growth

About half of the population growth in Third World cities is the result of natural increase — rather more than half in Asia, rather less in Africa. The main cause of rapid natural growth in developing countries has been the sharp decline in mortality, particularly in infant mortality, which has occurred over the last two decades. The accumulation of knowledge and skills in the various fields of medicine, hygiene and nutrition together with their diffusion throughout the Third World has been the principal reason for this fall in death rates, although there are still many countries, particularly in Africa, which have not yet experienced the full benefits. In contrast, birth rates are affected by a much more complex mix of biological, social and economic factors and, in general, have remained high. Annual growth rates have thus increased dramatically over the last twenty years and average 2.5 per cent for developing countries as a whole. Considerable variation exists, however, so that in Latin America and Africa many populations are increasing at annual rates in excess of 3 per cent, with some, such as the Ivory Coast and Kenya, nearer to 4 or 5 per cent. The significance of these rates of increase may be gauged from the fact that the population of the Third World is likely to double in only twenty-five years.

The variations in birth and death rates which exist in developing countries, when taken together with the demographic transition which the developed nations have experienced, make possible the production of a fourfold classification of growth rates (Figure 1.3). The majority of developing countries fall into the first two groups and it would seem that the most rapid phase of their population growth is either being experienced at present or is yet to come. However, over recent years evidence has appeared to modify this pessimistic prognosis (McNamara 1977). Between 1960 and 1977 birth rates in the less developed countries declined on average by about 13 per cent. Moreover, this fall in the crude birth rate has been fairly widespread, occurring in 77 of the 92 developing countries for which estimates were available; in addition the rate of decline is accelerating.

Although these general figures seem encouraging they do mask important variations in both regional and national trends. The greatest reductions in the crude birth rate have occurred in the countries with the smallest populations and in several of the largest nations, such as Bangladesh, Pakistan and Nigeria, the fall in birth rates has been minimal. But whilst the downward trends in fertility levels are welcome, they are not yet large enough to allay current fears over the anticipated pressure on world and national resources that population growth must create. It is important therefore that the determinants of the decline in birth rates be identified and incorporated into future birth control programmes.

It is fairly clear that the demographic transition in developed countries was paralleled by both mortality decline and socio-economic development. This relationship has consequently been simplified to one in which fertility decline is assumed to be dependent on the level of income per capita. However, the relationship is far more complicated than this and the circumstances that affect its character in the Third World today are considerably different from those which operated in developed countries. In general, five factors have been identified as being important in the current downtrend in Third World fertility rates. The first is improved health, particularly in infants, since the survival of children encourages parents to think positively about the size of their family. A second factor is the spread of education which makes both men and women more receptive to new ideas and more perceptive of the benefits of family planning. This phenomenon is closely linked to the third element which is the enhanced status of women.

Figure 1.3: Vital Statistics for Developing Countries, 1955

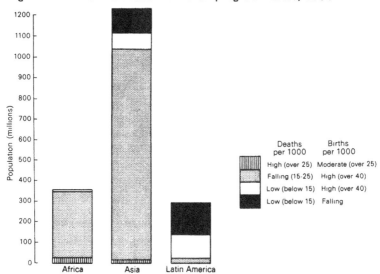

In addition to these specific family planning factors, there are two more general development features which can be linked with declining birth rates. One is the broader distribution of the benefits of economic growth. If the lower-income groups can be convinced that their living standards will rise, not just absolutely but relatively, then they will be more likely to change their opinions concerning family size. However, as discussed below, economic development in the Third World has not always been accompanied by an egalitarian distribution of benefits and the increased diffusion of such rewards remains one of the most important indirect ways in which governments can encourage family planning.

The other feature of modern development which has affected fertility is urbanisation. The move to the cities has drastically changed many of the traditional attitudes towards family size and function. In rural areas large families ensure a cheap labour supply but in the city they simply increase the dependency ratio and make housing more expensive. In addition, life in the city increases access to all of the other factors which are related to diminishing birth rates. At present, therefore, the indications are that lower levels of fertility are associated more with specific features of development rather than with the general level of economic wealth. McNamara (1977:25) provided convincing proof of this in his comparison of Korea and Mexico; for the substantially higher overall national income of the latter has failed to bring about either fertility reduction, or other socially desirable changes.

Despite such evidence, birth control programmes have continued to be advocated on the basis of the economic benefits which they are likely to bring about. This approach has been justifiably criticised because it is based on the assumed relationship between economic and demographic change which took place in industrial nations. However, the precise nature of this relationship is still imperfectly understood, and it would appear that economic development preceded the deceleration in population growth. As there were no birth control programmes during this period in the developed nations, one must assume that the improved standards of living, change in socio-economic values and increase in education brought about the reduced birth rate which occurred. If this is so, then the developing countries of the Third World are being asked to reverse the process and control fertility in order to increase economic benefits. In short, what the British or German family achieved voluntarily, the Indian or Nigerian family is expected to undergo in response to paper promises of prosperity.

There is no guarantee that developing countries will eventually follow the demographic transition experienced in the West, and the authoritarian attempts to impose admittedly humanitarian objectives on such societies place heavy demands on the individual family. This raises the important question of whether poor families in the Third World see demographic issues in the same light as the middle- and upper-income groups who determine national policies. To families in rural areas, the 'dependency burden' of children may well mean a less arduous life. Although similar agricultural logic cannot be applied in all situations, it does illustrate that the poor do not have large families without reason. Indeed, their very poverty forces them to make rational, pragmatic decisions.

At present the number of developing countries with government-supported birth control programmes is limited. In 1975 there were 34 with official programmes designed to reduce birth rates. More significant is the fact that in these countries only 10 per cent of married women of reproductive age have become 'accepters'. Even this is misleading since it does not distinguish between 'accepters' who have left the programme and those who re-enter to be recorded as new 'accepters'. Moreover, most of those participating in birth control are educated, middle-class women, who are not the main target of the programmes. A more serious criticism of birth control programmes is the assertion that they are a substitute for other kinds of development assistance; one which serves the interests of the donor as much as the recipient. Whilst this is perhaps an overstatement, there are many factors other than population growth involved in the prosperity and underdevelopment of the Third World and yet over the last two 'development decades' overall development assistance has decreased markedly whilst funds and agencies for population control have mushroomed.

Migration to Cities

Migratory movements of population are usually the result of an increase in population pressure on resources. This can occur in a variety of situations and need not have a direct relationship with either population densities or the size of the resource base. In most developing countries population pressure has been most intense in the agricultural sector where natural growth has exceeded the productive, and therefore the labour-absorbent, capacity of the land. In the past the displacement of population from certain rural areas did not always lead to urban growth within the countries concerned: sometimes a shift to other agricultural regions has taken place. On other occasions there have been international movements of population to industrially advanced areas where cheap migrant labour has been welcomed and exploited (see Power 1972, 1976). This type of migration is often the result of current or former colonial ties, for example, the West Indians and Pakistanis in Britain, or Algerians in France. However, the colonial connection is not a prerequisite and many Mediterranean workers, initially Portuguese or Italian but more recently Turks and Yugoslavs, have migrated to the industrial cities of Northwest Europe over the last two decades.

For much of the Third World, international migration of this nature has not been feasible, either financially or culturally. Instead, the rural migrants have increasingly moved towards the towns and cities within their own country. It is difficult to generalise about the direction of this migration. Whilst the largest cities seem to exert the principal attraction, so that most capital cities have large migrant components in their overall growth, the paucity of data, particularly for medium and small cities, makes definitive statements impossible. The available evidence does tend to suggest that city size alone is not the major factor in migration and that the relative proportions of rural and urban populations, together with natural growth rates, also exert considerable influence. Thus in Africa where there are particularly high rural populations, a modest movement to the urban areas will have drastic effects on their rates of population increase.

Even amongst large primate or capital cities the importance of migration *vis-à-vis* natural growth varies enormously. Abu-Lughod (1973a) has suggested that in the Middle East three different types of urban growth rates exist. These are attributed to recent shifts in the economic and political bases of the region. On the one hand the production and marketing of oil has induced tremendous migration to centres such as Riyadh and Kuwait City; in the latter non-Kuwaitis are approaching two-thirds of the total population. On the other hand, in cities such as Amman and Cairo, the various Arab-Israeli conflicts have brought about drastic refugee influxes. It has been estimated that 250,000 refugees have been added to the population of Amman since 1967, whilst almost half a million moved into Cairo from the devastated settlements of the Suez Canal zone following the 1973 war. In the other Middle Eastern cities the effects of economic and political change have been less marked so that in even larger centres, such as Damascus and Aleppo, natural growth has so far outstripped migratory growth. The important point, which Abu-Lughod clearly makes, is that the population size alone does not affect the rate of migration; broader economic and political factors play a much more influential role. Migration levels can therefore be seen to relate more closely to rates of population growth rather than absolute size (Figure 1.4).

However, the distinction between economic, political and urban influences is more extensive in the Middle East than elsewhere in the Third World where all of these elements tend to be so concentrated into one or two major cities that it becomes difficult to generalise about the complex motivations of individual urban migrants. Following an extensive examination of many migrational surveys, Brigg (1973) has concluded that the majority of independent migrants move to the city for reasons related to employment. This does not necessarily mean that all migrants have been out of work prior to their move, although unemployment and underemployment do tend to be high amongst

migrant groups immediately after their arrival in the city. It is during
this period that support from friends and relatives is most valuable.

**Figure 1.4: The Middle East: Migration, City Size and Urban Growth
Rates**

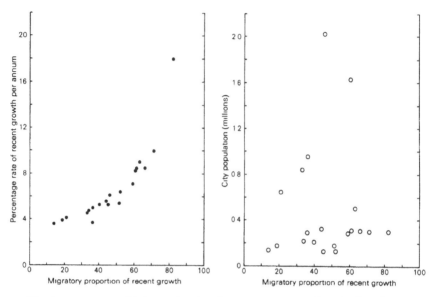

The importance of job motivation in movement to the city has in
the past led to the development of various economic models to explain
rural-urban migration; Todaro (1971) has perhaps expounded the most
sophisticated of these approaches. Such models can be criticised principally for their oversimplification of the migration process, in which the
individual is supposedly faced with a clear choice between rural and
urban life. In contrast, the actual decision-making process is extremely
complicated, with a multiplicity of factors affecting the expression of
urban values within the migrants' rural life and vice versa. The reasons
which actually influence individual mobility may differ before, during
and after migration. Certainly it seems that most migrants, when examining their move in retrospect, tend to simplify their motives down to
economic levels. Mukherji (1975) has shown in his studies of North
India that generalised perceptions of the value of urban migration
differed substantially from the immediate incentive to move which, in
this area, was drought. One must also concede Amin's (1974) argument
that the economic situation to which migrants are apparently reacting
is itself a product of much broader socio-economic processes. In the
Third World these processes are strongly influenced by the extent of

colonial experience.

Mehmet (1978) has suggested that migration is primarily the consequence of both the absolute and relative poverty of rural areas in comparison to the cities — a contrast which is a direct consequence of
urban bias in economic policies. But within the cities themselves there
is an additional bias towards a small elite whose political position allows
it to select the type of economic development which brings maximum
benefit to itself, giving rise to a wide discrepancy in household incomes
and huge levels of unemployment. The neglect of the political background to economic development has discredited several theories on
rural-urban migration, notably those which seek comparative typologies based on historical experiences within Europe and North America.
Zelinsky (1971), for example, assumed that the onset of modernisation would bring massive migration from the countryside into the
towns. He ignored the very visible fact that the labour migration
encouraged in most colonies was frequently very selective and thus
reasonably limited in scale. The physical evidence of this selectivity
can be seen in the present townscapes of North Africa where the sizeable foreign populations had, prior to independence, built extensive
modern residential quarters for themselves whilst restricting the
indigenous migrants to the decaying *medinas* or old quarters.

Elsewhere in the Third World, there is evidence to show that in
several of the largest South and Southeast Asian countries the level of
urbanisation has increased slowly in spite of the growing rural awareness of the modernisation process which is occurring in the cities. In
Indonesia, for example, the percentage of urban dwellers rose from 15
per cent to only 18 per cent of the total population between 1960 and
1975, in India during the same period the urban population increased
by only 3 per cent to 21 per cent of the total. Nor is the feature confined to national trends; in Sri Lanka the population of Greater
Colombo expanded by a mere 2 per cent between 1947 and 1975. This
was less than the rate of increase in the total population of the country
and is markedly at variance with existing theory on the nature of urban
primacy (Marga Institute 1976).

Not all countries in the Third World have experienced a heavy cityward movement of people and in some migrants form only a minor
fraction of the overall urban population, although the problem is
usually worse in primate cities. On the other hand, in some Asian countries, such as Malaysia and the Philippines, there is considerable evidence to show that the 'transitional shift' of population to the urban
centres is well under way (NEDA 1974/5). If such national variations

can occur in individual mobility, then the static assumptions of theories related to rural-urban continua, polarities or historical typologies are of less value than structural models which examine the wider political, social and economic processes involved in the shift between the peasant and capitalist ways of life.

Whilst detailed analysis of the migrational process is perhaps tangential to this text, discussion of the extent and persistence of the peasant attributes of migrant families is crucial to the proper understanding of urban problems in the Third World. Certainly this line of investigation is more fruitful than one which details simply the physical form of the move — whether it is stepped or direct. In general terms, rural migrants can be said to comprise the more vital elements of the rural population, being either young, skilled or prepared to take risks for the subsequent betterment of themselves and their families (Pryor 1979). Although most migrants have absorbed some urban, non-peasant values either through direct experience of town life, visits to urban-based relatives or exposure to mass media, many rural values do not disappear but tend to persist long after the migrants' initial settlement in the city. This cultural continuity strongly influences the nature of their urban lifestyle.

Rural values are maintained in two distinct ways, one of which has a much more direct repercussion on urban ecology. The less significant links are those back to the traditional rural home through visits and/or remittances. The extent of these contacts varies enormously throughout the Third World, but in some instances is much stronger than the relationships with their urban neighbours. Bruner (1961), for example, claimed that the urban Batak in Sumatra 'have more meaningful relationships with their rural relatives in the highlands than with their non-Batak neighbours in [the city of] Medan'. Suzuki (1964, 1966) discovered similar traits in his examination of Kirinti villagers in Istanbul. Amongst these migrants the main link back to the home village in Eastern Turkey was the communal *sandit* fund which was used to assist people and projects both in Istanbul and in the village. It is interesting to note that whilst Suzuki found very strong rural-urban links over great distances, there is less evidence to support this trait amongst later migrants to Ankara (Drakakis-Smith and Fisher 1975). In complete contrast, Jongkind (1974) has claimed from evidence gathered in Lima that regional associations in Latin America are essentially elitist, composed of well-adjusted and successful migrants who have united in regional associations not out of solidarity but more for purposes of prestige and display. In this context the regional association must be regarded as a thoroughly urban institution.

It would appear, therefore, that urban migrants are less completely protected by village or family organisations than previously has been assumed. Certainly the effectiveness of such groupings diminishes with the size of the city concerned so that even the strong family and clan systems of the overseas Chinese are rapidly disappearing in Singapore and Hong Kong. In the face of this diminishing effectiveness of regional associations other forms of adaptive relationships have emerged. Grindal (1973) has described one such system in Ghana, affecting the Sisala migrants to Accra and Kumasi. The original rural society of these people comprises a tightly organised tribal and religious network which regulates almost every aspect of their lives. After migration to the city the Sisala find the absence of these controls very disturbing and as a result are quickly and easily drawn into the strong emotional and economic security offered by the Islamic faith which is now predominant in the larger urban centres of Ghana. Complete Islamic urbanisation is usually achieved within a generation by the Koran-based education of the migrants' children.

Another form of adaptation to the pressures of urban and village life is circular migration — a phenomenon which has attracted increasing attention in recent years. In this system the migrant spends considerable time in his village where he retains his home and most of his family ties. In addition, he will usually hold on to any land he possesses, returning to help during the labour-intensive seasons of harvesting and planting (Forbes 1978). The continuous period spent in the city may vary considerably from a few months to several years, but in all cases the urban base is regarded as temporary and major ties are retained with the village. Bettelheim (1972) and Meillassoux (1972) have argued that this situation is encouraged by capitalist governments in order to maintain the responsibility for social security at the family and village levels. In some cities, this situation has given rise to distinctive cultural and morphological features which are only now being recognised and studied. Jellinek (1978) has described one such phenomenon in Jakarta known as the *pondok* system. A *pondok* is a lodging house inhabited by circular migrants engaged in one particular occupation and usually all from the same village. Each *pondok*, and there are many thousands in Jakarta, is run by a *tauke* who provides free, but very crowded accommodation, hires out the equipment necessary for carrying out the trade, supplies cheap meals and generally acts as a protector for the residents. Most occupants are recruited from the village through a network of kin or friends, and the prevailing atmosphere is one of mutual trust and assistance.

Whatever type of migrant association predominates, there is normally a strong spatial clustering within the city, frequently in areas of cheap housing, particularly if this is near to casual employment. Thus in Arab cities the old *medinas* are popular districts for new arrivals, and during the last decade many have experienced a rapid process of *taudification* (slum creation). Similar events occurred in the central tenement districts of most Asian cities, often in association with clan or village groupings. However, spatial clustering is probably most marked in the newer squatter settlements, irrespective of the country in which they occur.

The concentration of recent migrants, with their problems of economic and social adaptation, in slum and squatter districts has attracted much attention to these areas of cheap, often substandard, housing. Unfortunately this attention has largely been directed at the symptoms of distress rather than its underlying causes. Descriptions of squatter settlements are therefore far more frequent than explanatory analyses. Moreover, there has been a tendency within these studies to imply that the economic, social and political marginality of the urban poor is the consequence of their attachment to rural values and failure to adapt to the urban system. However, the semi-peasant lifestyle is not due to an overwhelming desire to stand by traditional values as much as the inability of the migrant to penetrate the veneer of structural relationships which comprise the modern, Western sector of the city and constrain all other activity. Migrants usually possess few of the skills or qualifications required for white- or even blue-collar work whilst unskilled factory jobs are usually already filled. Their consequent poverty restricts access to either the modern retail or housing markets and in this situation it is often the rural ties and values which enable people to survive.

The persistence of peasant values in the city is therefore a more complicated and important issue than it first appears because it encapsulates the process of subordination of the individual to the city as a whole. The simple question of how the structural relationships of the city permit rural migrants to shed their traditional lifestyle can thus be expanded to cover a wider range of issues. However, the city itself is a product of much broader developmental forces operating at both national and international levels and in order to analyse adequately the causes of even one of the many problems confronting the urban poor, it is necessary to examine the setting within which Third World urban growth has occurred.

Directions of Urban Growth

The Role of the City

Urban growth in the Third World has occurred and does occur under a great variety of economic and political circumstances; these have constantly changed, particularly during the present century. The mix of factors within which urban growth has taken place has produced enormous variation in both the morphological and social character of Third World cities and this is reflected today in the range of problems which face urban administrators. In the West many attempts have been made to explain the complex nature of urban growth by classifying towns and cities according to the functions they perform or to the urban attributes which they possess. In the Third World the sophisticated information needed to produce such classifications is lacking. However, as Slater (1976) and also Castells (1977) have pointed out, the concern with accumulation of data and mechanistic techniques of analysis has ignored the most important issues, namely the structural processes through which present patterns and systems evolved. Until recently, therefore, much investigation of urban phenomena in the Third World was descriptive rather than analytical with some studies having degenerated into crass simplifications of regional 'types'. Abu-Lughod (1973b:8) provided eloquent support for this in her criticism of the concept of the 'Islamic City', a stereotype which was usually derived from case studies of one city or region and was then assumed to apply to the entire Islamic world throughout its history. She noted that there was a 'tendency to focus more upon the persistence of forms rather than on changes'. Moreover, such changes were assumed to have commenced only with the penetration of Western colonialism.

Assumptions and simplifications such as these form the basis of much of the work undertaken to date. In particular there has been a tendency to examine cities in the Third World with Western theories and methods in mind. A good example is the search for urban hierarchies, particularly those based on Loeschian or Christallerian networks, that ignore the 'informal' relationships within which the great majority of urban dwellers live and work. Frequently some sort of network or hierarchy has been 'discovered' simply because it was looked for. But, as several studies have shown, contemporary urban systems in the Third World are the product of processes for which Western concepts alone offer inadequate explanation (Santos 1977b). This criticism, and the search for more useful forms of analysis, evolves primarily from a historical approach to the development of spatio-structural relationships.

One of the first major attempts to examine the nature of the differences between modern and traditional cities in terms of formative processes was by Sjoberg (1960) who based his arguments upon the effect that technological change has on city structure. In the resultant taxonomy of urban types, the most influential distinction which emerged was his separation of pre-industrial and industrial cities; a distinction which, although based primarily on historical evidence, was extended to cover the contemporary differences between cities in the developed and the developing world. The principal fault with Sjoberg's concept, as with so many others, was that it failed to distinguish between growth, development and modernisation, all of which were supposedly aligned along a continuum directed towards the ultimate goal of the Western urban system.

In many related writings on the same subject the Western-style city is seen both as the agent and goal of change (for example, Reissman 1964, Rostow 1966). In this literature urbanisation in the Third World is viewed as essentially the same process as that which occurred in developed countries, involving similar socio-economic shifts from rural to urban values. However, not only is the current demographic situation very different, but the whole thesis ignores the distortions which have been introduced by the incorporation of the Third World into the global capitalist system. The underdevelopment maintained within this unequal, exploitative relationship between the First and Third Worlds has prevented any mechanistic transition to a 'mature' economy and has resulted in what Castells (1977) has termed dependent urbanisation, the effects of which are evident in both the internal and external spatial organisation of cities. The primate city was above all the creation of, and agent for, this capitalist penetration.

As long as Western urbanism was assumed to be the desired goal of developing countries, however unsuitable or untenable this was in reality, government planners saw little wrong with the way in which urban systems were evolving. To such individuals, and many were indigenes of the Third World, slums and unemployment were looked upon as an undesirable but inevitable consequence of the progression towards economic 'maturity'. Recently, writers such as Frank (1971), McGee (1971) and Gutkind (1972) have emphasised the important contrast in economic and social processes, couching their arguments largely in political terms. On the whole, however, studies of urbanisation process have been characterised by a neglect of the political underpinnings of economic and social change. Only with the post-1945 upheavals in the colonial structure of the Third World did this situation alter, since the massive cultural and political fluctuations were almost inevitably concentrated in the metropolitan foci of the existing power systems. The work of Balandier (1966), Horvath (1969, 1972) and King (1976) on the nature of colonial urbanisation and the character of colonial cities, thus takes on enhanced importance because many of the issues to which they draw attention have persisted through to the urban structure of the post-colonial era.

Structural Relationships and the Form of the Colonial City

Colonialism is not peculiar to European or industrialised societies. Whilst its spread on a global scale certainly reached a maximum during the uninhibited capitalism of the Industrial Revolution, colonial urbanisation has been a feature of all empires, from Greek Miletus to Portuguese Macao and beyond. As Luthy (in Horvath 1972:48) has remarked, 'the history of colonization is the history of mankind itself'. North Africa in particular has experienced a regular succession of empires and its present urban structure is a virtual palimpsest of colonial settlement patterns from the classical period, through Arab and Ottoman eras, to the relatively recent developments of European colonisation and independence. Blake and Lawless (1974) offer a fine description of this process in Tlemcen, a relatively small town in Western Algeria, where imperial vicissitudes have had a marked effect on both its morphology and its role in the regional hierarchy of settlements. But even within the period of recent colonialism, the physical manifestations of urban development have varied enormously in both form and function so that it is somewhat futile to search for a stereotype 'colonial city'. Most well known are the large coastal entrepôts, such as Bombay or Singapore, which tapped the resources of their colonial hinterlands and acted as distributors for the manufactured goods of the metropolitan powers. However, several other types of urban settlements also existed, ranging from recreational hill stations to strategic military bases and communication centres, such as railway towns or coal-bunkering depots, like Aden.

Despite this superficial functional variation, all colonial settlements were designed primarily to operationalise the economic exploitation of their hinterlands. Socially, therefore, urban populations could be stratified into several groups based on the mix of traditional and capitalist forces operating in any particular location. In general, however, three broad categories could be distinguished: those organising or profiting from colonial capitalism, those labouring within it, and those not directly involved but drawn by the prospect of employment. Morphologically this was reflected in distinct socio-cultural zones within the colonial city, a trait strongly encouraged by the segregationalist principles that influenced urban planners. Administrative civil lines, labour lines, the military cantonment and 'indigenous quarters' were the most obvious and lasting of these divisions.

As Castells (1977) has observed, urban form is a function of the political, social and economic forces operating in the city, so that although there is considerable physical variation in urban morphology in developing countries, several common features can be identified. King (1976) has claimed that three principal variables conditioned the socio-spatial nature of colonial cities. First, the contact between two different cultures; second, the contrast in economic and technological levels; and third, the uneven power structure in which the metropolitan society is dominant. The dominance-dependency relationship which this power system fostered was reflected in the structure of colonial society which, as Balandier (1966) has noted, was characterised by segregation along both ethnic and socio-economic lines. The power of the urban administration in colonial cities, which was far greater than in the metropolitan country where commercial interests were vested in a different set of individuals, enabled this social segregation to be expressed in physical terms. The component sectors of the colonial city were kept separate, deliberately preventing the development of those characteristics of diffusion and interaction which are invariably assumed to be part of the Western city. In short, the colonial city was characterised by a dualism which permeated all aspects of life. This dualistic framework, as developed by Geertz (1963), amongst many others, has also provided a methodological base for later analysis of the post-colonial urban structure of the Third World, a conceptual transfer which is validated by the economic and cultural dependence on metropolitan nations that has persisted long after political autonomy has been obtained.

Socio-spatial Relationships in the Post-colonial City

Without doubt, the overwhelming influence on the socio-spatial structure of cities in the Third World is continuing capitalist exploitation. A dominant-dependent relationship has clearly emerged at all levels of the urban hierarchy between those directly participating in this exploitative process and those tenuously involved on the operational periphery. Nowhere is this more evident than in the employment structure of Third World cities. The following section will examine the principal characteristics of this employment situation and some of the concept-ual theories which have accompanied recent investigation. The relation-ships and forces involved in the discussion have a direct bearing on most aspects of urban life in the Third World and will act as conceptual underpinnings to later analysis of housing problems.

The employment characteristics of developing countries provide one of the principal distinguishing features between urbanisation in the First and Third Worlds. In the former, urban development was accom-panied by a pronounced shift from agricultural to manufacturing occu-pations with a subsequent increase in tertiary employment. There is scant evidence to support the existence of such a process in the Third World. Castells (1977) has argued that urbanisation in the Third World is not the result of industrialisation *per se* but of the process of indus-trialisation in advanced capitalist countries. As a result, urbanisation in the Third World is accompanied by increased industrial output but not by increased industrial employment. Mehmet (1978) has explained this largely in terms of local elites pushing dependent development for their own benefits. He argues that economic planning in developing countries is intended to maximise investment returns rather than expand or generate employment incomes. In addition to increasing the degree of relative and absolute poverty, this policy also results in reduced employment opportunities. There are several reasons for this, ranging from the capital-intensive nature of industrial investment through elitist and irrelevant educational policies that excessively emphasise tertiary education, to non-competitive labour markets which are highly selective of certain social strata or cultural groups. The result of these policies has been a severe shortfall in jobs in the secondary sector. This is characteristic of most cities in the Third World and poses increasingly severe problems of underemployment and unemployment. It is true that overall employment in the cities has expanded at a much faster rate than in rural areas; Bairoch (1973) has estimated that between 1950 and 1970 the total growth in urban employment was 160 per cent, compared to only 40 per cent for employment in rural areas. However, the rise in urban population has been even more rapid and extensive unemployment has resulted (see Table 2.1).

Although the figures contained in Table 2.1 must be considered with a degree of caution because of the variation in definitions used in each individual country, in no sense do they overstate the seriousness of the urban employment situation. Indeed, most of the urban data relate to capital or primate cities where unemployment is likely to be propor-tionately lower than in provincial, middle-order or small settlements.

In addition, although national definitions may vary, the statistics relate to unemployment alone and do not incorporate the effects of under-employment. This phenomenon is very difficult to measure but Bairoch (1973) estimates that on average between one-fifth and one-quarter of urban working populations can be classified as underemployed.

The absence of longitudinal data makes trends difficult to discern but, in general, urban unemployment seems to have risen steadily over the past twenty years. Much of this has been due to the emphasis on technically sophisticated manufacturing industries, the labour demands of which are limited in number and oriented towards skilled or educated workers. It could be claimed that the situation is not always so depressing since many capital-intensive investments spawn developments in associated small-scale industrial enterprises. However, Gerry (1977), McGee (1977) and several other investigators have pointed out that this is a naive interpretation of events since peripheral employment is highly exploitative. The next stage of the analysis thus involves the examination of the broad spectrum of employment forms within the structural relations which characterise most Third World cities.

Although a great deal of the 'surplus' labour drifts into the traditional or 'informal' sector (which is used in the discussion simply as a convenience phrase), very little interest has been shown in this type of employment. Until recently, many, like Bairoch (1973), assumed that it was virtually coincident with service or tertiary occupations. McGee (1977) and Dick and Rimmer (n.d.) have argued that attitudinal change has been brought about by several events. First was the realisation that the employment situation in Third World cities was unlikely to improve and that population would continue to grow faster than the creation of jobs in the modern, industrial sector. As a result of the unequal distribution of benefits, overall economic growth has not necessarily brought about improvements in employment. Thus development strategists have been forced to face the fact that the labour-intensive activities of the informal sector are likely to play an increasingly important role in the urban growth of the Third World.

The second reason for the growing intellectual and administrative sympathy towards the informal sector has been the increased awareness in developed countries that economic growth does not necessarily equate with development (Logan 1972, Mehmet 1978). The consequent reaction against 'big business' has taken the form of extensive support for small-scale operations, intermediate technologies, and the conservation of energy and resources. 'Increasingly sociologists have come to understand and appreciate the indispensable role played by small

systems in mediation between the individual and the large scale
society . . .' (Abu-Lughod 1973a:8).

The role played by the informal sector is, however, even more
important than that of a mediator because in most cities it is rapidly
becoming a permanent way of life for the majority of the population.
The group created in this process, McGee's protoproletariat (1976b),
does not fit easily into the usual Marxist social framework of bourgeoisie, proletariat and lumpenproletariat, nor is its revolutionary implication clear. For these reasons it has attracted close attention from a
number of neo-Marxist writers. One of the most difficult problems
which has emerged in the growing debate on the informal sector is its
composition and definition (see Rimmer *et al.* 1978, Gerry 1977,
Bromley 1977). As yet there is no consensus on this, although three
broad approaches can be identified. The first utilises structural dualism
to separate types of economic activity and has spawned a wide variety
of descriptive nomenclature. A second approach involves classification
by mode of production, whereby the individual is allocated to the
capitalist, socialist or peasant sector of the economy according to the
nature of his work. This is characteristic of the neo-Marxist position
and in the field of housing supply is represented by Burgess (1977).
The final type of approach is that of Hart (1973) who has used the
source of income as the basis of his classification.

All of these definitions have their faults, but given the relatively
recent emergence of research on the subject, this is to be expected.
The most frequent criticism is that the definitions and models differ
substantially from reality. As several studies (Mazumdar 1976, McGee
and Yeung 1977, Rimmer *et al.* 1978) have shown, entry into the
formal sector is not easy and involves extensive use of family and
village ties, as well as cash payments. Nor does movement between
occupations readily occur. Characteristics such as these form the basis
for criticism of the 'informal' terminology since, in most aspects, the
organisation of activities is highly structured. An additional difficulty
posed by dualistic frameworks is that many families and individuals
overlap between sectors. Squatters from 'informal' housing may be
employed in factories or shops and may borrow money from formal
institutions to build their homes. On the other hand, many public
housing tenants often seek to supplement their income by engaging
in 'informal' hawking activities. On the production side, this overlap
is reflected in subcontracting arrangements from formal firms to
small-scale or even domestic units. Dick and Rimmer (n.d.) claim
that this confusion occurs because not all components of 'economic

dualism' are dichotomous, but that some, such as the scale of opera-tions, are characterised by a continuum. When combined with organisa-tional and technological features this approach offers a more fruitful improvement in structural generalisation than does the mere incorpora-tion of additional features peculiar to only a limited number of cities (see Figure 1.5).

Figure 1.5: An Integrated Alternative to Dualism

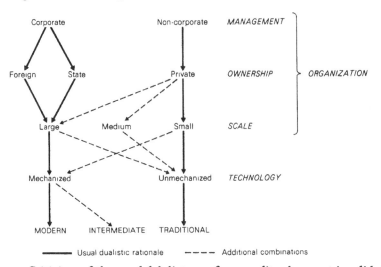

Criticism of the models' distance from reality does not invalidate their use. The simple bipolar construct is designed to help the under-standing of a real but complex situation, not to reproduce it (see Missen and Logan 1977). A more serious criticism of structural models in general is the allegation that they are essentially descriptive rather than analytical, and tend to neglect the examination of both internal and external linkages. Supplementary explanations of the processes involved have been put forward in both dependent-dominant theory and also in the concept of peripheral capitalism (see Oxall *et al*. 1975, Obregon 1974). Dependency theory emphasises the exploitative integra-tion of Third World economies into the international capitalist organisa-tion — a relationship which some claim has been in existence since the emergence of international/imperial banking systems in medieval Europe (Wallerstein 1966). More recently the persistence and growth of the inequalities associated with this exploitative relationship has led to the development of a body of theory known as peripheral capitalism which is particularly concerned with the nature of the relationship in developing societies.

Peripheral capitalism is a combination of capitalist and petty capitalist forms of production under the control of the former. The function of the petty capitalist sector in this relationship is to provide an economic and social environment which permits the continued dominance of the capitalist element. Thus its activities revolve around the small-scale operations which are not profitable enough for the modern, industrial firms. The underemployment and low incomes resultant from this situation ensure the continuation of a cheap supply of surplus labour which can be used and discarded when needed, thus keeping factory wages low. The petty production sector also enables fluctuations in demand to be absorbed within the existing system by subcontracting to informal sector producers at peak periods. In this way profits are retained without the expense of new capital investments. It is also claimed that the existence of a large body of petty capitalists is supported by the public sector, both national and international, because it offers opportunities for minimising the overheads of social welfare without jeopardising the political quiescence of the urban poor. This criticism has been made by several observers with respect to aided self-help housing and will be discussed more extensively in later chapters.

Gerry (1977) has attempted to combine the attributional classification common to dualistic structures with characteristics based on mode of production. The resultant taxonomy (Table 1.2), whilst retaining many of the faults inherent in descriptive categorisations, nevertheless provides a more utilitarian and explanatory framework than have most previous models. This is particularly useful when policy recommendations are being considered in relation to the informal sector. In a way this is ironic because Gerry holds the view that programmes aimed at lifting the restrictions on informal activities, such as hawking or trishaw operating, ultimately serve only the interests of the capitalist elites, for reasons outlined above.

However, ameliorative policies towards the informal sector are not yet widespread and to abrogate such programmes at the outset is to condemn the urban poor to further misery and exploitation. This is not to say that mechanical allocation of funds or rescinding of legislation is sufficient. Santos (1972/3) has argued that although the awareness of an informal sector has increased dramatically in recent years, the understanding of it has not. He claims that 'good' planners are those who suggest objective and viable solutions which do not disturb the system's basic continuity, and supports Slater (1977) in suggesting that 'the problem of poverty is not a question of integrating the poor population into an oppressive structure . . . but of transforming this structure'.

Table 1.2: Some Characteristics of the Urban Labour Force

Strata	Mode of Reproduction	Functional Relationship with Capitalist Mode of Production
Workers in capitalist industry (formal sector)	Repetitious sale of labour in the capitalist production process	Real subjugation of labour by capital: labour directly functional in capitalist production and accumulation
Casual workers in capitalist industry (industrial reserve)	Intermittent sale of labour with some petty commodity production and/or services	Alternation of real and formal subjugation of labour by capital: labour incorporated or surplus according to cycle of capitalist accumulation
Workers exercising skills within a co-existing mode of production which is subordinate (informal sector)	Petty commodity production	Formal subjugation of labour to capital on a relatively permanent basis: simultaneously functional in both direct and indirect senses
Unsuccessful sellers of labour (unemployed, lumpenproletariat)	Combined elements of above, also begging, extortion, theft etc.	Minimal relations with organised capital: occasionally politically functional but usually economically dysfunctional

Source: after Gerry (1977).

Conclusion

How does this conceptual discussion relate to the question of housing provision for the urban poor? The response must be that it relates in every possible way. Contrary to the tenor of most studies to date, low-cost housing construction and its attendant problems do not form a unique and separate segment of the development process. They are the product of complex linkages which extend throughout the entire socio-spatial field — from cultural traits to political psychology. Despite this very obvious relationship, most examinations of 'housing problems' have been pursued in isolation from other facets of the development process — a situation which has given rise to oversimplified and somewhat naive interpretations of the real nature of the problems facing the urban poor. As a consequence, investigations into housing provision have tended to be descriptive rather than analytical, although this could also relate to their historical roots in physical planning and land use studies. An even more important result of the conceptual isolation has been the superficial assumption on the socio-economic homogeneity of the urban poor and their housing problems, an assumption which has led to the search for the single universal remedy to housing shortages in the Third World. In the past the mass provision of high-rise estates fell into such a category; more recently these have been replaced as a panacea by aided self-help schemes, particularly site and service projects.

The most urgent research need at present is for a more thorough approach to structural conceptualisation, so that the main sources of housing provision can be clearly identified, together with their characteristics and interrelationships. This structural framework must also be put into a developmental perspective in order to examine its linkages with the wider socio-spatial systems, urban, national and international, of which it is part. Implicit in this operation is the incorporation of a positive dynamism – the identification of ways in which such relationships and linkages have been, and can be, changed.

The following chapter examines several of these themes in relation to housing provision for the urban poor. First, it discusses current attitudes on the role of low-cost housing in development planning, identifying the major constraints on increased investment in this sphere. Second, it outlines a structural framework through which a positive analysis of the present situation can be undertaken, examining closely its conceptual validity. Third, within the structural model the principal sources of low-cost housing are identified and their interrelationships briefly discussed. The framework and components thus established form the basis of subsequent chapters in the book. Each will examine one major source of low-cost housing, real or potential, in terms of its nature, evolution, future role and the changes necessary to increase its output of housing for the urban poor. The final chapter will attempt to synthesise these conclusions into a model which outlines the place of this type of housing provision in the overall development processes of the Third World.

2 HOUSING AND DEVELOPMENT PLANNING

Assessing the Dimensions of the Housing Problem

It is customary to preface discussions on Third World housing with
some form of overall assessment of needs. The calculation of these
needs usually involves demographic data on population growth rates
and household formation, together with an assessment of current
dwelling units in terms of their numbers, condition, size and facilities.
The unreliability of data of this nature and the incompatibility of
national definitions make international comparisons of such dubious
value that many assessments have had recourse to surrogate criteria on
density or overcrowding to illustrate variations in housing standards.
Whilst easier to compile, these simple tables provide very little useful
information. Most incorporate demographic data only and take no
account of housing needed to replace existing substandard stock. It is
this latter problem which has proved most intractable in statistical
comparisons, since it is impossible to draw up an international standard of habitability (for some discussion, see Fraser 1969). A final
disadvantage in calculating housing needs, by whatever method, is that
the estimates produced are so daunting in relation to the physical
and fiscal capacities of most developing countries, that housing investment is discouraged rather than encouraged.

In view of the disadvantages there has been an increasing tendency
away from 'need'-oriented calculations to those based on 'demand'.
Effective housing demand is related primarily to an ability to pay for
the commodities offered and is determined by factors such as household income, expenditure patterns, housing prices and construction
rates. If these calculations were used primarily as a basis for identifying
the differing requirements of various socio-economic groups, then this
would be a useful step in the decision-making process. Unfortunately
experience does not bear this out, and effective demand is more often
used as a justification for directing government housing programmes
towards the middle-income groups in order to avoid rental deficits.

Whilst the relative merits and demerits of need- or demand-based
calculations should be debated, they are perhaps secondary to the
more important issue which concerns the real value of global comparisons of this nature. In view of the unreliability of most of the data, this
value would appear to be limited. A more useful exercise would be to

compare housing standards between socio-economic groups within individual countries, but even in this respect quantification alone will not reveal the reasons for such contrasts. Explanations must be sought in the activities of the people involved, whether they are residents, builders or administrators, and in the structural relationships of the city, rather than in sterile analyses of suspect statistics. This chapter will examine the place of housing in development planning with this principle firmly in mind.

Housing Provision in Development Plans

Economic Attitudes

Although housing investment has long been considered by many observers to be an important part of Third World development, the advocates of this approach have often found it difficult to justify their position to sceptics. Early statements tended to adopt the simple humanist stance that housing for the urban poor was one of the most effective ways of improving their overall living conditions, an attitude which David Ward (1976) has claimed is basically Victorian in that it envisages housing improvement as an end in itself rather than a means to the broader end of eradicating poverty.

Humanist views alone have had little influence on decision-makers so that housing protagonists have tended to expand their arguments to incorporate quasi-economic and political reasoning in order to enhance their acceptability. Grebler (1973) has noted that this modified approach places great emphasis on the high social utility of low-cost housing programmes through their potential for income redistribution, for the reduction of disease and delinquency, and for moderating the impatience of the urban poor with the persistent inequalities of urban life. In addition, it is also argued that the relatively high labour-intensity of residential construction results in increased job opportunities. This is considered to be particularly important for migrants because employment in the building industry is supposedly easy to obtain and provides an economic apprenticeship where urban skills can be acquired.

These propositions have often been put forward with more emotion than reason so that conventional economists have found little difficulty in refuting them. It is frequently pointed out, for example, that poor housing is no more likely than unemployment to foment unrest, and that income redistribution can be more efficiently achieved by methods other than investment in low-cost housing. It is also argued that housing shortages are just one of many problems which result from rapid urban growth, and developing countries are urged to invest in areas which offer more tangible or immediate returns. The assumption is that general economic growth will eventually bring about improvements in other fields, such as housing. As Grebler (1955) once expressed it, 'the only road to greater material welfare is through greater economic productivity'. In the conventional economic strategies of the 1950s and 1960s, therefore, housing was considered to be a social overhead which absorbed rather than produced resources.

A practical illustration of this planning philosophy occurred in Malaysia during the period of its second Five Year Plan which lasted from 1971 to 1975. The main aim was to continue with the modernisation of the economy and the restructuring of Malaysian society so as to eliminate the identification of race with economic function. In short, Malays were to be pushed into the commercial and industrial sectors of the economy in order to challenge the hegemony of the Chinese and Indians. This had been a national objective since independence in 1957 but was given increased impetus in the wake of racial riots in 1969 when extensive and bloody rioting between Chinese and Malays occurred in several Malaysian cities. The government placed the blame for this conflict on the income disparity against Malays and has sought to accelerate measures to redress the imbalance. Unfortunately, as Mehmet (1978) has pointed out, increased Malay participation in the secondary sector has been brought about largely by their employment within the public utility companies, usually in very poorly paid jobs. As a result the Malay share of national income rose by only a small proportion since independence. Worse still, the increase has been very unevenly spread throughout the Malay population with most accruing to the already wealthy, so that the poorest groups have continued to lose ground (Figure 2.1).

Leaving aside this structural discussion, the way in which the specific goals were to be achieved deserves closer analysis, because it reflects the current attitudes towards social investment prevalent in a wide range of developing countries. The 'modernisation' of the Malays and their increased incorporation into commercial and industrial life, in effect meant urbanisation for a hitherto predominantly rural community, but Malaysia was already one of the most urbanised countries in Asia, with at least one-third of its population living in the urban areas. The new emphasis further accelerated the pace of urbanisation and yet the amount of money invested in the social services fell from 17.7 per cent to 14.7 per cent of the national budget.

Figure 2.1: Malaysia: Income Distribution amongst Ethnic Groups, 1958 and 1970

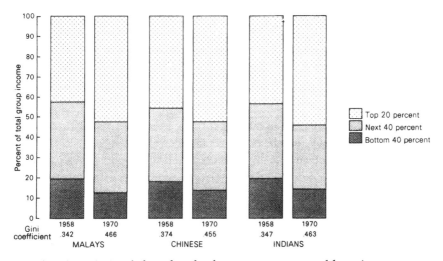

   The plan admitted that already there were severe problems in housing provision for the major urban areas, and observed that most community services had not kept pace with urban growth. It was claimed that greater attention would be given to resolving these problems, but in fact the amount of money allocated specifically for housing fell in absolute terms from M$197 to M$172 million — a virtual halving of its proportional allocation in the budget. Recommendations such as these indicate the limitations within which social development is usually planned. The 'modernisation' of the Malay community required concomitant investment in the improvement of the physical structure of the cities in order to cope with the ensuing influx, but this was not forthcoming. The Malaysian government apparently believed that a concentration of investment in the industrial and commercial sectors, together with legislation to encourage increased Malay participation in these spheres, would bring about the desired ethnic integration. It ignored the fact that limited physical resources forced the increasing numbers of Malay migrants into large squatter settlements in and around the major towns. However, as Malay elites were already benefiting from the new economic policies, such action seemed justified in their eyes. This rather narrow attitude has ostensibly been abandoned in the third Malaysia plan which covers the period up to 1980. The principal development goal is now the eradication of poverty wherever it occurs, but as poverty is more characteristic of the Malay community than either the Indian or the Chinese, the original bias still remains. On the other hand investment in the social services, including housing provision, has increased substantially and the government seems to be more aware of the specialised needs of the urban poor as a result of past failures.

Despite the force with which the hardline economists have expressed their views and the extent to which their recommendations have been followed in the Third World, there is scant evidence that a narrow focus on economic growth has resulted in a broad permeation of benefits throughout society. Indeed, the tendency to date appears to be toward greater rather than less income disparity as growth occurs (Ahluwalia 1974, Hopkins and Scolnik 1976, Hasan 1978) (Table 2.1). This is primarily the result of the elitist control in development planning which enables the advanced capitalist countries to continue to exploit Third World resources. The urban bias in the control system has resulted in enormous income disparities between rural and urban populations so that in Malaysia, for example, 88 per cent of the households below the poverty line are rural. In many cases income has declined in absolute terms. However, this is not to say that the position *vis-à-vis* the urban poor is substantially better, since unemployment and underemployment have combined to keep the income of most households very low, particularly in relation to urban price levels.

In recent years, the polarised polemics of development planning have begun to give way to an appreciation of the broader societal effects of economic growth. As far as housing is concerned this trend has modified and tempered many of the more emotional arguments of earlier housing protagonists, and has resulted in a much firmer rationale for increased government investment in low-cost housing. It has shown, for example, that although the construction industry is not necessarily an employment sponge for unskilled migrants, it does provide an erratic but important source of jobs for the urban poor (Whiteford 1976, Lomnitz 1977). Stretton (1978) has documented the situation in the Philippines and has shown that many construction workers have experience in the building industry before they enter the city, and that their incorporation into the urban workforce is usually by village or family ties with one of the influential foremen or brokers who organise the labour supply. In times of recession these labourers usually return to their village to work on the land, secure in the knowledge that they will be recruited again when further construction employment arises. However, employment in the construction industry does not always mean employment in housebuilding. Strassman (1970) has noted that only when countries achieve annual GDP growth rates in excess of 6 per cent

Table 2.1: Economic Growth and Selected Inequality Indicators

Country	GIP 1977 (US$)	GNP % Annual Growth 1970-76	Gini Coefficient	% of GNP held by poorest 40% of households	% urban unemployed
Chad	130	-1.4	.3545 P		
Ethiopia	110	-0.2			
Ivory Coast	710	1.9	.5160 E	16.0	
Kenya	270	0.9	.5974 E	16.3	20.0
Malagassy	210	-2.3	.5235 P	16.0	
Malawi	140	3.2	.4490 H	16.0	
Rhodesia	500	1.5	.6239 E		
Senegal	420	0.5	.5640 P	8.5	
Sierra Leone	200	-0.8	.5813 H		
Somalia	110	-0.6			
South Africa	1,340	1.4	.5606 P	16.0	
Sudan	300	2.3	.4270 H		
Tanzania	200	1.7	.4815 H	16.0	7.0
Togo	300	1.1		16.0	
Uganda	260	-3.1	.3817 E		
Upper Volta	110	0.4		16.0	
Zaire	130	0.4		16.0	
Zambia	450	0.7	.4881 H	16.3	12.9
Algeria	1,110	3.8	.4129 H		26.6
Egypt	310	3.1	.4728 H		
Iran	2,180	3.2	.6068 P	8.5	5.5
Iraq	1,530	7.1	.2957 G		
Israel	2,920	3.3	.4859 H	11.4	
Tunisia	860	6.9			
Turkey	1,110	4.7	.5443 H		
Afghanistan	190	2.6			
Bangladesh	90	-0.8	.3238 H	15.2	
Burma	140	0.9	.3720 H		
China, Republic of	1,180	5.5	.3160 H	21.9	
Hong Kong	2,590	5.2	.4300 H	15.7	3.2
India	150	0.5	.4606 H	17.2	8.5
Indonesia	300	5.3		15.2	7.0
Korea, South	810	8.7	.3479 H	16.3	
Lebanon	1,070	3.7	.5175 H	9.5	
Malaysia	930	4.7	.4973 H	10.6	11.6
Nepal	110	0.6		16.0	
Pakistan	190	1.1	.3195 H	15.2	
Philippines	450	3.9	.4755 H	11.9	13.1
Singapore	2,890	6.8		9.5	9.1
Sri Lanka	200	1.2	.3730 H	18.2	14.3
Thailand	410	4.2	.4904 H		2.8

Country	GNP 1977 (US$)	GNP % Annual Growth 1970-76	Gini Coefficient	% of GNP held by poorest 40% of households	% Urban unemployed
Argentina	1,730	1.8	.4220 H	14.1	5.4
Brazil	1,390	7.4	.5534 H	7.0	
Chile	1,170	-2.3	.4868 H	13.0	6.1
Colombia	710	3.3	.5357 E	3.5	15.5
Costa Rica	1,240	3.0	.4287 H	12.0	5.6
Dominican Republic	840	5.7	.4710 H		
Ecuador	770	4.8	.6567 E	8.5	6.6
El Salvador	570	2.1	.4508 P		5.4
Guatemala	790	3.0	.2870 H		
Honduras	450	0.5	.5979 H		7.8
Jamaica	1,150	-0.5	.5581 H	7.3	19.0
Mexico	1,110	1.7	.5580 H	12.3	
Panama	1,220	1.3	.5368 E	7.0	
Peru	830	2.7	.5714 E		9.3
Puerto Rico	2,460	-0.0	.4053 H		5.2
Uruguay	1,450	0.7	.4809 E		10.9
Venezuela	2,820	3.1	.5908 E	10.3	6.5
Australia	7,340	1.9	.3057 H	20.1	
Fiji	1,220	4.4	.4232 H		
Japan	5,640	3.9	.3060 H	21.0	
New Hebrides	490	1.6			
New Zealand	4,370	1.7	.3295 E		
Papua New Guinea	480	1.5			
Bulgaria	2,590	4.0	.2058 E		
Czechoslovakia	4,090	2.5	.1831 E		
Denmark	8,050	1.5	.4230 E		
Finland	6,150	3.4	.4546 E		
France	7,290	3.3	.4984 H	14.1	
Germany, Federal Republic of	8,160	2.0	.4534 E	16.8	
Greece	2,810	4.1	.3620 H		
Hungary	2,570	2.6	.2026 E		
Netherlands, The	7,160	2.6	.4270 E	18.1	
Norway	8,540	4.5	.3478 E	19.2	
Poland	3,150	5.3	.2532 H		
Spain	3,190	4.2	.3754 H		
Sweden	9,250	2.1	.3900 E	19.7	
United Kingdom	4,430	1.7	.3200 H	18.9	
Yugoslavia	1,960	5.8	.2337 E		
Canada	8,450	3.5	.3173 H	16.8	
United States	8,640	1.7	.3084 P	15.2	

E = Economically active population
P = Total population
H = Households

The inequality indicators represent the latest available data.
Lebanon GNP data for 1974 only

Source: Bairoch (1973), Grimes (1976), World Bank (1979)

does housing become an important element in overall construction, but he also argued that an earlier emphasis on construction in order to give greater emphasis to employment in development strategy is quite feasible. On the other hand, Strassman (1976) also cautions that the 'employment effects' of housing investment vary with city size, type of housing constructed and the related costs of land and credit.

Most other economic arguments in favour of housing programmes revolve around the multiplier effect which construction is said to have on the economy as a whole. Gorynski (1971), for example, has claimed that the building industry purchases almost three times as much material from the non-industrial sectors of the economy as does manufacturing. Makanas (1974/5), in a detailed study of the Philippine construction industry, has supported this position and argued that an increase in the production output of residential buildings will induce an expansion of the entire system of industries. Whilst this particular assessment of the role of residential construction is important, its place in developmental planning strategies is subject to the caveat that some governments view it as an economic safety-valve which, whilst providing employment and general economic stimulus during periods of stagnation, also furnishes opportunities for expenditure curbs in times of inflation. It might also be noted at this point that such manipulation of housing investment is not the prerogative of the public sector. Johnstone (1978) has evidence that in the Malaysian private sector, housing development is usually undertaken by large companies with multiple interests. In times of economic recession in the primary industries of tin and rubber, investments flow across to the housing section; in contrast, when profits are high in the industrial operations, construction development all but ceases as investments are reversed.

In view of the wide-ranging effects which housing investment can have on economic development, one must concur with Cullingworth (1967:27) that 'housing policy cannot be regarded merely as a social policy having little impact on, or connection with, economic growth'. Implicit in this view, although not always recognised as such, is the fact that housing investment can be used as a positive influence in development planning to affect both the pace and direction of growth. It has been claimed, in this respect, that one of the principal benefits of improved housing is the increased productivity which it encourages within individuals (Grebler 1963, 1973). Features such as improved health, greater privacy and the accompanying rise in levels of aspiration, all allegedly combine to increase the individual's mental and physical capacity for work.

Apart from its moral repugnance, a major technical criticism of this theory is its implication that the existing housing of the urban poor in the Third World has adverse effects on productivity, a characteristic which few, if any, studies have verified. Nor has it been possible to assert with any degree of conviction that government rehousing programmes have led to the substantial improvements expected. This is largely because most public housing in the Third World is far too expensive for the really poor, so that it is hardly surprising that Burns and Mittelbach (1972) found little support for the productivity theory of housing in their case studies in developing countries. Indeed, in Hong Kong, one of the few cities where extensive squatter resettlement has occurred, there is evidence that many rehoused families experience more mental stress and physical discomfort after relocation than in their original accommodation (Mitchell 1972, Newcombe and Millar 1977).

Political Considerations

Whilst economic arguments have dominated most discussion on the value of low-cost housing investment, there has been a growing awareness amongst the elites of the Third World of the political utility of such policies in maintaining the status quo in the distribution of power and resources. This role has recently assumed new and vital proportions in the wake of the increased rhetorical and financial support which the multinational organisations have expressed for aided self-help and improvement programmes. In these circumstances it is useful to examine the growth of the political rationale for housing investment in a little more detail since it is likely to become the major influence on policy formation in the near future.

It has long been recognised that gestures of welfare investment are an effective way of easing some of the frustrations that the urban poor experience as a result of continued socio-economic inequalities. Opinion is divided on the extent to which this frustration could be expressed in violent reaction to the status quo. Some observers have been strongly influenced by their own value-judgements and have found it difficult to conceive that the urban poor would not take up arms against governments that allowed such squalid living conditions to persist. Oberschall (1969:8) has asserted that such attitudes are the consequence of overstating the concept of rising expectations and he distinguished between 'unfulfilled hopes and desires [which] do not have the explosive social implications that a rise in food prices or a drop in purchasing power have, when expectations are frustrated'.

Several studies have gone further than this in their denial of the revolutionary potential of the urban poor and have argued that in many instances the new migrants to the city exhibit conservative political characteristics. Turner (1969b) in Lima, Weiner (1967) in Calcutta and Stone (1972) in Kingston, Jamaica, have all analysed voting patterns and concluded that the urban poor vote even more conservatively than the urban middle class. Their common conclusion is that squatters are not potential revolutionaries but are more likely to be responsible citizens if given the opportunity to participate in the planning of their city. Such judgements are, however, based upon biased data since voting patterns in developing countries are seldom representative of the squatter population, either through franchise limitations or because of ignorance of voting procedures. Moreover, the nonconformist and potentially revolutionary elements within the squatter society are more likely to abrogate any voting rights which they may have, if they consider all candidates to be representative of the established power groups. In a way, therefore, suggestions of overwhelming conservatism are as sweeping and as generalised as those of the protagonists for revolutionary upheaval, and derive largely from the internal organisation and cohesion which have been noted in most Latin American squatter areas. Although some see this organisational ability as evidence of revolutionary potential, most seem to agree with Turner's assessment of squatter areas as potential 'urban safety belts'.

More detailed studies of the political organisation within squatter communities, however, show that the orientation of each local area is strongly influenced by its own recognised leaders. Havens and Flinn (1970) have indicated that within Colombian shantytowns formal, reputational and real power rests in the hands of a small group of religious leaders and *gamonal* (small businessmen). The conservative influence of the former has been duplicated for squatter settlements in some other parts of the world particularly those in Muslim societies (Sewell 1964, Soedjatmoko 1971), but there is no uniform relationship and in many societies, such as the Philippines, religious leaders are in the forefront of political protest. The domination of the poor by small businessmen is more consistent because of their control of the availability of consumer goods and credit facilities. This economic influence is further strengthened by the consequent pre-eminence of the *gamonal* in the *compadrazgo* (godparent) system of the shantytowns.

Buchanan (1963) and also Gutkind (1972) have abandoned wholesale generalisation of the urban poor as either revolutionary or conservative and have instead identified two broad subgroups. The first comprises those migrants in regular employment who, it is suggested, have little to gain from violent upheaval and tend towards caution and compromise. Thus, although this group is economically important, it does not have much political power. The second subgroup is composed of the lumpenproletariat – the unskilled, unemployable 'mass of hungry, rootless and detribalized wretches living in the shantytowns and squatter settlements' (Buchanan 1963:6-7). The validity of this dual approach to the analysis of the urban poor rests upon the proven existence of a large lumpenproletariat, a phenomenon for which previous studies, even in Africa (to which both Buchanan and Gutkind largely refer), show conflicting evidence. A considerable amount of support exists for the theory that the lumpenproletariat, when present, will provide the most powerful source of urban revolutionary potential. Fanon (1963) and Worsely (1964) were particularly vigorous proponents of this view and Fanon (1963:103) has written vividly of 'that horde of starving men, uprooted from their tribe and . . . clan [which] constitutes one of the most spontaneous and most radical revolutionary forces . . .'.

The arguments against this theory are, first, that large numbers of lumpenproletariat have yet to be shown to exist on an extensive scale; and second, that if they do exist, why has widespread urban violence in support of improved living conditions not yet appeared? Buchanan (1963) has argued that the group needs to be politically trained and organised before its revolutionary potential can be realised, pointing to the incorporation of the casbah into the FLN campaign in Algeria, and to the anti-Lumumba mobs in Leopoldville as examples of channelled violence. However, these are instances of the urban mob being utilised for political ends; examples of spontaneous urban violence in support of general socio-economic improvement are much more infrequent and tend to revolve around racial or tribal rather than class jealousies.

In historical terms, many revolutionary upheavals have been shown to involve the middle class more than the poor (Rudé 1971). To a certain extent, studies in the Third World have borne out this relationship. Havens and Flinn (1970) concluded from their analysis of power structures in Colombian *barrios* that the individuals most conscious of current inequalities, class differential and the need for change, are those who have experienced some upward mobility. Similar situations have been noted in Africa (Gutkind 1972) and India (Weiner 1967:49), causing Weiner to comment that 'in order to be discontented with the city one has to be integrated into it'.

It would appear that homogeneous characterisations of the urban poor as either revolutionary or conservative are misleading. Clearly, there are substantial differences between the regularly employed, who have definite aspirations concerning upward mobility, and the depressed unemployed. The role of underemployment as a transitional element within this polarisation is not yet clear, nor is there evidence for either of the extremes possessing greater revolutionary potential than the other. Simply to deny *any* revolutionary possibilities on the grounds that little violence has yet occurred, would be unwise because the ranks of the urban poor will undoubtedly swell in future years, given the present trends in population growth and industrial employment. It may be, as Whiteford (1976) has pointed out, that the present generation will not challenge their position in the social order too strongly and will be content with the token improvements currently handed down. This is unlikely to be true of their children who are much more politicised and who are now reaching maturity in many cities.

Whilst not quite in the exploitative category, Singapore is illustrative of the political relationship between motivation and housing investment which occurs in much of the Third World. When the island became an independent republic in 1965, its population comprised a volatile mixture of Chinese, Indians and Malays, many of whom had been born outside Singapore and had little sense of identity with the new state. The ruling People's Action Party headed by Lee Kuan Yew has invested heavily in government housing programmes over the last fifteen years, specifically to enable as many people as possible to acquire a stabilising interest in their community. Thus, the emphasis within the building programme has been on relatively high-quality flats for owner-occupation through innovative financial schemes (see Chapter 5). As a result, there is evidence that the poorest elements of Singaporean society have not been the principal beneficiaries of the programme (Buchanan 1972, Hassan 1977, Drakakis-Smith and Yeung 1977). However, there is no doubt that the government has achieved its principal goal of a stable, conservative, bourgeois community. Significantly, the Malaysian racial riots of 1969 had relatively few repercussions in Singapore.

The Realities of Housing Investment

Whilst it is not difficult on theoretical grounds to justify increased investment in housing provision in the Third World, there is as yet little evidence to indicate that many governments in developing countries are convinced by these arguments or have altered their investment priorities. In an extensive multiple regression analysis of 36 nations, Grebler (1973) has shown that housing investment as a proportion of GDP is most closely related to economic factors, notably the level and rate of increase of per capita real income. This relationship is non-linear and although housing investment increases as economic growth takes place, it levels off once the highest echelons are reached. Countries typical of the highest investment category include South Korea, Spain, Israel and Greece.

Whilst economic factors currently exert substantial influence on government housing programmes in the Third World, Grebler's study indicates that these account for only 60 per cent of the variation in investment totals. Clearly, many other considerations affect policy decisions, although, somewhat surprisingly, population growth itself does not appear to be one. Empirical assessment suggests that there are two main factors which either influence present policy formulation, or are likely to do so in the future. The most important of these is political motivation which has already been discussed in general terms and which will be examined in detail in later chapters. The second is the organisational ability of the public sector to carry out policy decisions. The allocation of funds for housing is futile unless logistical and technical requirements can be met at the same time. At present, the administrative, planning and construction systems in most developing countries are unable to fulfil these requirements and, in an effort to cope with accelerating housing shortages, many governments have turned to the successful solutions of the West. The resultant desire to replicate the prefabricated high-rise buildings of Europe or North America has led to large-scale imports of materials, techniques and personnel. Most of the units constructed in this way are expensive and beyond the reach of the poor, even when subsidised. Such situations only serve to discourage further investment in low-cost housing provision.

Most urban planners and administrators in the Third World are familiar with the arguments for and against increased housing provision, but the combination of previous failures with alternative and apparently more attractive priorities has resulted in the dismal investment situation which exists at present. To a large degree, the disillusion with housing investment is the result of the limited appreciation by administrators and policy-makers of the various alternatives open to them for spending their restricted financial resources. Few are aware of the potential sources for low-cost housing and the contrasting roles each of these performs at different stages in the development process. The remainder of this chapter outlines a structural framework within which the major alternative sources of low-cost housing are identified and briefly described. The present and potential roles of these alternatives in meeting the needs of the urban poor, together with their interrelationships, are then taken up in detail in individual chapters.

A Typology of Housing Provision for the Urban Poor

Figure 2.2 is a structural model which illustrates the main sources of urban housing in the Third World. It is a simple bipolar format derived primarily from the dualistic theories discussed in the previous chapter, and as such it is open to the same criticisms. The typology is not intended to reproduce reality; its components represent a simplification of the real world and may not coincide with the principal sources of housing supply in each and every city in developing countries. Nor, at this stage, does the model indicate the relative importance of the constituent parts, although it is clear that throughout the Third World the conventional sector, whilst holding most of the material and financial resources, constructs very little housing directly for the low-income groups.

Figure 2.2: Major Sources of Housing for the Urban Poor

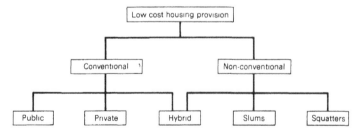

The model could be elaborated in several ways, principally by the incorporation of additional components which would permit it to resemble more closely existing situations. But there is no single reality common to all cities and structural elaboration of this nature is more appropriate for studies of individual countries where a better understanding of the specific forces governing housing supply is necessary. Examples of such elaborative features might include the pavement dwellers of Calcutta or Jakarta (Moorhouse 1972, Suparlan 1974), the *pondok* lodgings of Indonesia (Jellinek 1978), or even company housing in corporate Japan (Umezawa and Honjo 1968). As it stands, therefore, the model is not intended to be an analytical tool for assessing the housing situation in individual cities or countries, although it could fulfil this role. It is primarily a general-purpose model aimed at simplifying the analysis of urban housing provision in the Third World as a whole; as such, the individual components need to be defined and distinguished as distinct, valid entities.

Conventional : Non-conventional

In earlier expressions of this model (Drakakis-Smith 1975, 1976a) the terms 'formal' and 'informal' have been used to distinguish between the two main poles of housing provision but, as the previous chapter has shown, these inadequately describe the attributes of each sector. 'Conventional' is used here in the sense of 'being in accordance with accepted artificial standards' (Garmondsway 1965), a particularly apt definition for housing provision in developing countries as most of the criteria by which housing becomes acceptable are unrelated to the realities of existing socio-economic circumstances. Housing is conventional, therefore, if it is constructed through the medium of recognised institutions, such as planning authorities, banking and real estate systems, and is in accordance with established legal practices and standards. By and large, this consumer-based definition corresponds with an industrial mode of production which utilises wage labour, is capital-intensive, and employs relatively sophisticated technology. However, a considerable number of conventional dwellings are constructed in the private sector by small groups in more traditional ways.

Non-conventional housing, by implication, is that which does not comply with established procedures. It is usually constructed outside the institutions of the building industry, is frequently in contravention of existing legislation, and is almost always unacceptable in terms of prevailing bourgeois *mores*. Although the mode of production is often the labour of the individual or household intending to occupy the accommodation, this is not always the case and petty capitalist construction firms also operate within this sector.

These characterisations of conventional and non-conventional housing represent the extremes of the dichotomy and a broad transitional zone, or continuum, of 'hybrid' dwellings links the two. In this way the model avoids undue rigidity for it is not intended that all housing which is not conventional must be considered non-conventional, or vice versa. The hybrid categorisation is intended to cover those units of shelter which incorporate features from both of the major sectors. In most instances, the housing is similar in appearance to that of the non-conventional sector but contravenes fewer legal standards (Plate 1); as a result, the units become socially and politically more acceptable. At the same time, the category also includes housing which is ostensibly conventional in nature but which has some degree of illegality. Cities in the Third World often contain large, high-rise apartment blocks apparently constructed within the normal institutional and juridical framework but which have no formal occupation permits.

As the basic characteristics of hybrid housing are essentially those of the conventional and non-conventional sectors, it will not be analysed separetely. This does not mean that such shelter is insignificant. On the contrary, in cities where building standards are stringently defined, but loosely or inconsistently enforced, hybrid housing may be quite extensive, providing it is socially accepted or officially tolerated. Although the physical nature of this intermediary group seems chameleonic, its implications for policy formulation are distinct and important. The relaxation of rigid juridical, administrative and social codes is one of the most positive and practical ways of widening the range of options open to the urban poor.

Squatters

Squatter settlements are the most familiar type of non-conventional housing constructed by the urban poor — largely because they tend to be a very visible element in the urban landscapes of the Third World. Despite this apparent familiarity, there is little consensus on the definition of squatting. The visual impact of shantytowns, with their apparent chaos and squalor, has given rise to a descriptive terminology based primarily on the physical appearance of the dwellings. Although such an approach must be influenced by the cultural values of the observer, it has gained substantial support and has given rise to a distinct nomenclature. Two of the most frequent euphemisms employed to describe the settlements concerned are 'uncontrolled' and 'temporary'. No doubt the latter represents wishful thinking on the part of planners and administrators but it bears little relation to reality. In many Third World cities squatting began during the inter-war period but large-scale population movements did not commence until the latter part of the 1940s. A large number of those migrants who entered the city at this time are still resident in the same squatter settlements, although over the years a few have received partial recognition from the authorities. Some form of toleration exists in many cities and, because of the basic illegality and insecurity of squatter settlements, gives the authorities a considerable degree of direct and indirect control over the inhabitants. For this reason, no matter how temporary or established a squatter community may be, almost all are vulnerable to legitimate demolition and clearance with minimal warning and little compensation.

Whilst the epithet 'spontaneous' is an improvement over 'uncontrolled' or 'temporary', going beyond physical appearances and attempting to convey some of the vigour of squatter life, it is an inappropriate description of the process of formation of squatter settlements. Most have been built up slowly over the years by a process of gradual infiltration – accretions based on kinship or village relationships. Even the well-publicised squatter 'invasions' of Latin America are neither as impulsive nor as disorganised as they seem to be, and Turner (1968) has shown clearly the considerable amount of planning and selectivity which characterises such actions.

Throughout this book the term 'squatter' will be used in preference to euphemisms such as those mentioned above. In almost all countries squatting has strict legal connotations, referring either to the occupation of land without the permission of the owner, or to the erection or occupation of a dwelling in contravention of existing legislation. This juridical interpretation clearly defines the nature of the relationship between the squatters and the authorities, one which provides the latter with complete legal justification for any action it chooses to take. The insecurity generated amongst squatters by this situation has important effects on their lifestyle. On the one hand it inhibits their participation in the normal life of the city – even in activities and services to which they are legally entitled. Perhaps more important, the illegal nature of the housing in squatter settlements also encourages the pursuit of clandestine occupations – further compounding the nature of the relationship with the urban administration.

The adherence to a juridical approach does not necessarily mean that squatting is any easier to define. A multitude of building and tenancy regulations exist in most countries, many of which are not enforced. This is where the distinction between squatter and hybrid housing becomes rather blurred. In addition, land claims may be complicated by the existence of several conflicting codes from the post-colonial, colonial, pre-colonial and even pre-urban periods. Nor does a legal definition sit easily with the notion that squatters are closely bound to the 'informal' sector, a point which will be discussed at greater length below. As a consequence, the appearance of a squatter settlement will not necessarily match its legal status — the degree of toleration exercised by the local authorities plays a crucial role in this respect. It is evident, therefore, that no comprehensive and completely satisfactory set of criteria can be drawn up for defining squatter settlements. The juridical approach simply identifies one of the most important of the intricate mix of features characteristic of such communities.

Slums

Slums are defined here as legal, permanent dwellings which have become substandard through age, neglect and/or subdivision into micro-occupational units such as rooms or cubicles. International standards of habitability are impossible to establish even within the Third World alone, and this makes the identification of slum districts and their populations an extremely individual affair. The situation is further confused by the common misuse of the term 'slum' to encompass virtually all types of housing occupied by the urban poor, including squatter settlements.

Slums and slum formation are recognised within this analytical framework as being worthy of study in their own right. Massive numbers of urban poor are housed in such units throughout the Third World and yet they receive scant attention from planners or administrators. In some ways this is understandable since slum formation is not a particularly visible process, occurring as it does within existing buildings. Compared to squatting it is insidious rather than spectacular. As a consequence the available statistics are even more meagre and unreliable than those for squatter settlements.

In contrast to squatting, slum formation is not usually illegal. Old buildings persist in most cities because the authorities cannot afford to decrease their already inadequate housing stock by demolition. In the Third World dilapidation is more often due to the financial incapacity of landlords to maintain their property rather than any deliberate attempt at exploitation, although the latter does take place. The main reason for inadequate maintenance is usually rent control which drastically affects landlord incomes in old property. The major way in which slum conditions are created is, however, internal subdivision of both old and new dwelling units. In many instances this is largely independent action undertaken by the incumbent residents in order to incorporate new arrivals or newly created households; many new tenements built in Asia often contain provision for future internal partitioning. Whilst subdivision is sometimes encouraged by the landlord, most money transactions usually benefit the chief tenant so that the whole process is essentially the same as that which takes place in squatter settlements – an informal arrangement which operates outside conventional housing institutions and often excludes legal property owners. However, with the replacement of old tenement floors by modern apartment blocks, the style of leasing, and therefore the role of the landlord, is changing rapidly.

Slum formation differs from the formal provision of low-cost homes by the private sector, in the sense that few new dwellings are constructed; the process primarily involves the rearrangement of space within existing structures. The subdivision which occurs involves increased densities and sharing of facilities and it is from statistical changes of this nature that most inferences on slum formation and characteristics must be drawn. However, even these limited data include pitfalls for the unwary, since subdivision increases the number of rooms as well as the number of occupants so that room densities might not increase significantly. More useful measurements are those which indicate either ground densities, the extent of sharing or simply the number of occupants per dwelling.

Although analytical research on slum formation remains relatively rare, numerous descriptive investigations have followed the initial awakening of social consciousness in the Victorian era. The pejorative assessments which invariably emanated from such studies, have indelibly affected current appreciation of tenements and slums and their place in the urbanisation process. Only in the last decade, spurred by the work of investigators such as Oscar Lewis (1966), has new debate been stimulated on this important issue. The discussion of slums in Chapter 4 will therefore be arranged largely with reference to Lewis's conceptual approach.

Public Housing

In many developed countries the government is an important source of housing for the urban poor, but this is true of very few countries in the Third World. Only in relatively wealthy cities with controlled population growth, such as Hong Kong or Singapore, does the public sector provide houses for a substantial proportion of the population. Elsewhere, as earlier sections of this chapter have noted, government investment in housing is limited and has invariably been wasted on expensive projects designed to impress electorates rather than meet any real needs. It is largely for this reason that government housing schemes, although relatively few in number, tend to be visually prominent in the townscapes of developing countries. The high-rise apartment blocks which fulfil this psycho-political role satisfy few needs of the urban poor themselves. Any examination of government responses to the housing needs of the urban poor must therefore be firmly placed within this context.

Positive housing policies, as opposed to the indifference characteristic of many governments, can be classified into three broad groups – reactionary, alien and indigenous. Reactionary responses are those which are concerned simply with eradicating slum and squatter settlements because they disfigure and disrupt the city. Such policies cover a wide range of activity but normally involve no construction of housing for the displaced families. In some countries, reactionism takes the form of preventative measures which attempt to check the flow of migrants to urban areas. In others, demolition of existing squatter dwellings is the most prevalent government activity. The assumption underlying the latter is that the affected households will return to their supposed rural origins. This does not occur since most of the poor are strongly committed to urban life and after eviction they move into other low-income districts to begin their personal urbanisation process all over again.

In cities where more progressive rehousing policies prevail, most government programmes are unfortunately alien in nature, in the sense that they seek to apply standard Western solutions to the urban housing problems of the Third World. Such schemes are characterised by their reliance on capital-intensive, technologically sophisticated industrial methods and invariably take the form of massive high-rise blocks. Whilst the urban poor are often disturbed by the cultural change involved in relocation to high-rise housing, the principal defect of this type of programme is the cost. Even if generous subsidies are made, rents are usually relatively high with extra charges frequently being made for water, electricity and similar basic facilities. In addition, hidden expenses are also involved if the new buildings are located in the urban periphery, since the costs of the journey to work are increased and the number of part-time jobs for children and wives is drastically diminished. As a result of this cultural and financial pressure, the urban poor who manage to gain access to such accommodation frequently sell out or sublet to middle-income families eager to alleviate their own housing problems. In some instances entire blocks remain unleased or unsold and are eventually allocated to employees of the civil or military services who already receive favourable credit facilities on the open market.

Despite the obvious defects, Western planning principles have continued to characterise most government responses to low-cost housing needs. However, over the last decade it has been argued that a cheaper, more practical and more satisfactory way to improve the living standards of the urban poor is to use the energies of the people themselves in aided self-help schemes. The protagonists of this approach argue that if the government prepares the land, provides basic infra-structural services and, possibly, cheap materials, then the residents themselves will build acceptable accommodation.

The aided self-help concept, or indigenous approach, is based on the premiss that all non-conventional housing is a normal response to housing shortages and indicates the determination, effort and ability which the urban poor invest in order to consolidate and improve their life in the city. It is possible to argue with this premiss on the grounds that it is immoral to consider as normal the unequal distribution of economic and social resources which gives rise to squatter settlements, and that aided self-help programmes simply maintain this inequality. Such criticism seems to have had little affect on government policies, because aided self-help schemes of various types have increased drama-tically throughout the Third World since 1970. This is largely due to the financial and technical resources which the multinational organisa-tions, such as the World Bank and United Nations, have made available specifically for such schemes. Aided self-help projects have therefore become part of highly organised government programmes, despite their populist origins. It is for this reason that they have been classified as conventional rather than non-conventional. Virtually all aspects of aided self-help housing construction have been rigidly institutionalised, albeit in modified form, in order to make the finished product con-formist enough to be acceptable to the authorities. The deleterious effects of this process are only now becoming appreciated (Ashton 1976) but the formalised structure within which the programmes now operate is likely to prevent improvement.

Private Housing

Conventional private housing is that which is constructed through normal institutional channels and is offered for sale or rent on the open market. At present, although the private sector builds most of the con-ventional housing in Third World cities, relatively few of these new units fall within the financial reach of the urban poor, with the obvious exception of housing constructed under contract for the government. On the other hand, as existing private sector housing ages, suffers neglect and/or subdivision, and generally becomes substandard, it plays an increasingly important role in housing the lower-income groups. The process by which private housing deteriorates into slums is very complex and as this book is primarily concerned with policy change in relation to newly created accommodation, the broad mass of existing private housing will not be directly considered.

It is widely assumed that the private sector plays, and will continue to play, a minor role in housing the urban poor. In general this is true since the profits which can be made from low-cost housing construction are relatively small, but then not all private construction is undertaken by large-scale firms, using modern capital-intensive techniques and looking for large profits. Although such firms are usually dominant in terms of the value of output, they tend to comprise a relatively small proportion of the total number of construction firms. The majority of private companies consist of relatively few workers, building houses on direct commission from the purchaser or architect rather than on speculation. Many countries also have considerable numbers of unregistered builders organised by foremen who in turn are legitimately employed, again directly by purchasers or architects, to construct houses which in every other respect comply with both legal and social standards (Lomnitz 1977, Stretton 1978).

The private sector, therefore, contains far more potential for low-cost housing construction than is generally recognised. Admittedly, it is unlikely that private firms could or would produce homes for the most destitute of the urban poor, but there might be a more suitable market amongst the more fortunate low-income households characterised by stable employment, rising aspirations and an ability to accumulate savings. It must be noted at this point that private sector concentration on the lower-middle-income families is unlikely to lead to a downward filtration of vacated dwellings. In Third World cities there is such a general shortage of accommodation that any increase in production will be absorbed by the middle-income strata with little release of unwanted housing.

The identification of the target population for increased private sector production is of crucial importance, since profit margins on individual units will be small and large developers would require as extensive a market as possible. On the other hand, smaller producers may be content with a more modest output. The size of the target population will depend on the price households can afford to pay, the cost at which the units can be produced and the profit margins permitted. In general terms, these three factors can be brought closer together by a reduction in building costs and cheaper credit facilities; assuming, of course, that any economies will be passed on to the consumer. Chapter 6, in which these problems are discussed in detail, reaches the conclusion that these goals can only be achieved through government assistance and supervision.

Conclusion

In the previous chapter it was noted that one of the main criticisms made of dualistic models was the failure to incorporate the features of production, thereby diminishing their explanatory potential. The structural model outlined in Figure 2.2 also appears open to this criticism since it is based primarily on the consumption characteristics of housing provision. It is not the intention of this analysis to ignore production, for such an omission would make the present situation in the Third World virtually incomprehensible. On the other hand, there have been relatively few field studies of the modes of housing production, so that current theories do lack a substantive factual base and need to be treated with some caution. Nevertheless, recent developments in the mode of production approach do offer important alternatives in assessing housing provision and it will be useful to re-examine the typology postulated in Figure 2.2 from this point of view.

Several production-based models have emerged in recent years, but the most useful in terms of analysing housing provision is that of Burgess (1977) who distinguishes three basic modes of production – the industrial, the manufactured and the 'artisanal' (*sic*). Individual production covers construction activity in which the relationship between consumption and production is governed by commercial exchange and market values. The second category, manufacturing, refers to activity in which small groups of hired workers undertake housing construction for an architect or builder. It is characterised by a mixture of capital-investment and intensive labour usage. 'Artisanal' construction covers situations in which the producer and consumer are one and the same. Only rudimentary technology is involved in the construction process which is also characterised by its use of recycled materials and large amounts of labour.

Burgess's classification, like much neo-Marxist theory, tends to romanticise the self-sufficiency of the urban poor. It assumes without justification that most squatter housing is self-built. This may well prove to be the case, but at present the evidence for such a statement is contradictory and much more research is needed on the operations of this type of petty capitalism before firm conclusions can be reached. In addition to this criticism, there seems to be no place in Burgess's model for government housing construction, the production of which is usually industrial in nature but the distribution of which is sometimes affected by forces other than market values — for example, if rents are subsidised or allocations made to certain categories of the population.

Despite these criticisms Burgess's model does offer a useful structural framework within which to examine the characteristics of low-cost housing production and as such it complements existing methodology which is largely consumer-based. But many neo-Marxists would have consumer-oriented models completely replaced with those based on various forms of production, even though there are many elements within the present situation which cannot be explained solely by reference to production characteristics — the pavement dwellers in Jakarta are a case in point since no physical production is involved. A structural model which incorporates features of both consumption and production would seem to be the most useful, and Lea (1979) has attempted to do this in his analysis of self-help and autonomy in housing provision. Figure 2.3 attempts to relate Burgess's modes of production to the structural model outlined earlier and it is evident that there is a substantial degree of compatibility. The area of least agreement is in the rather vague intermediary zone where small-scale units of varying degrees of conventionality are produced through several modes and forms of production. Outside this area of uncertainty the industrial mode of production corresponds closely with the public sector and larger private firms, whilst slum and squatter housing is usually the product of artisan labour. In view of this correlation the original model seems adequately constructed to incorporate elements of both consumption and production into subsequent discussions.

Part of the difficulty in attempting to relate these models or production and consumption lies in the fact that each assumes a degree of discreteness for its component parts which is not borne out by reality. Overlaps occur in many ways. Squatter housing, for example, is not always constructed of scrap or recycled materials. Much is built from better-quality wood, metal, concrete or brick purchased from commercial dealers perhaps with money earned in 'formal sector' employment. Similarly, loans for improvements or new construction may be sought from institutions such as banks or government schemes rather than the usual source of family or friends. Not only are the conventional and non-conventional housing sectors linked, therefore, but considerable and complicated interrelationships also exist between them and other elements of the 'dual' economy. In this respect the influence of the government is often underestimated but, as Rew (1977a) and Lamb (1976) have shown, bureaucratic control of and access to resources for housing of all kinds is pervasive. Such links have long been suspected but it is only in recent years that any substantial corroborative evidence has emerged to indicate their extent (for example see Johnstone 1979). Although further investigation may well induce considerable change in attitudes towards squatting, it is beyond the purpose of this book to discuss such changes in detail and, indeed, at this point such discussion would only serve to complicate the simple model put forward as a basis for describing the major features of low-cost housing provision.

Figure 2.3: Consumption and Production Models of Housing Provision

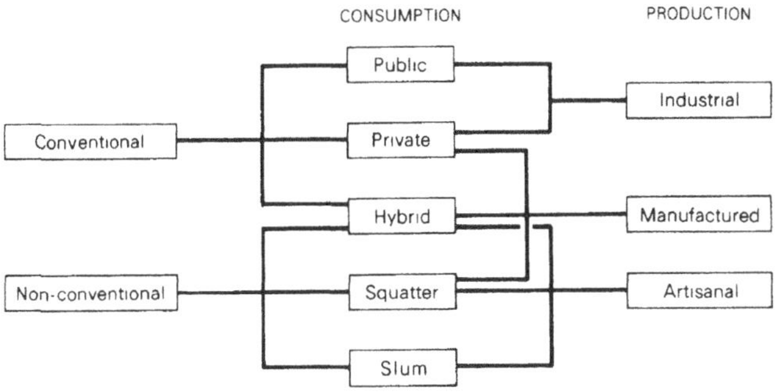

This brief examination of the structure of low-cost housing provision and its current role in development planning has identified several crucial elements which must be considered in any further analysis. The first is that housing cannot be dismissed as a mere 'social overhead'. As the following chapters will indicate in their various case studies, all decisions on housing investment in the Third World are closely correlated with the level of economic development and with political attitudes. A paradoxical situation exists in which governments, whilst regarding low-cost housing provision as a purely social consideration, nevertheless make their investment allocations on political and economic grounds.

The second factor which emerges from the overview is the heterogeneous nature of low-cost housing supply in developing countries. The mix of the four major components identified here varies throughout the Third World as social, economic and political circumstances change. At the lowest level, the individual household responds to such changes by revising its priorities *vis-à-vis* housing: the initial need for job proximity is therefore superseded by a desire for security of tenure and, in turn, by aspirations for 'modern' amenities and facilities. However, whilst individual responses adapt to new conditions, national housing policies tend to remain cataleptic and inflexible even under rapidly changing circumstances. Within this stasis meagre financial resources are un-enthusiastically spent on conventional Western 'solutions', usually with few benefits for the urban poor. In recent years, the new conventions of aided self-help have been adopted, with more immediate success but within equally rigid policy structures.

A deeper appreciation of the mechanisms by which low-cost housing is provided should enable more efficient use to be made of limited investment funds, but only if national responses to the needs of the urban poor become as dynamic and flexible as those of the individual family itself. The following chapters will examine, with the aid of case studies, each of the identified sources of low-cost housing in order to evaluate their respective roles in past, present and future housing policies. The more complex task of relating this fluid mix of compon-ents to the general development process will be left to the concluding chapter which will attempt to summarise the major relationships in a series of simple models.

3 SQUATTER SETTLEMENTS

Introduction

Although the structural framework outlined in the previous chapter has established the basic nomenclature that will be used throughout this book, further discussion is perhaps required for squatter settlements because of the proliferation of alternative descriptive terms which has emerged in recent years. In essence euphemisms such as 'uncontrolled' or 'spontaneous' have been put forward in order to avoid the use of two of the most common terms, viz. 'shantytown' and 'squatter settlement', which are currently regarded as disparaging. To a certain extent this criticism is valid although in the latter case the deprecatory connotations are not implicit in the etymology of the words *per se*.

There has undoubtedly been a pejorative bias in many assessments of squatter settlements to date, a factor which is not unconnected with the dilapidated appearance of most communities. Atman (1975) typifies this approach when he described squatter *kampungs* in Indonesia as 'the slum dwellings of homeless people'. But how can the inhabitants of a dwelling, however meagre, be considered homeless? It is similar refusals on the part of urban authorities to consider squatter houses as 'homes' which has adversely affected housing policies towards the urban poor for so many years. It was noted in Chapter 2 that the word 'squatter' is deliberately retained and used throughout this book because it reflects the illegal nature of most settlements and conditions the nature of their relationship with urban governments. In many ways the authorities are relatively content to allow such settlements to persist since, on the one hand, the low cost of squatter housing and the money earned from clandestine occupations ensure that large masses of the urban poor survive with minimum demands on the public exchequer. On the other hand, the illegal nature of so many aspects of squatter life enables the authorities to retain a strong, although not always tight, control over the inhabitants. Indeed, many government officials are deliberately lax in enforcing laws and regulations, provided they receive financial recompense. It is important to note, therefore, that extensive urban squatting is not always a manifestation of weak political or administrative control. As long as some laws are contravened the squatters remain in a precarious position *vis-à-vis* the urban authorities.

The use of juridical criteria to define squatting does not necessarily ensure that precise statistical and cadastral information can be obtained. In many countries and cities the legislation pertaining to residential construction is confused and contradictory. In Malaysia, for example, Johnstone (1978) has shown that whilst the official definition of squatting relates only to the illegal occupation of land, much of the 'makeshift' and 'low-quality' housing also contravenes legislation related to materials and mode of construction. Elsewhere it is not uncommon for squatter settlements to be partially legalised in pre-election manoeuvres, producing a situation in which the residents may be recognised as legal occupants of the dwelling but are still only tolerated on the land itself. In Ankara, for example, squatters in the older central areas experienced this process as long ago as 1953 when they were granted limited tenurial rights but were forbidden to materially improve their dwellings in order to discourage speculators. The effect has been to freeze the dilapidated condition of the structures for over twenty-five years. Not all of the concessions to squatters in Turkey have been so limited and many former squatter communities now constitute accepted, enfranchised residential districts. However, in most instances the original Turkish name for such settlements, which is *gecekondu* (in literal terms this means 'built overnight'), has been retained in official plans and gazetteers. The term is usually, but inaccurately, translated into English simply as 'squatter' and misleadingly appears thus in all statistical collations. In similar fashion, the *bustees* of Calcutta are also alleged to comprise squatters, but according to Sivaramakrishnan (in Saini 1973) they are primarily tenancy settlements where land is owned by landlords who rent it to *thika* tenants who in turn build on the land and then either live there themselves or rent the accommodation to others.

Such caveats illustrate that even apparently straightforward legal definitions have drawbacks and inconsistencies. It follows that with the weak enforcement of legislation, the status of a squatter settlement is likely to differ substantially from its appearance and well-being, the nature of which is the product of a *mélange* of socio-political factors. A wide range of squatter communities therefore exists throughout the Third World, with considerable variation occurring even within the same city. Whilst this differential will be discussed in greater detail below, it draws attention to an important distinction which has emerged over recent years in government policies towards squatter settlements. On the one hand, there are the 'obvious' squatters at whom official attention, whether indifferent, punitive or progressive, is directed; on the other hand, there often exists a sizeable minority of make-shift legal housing which poses special problems for the urban authorities. As these dwellings do not blatantly infringe existing legislation, they fail to attract the attention of 'progressive' policy-makers and tend to be easily absorbed by private commercial developers and speculators.

The lack of any widely accepted English word to describe squatters could be attributed to the paucity of such communities in the developed countries, but this has not always been the case. The squatter phenomenon is peculiar neither to the Third World nor to the post-1945 era (see Mumford 1961, Parsons 1968). In general, the capacity of cities to absorb migrants has varied according to the economic situation in the cities themselves and their surrounding rural areas. When the disparity between the two was great then migration was usually heavy, irrespective of whether or not the city was economically or physically able to cope with the influx. In late medieval Europe, for example, trading activities attracted large numbers to the cities and urban historians have noted the subdivision of houses, suburban squatting and high rents which were features of the period (Smith 1967, Koenigsberger and Mosse 1968, Russell 1972). Stow wrote of sixteenth-century London that the common field outside the city gates was 'encroached upon by the building of filthy cottages, and with other purpressors, inclosures and laystalls (notwithstanding all proclamations and acts of Parliament made to the contrary) . . . which is no small blemish to so famous a city to have so unsavoury and unseemly an entrance or passage thereunto' (in Kingsford 1908:2).

It is difficult to find comparable evidence of squatting during the Industrial Revolution. On the one hand, new, cheap methods of construction saw most migrants legally if not luxuriously housed. Later developments in urban transport, such as the railway, tramcar and omnibus, all helped to encourage and enable middle-class dispersal to suburbia, thus vacating the central dwellings for subdivision into artisan slums. However, more recently evidence has appeared to contradict assumptions on the paucity of squatting. David Ward (personal communication) contends that many American towns had large, but temporary, squatter districts particularly during periods of rapid growth. He cites the frontier settlements in the American West as examples of such developments. Squatting has subsequently tended to reappear wherever cityward migration has reached unusual proportions, particularly at times when recession has prevented full economic and physical absorption of the population. This type of situation arose during the Depression in both Europe and America where brief squatter communities appeared in several large cities (see Beck 1971).

In contemporary Europe pockets of squatters can still be found in many of the capital cities. Athens, for example, experienced extensive refugee settlement during the 1920s and 1930s as a result of both external and internal conflict (Papagiourgiou 1968). Even in the communist states of Eastern Europe squatter housing is evident despite the extent of government building programmes. Simic (1973:97) has described one such site in Belgrade where 'on the very banks of the Sava and Danube stand . . . shanties assembled from every imaginable kind of salvageable material'. But some of the most miserable squatter settlements in Europe are undoubtedly in France where immigrant Algerian workers can be found in *bidonvilles* adjacent to the massive construction sites on which they are employed. The wretched plight of these exploited but essential workers is in many ways as bad as any in the Third World (see Power 1973, 1976) and illustrates how metropolitan colonialism has persisted despite the nominal political independence which has occurred. The position of *bidonville* residents in France contrasts ironically with that of some other Western European squatter communities, particularly the slum collectives of young people who settle in vacant or condemned buildings in an effort to achieve 'human environments under corporate administration' (Anderson 1972:115). In essence these new squatters are attempting to re-establish the closeness of rural and village relationships which have long disappeared from contemporary European urban society. Amongst the squatters of the Third World such values are still very strong, and constitute one of the most important resources that the urban poor have at their disposal to counteract the strains and pressures which migration to the city imposes on both the individual and the family.

Statistical Dimensions

Accurate statistics on the extent of urban squatting are difficult to obtain. In part this is a consequence of the problems of definition outlined earlier in this chapter, although inadequate methods of data collection also affect the situation. Most authorities undoubtedly underestimate the size of their squatter populations either by ignoring communities outside the official city limits or because of the enumeration difficulties posed by the morphological irregularities of many squatter settlements. Moreover, many squatter huts are used not for residence but for storage, or else have been abandoned by their owners in *de facto* terms whilst nominally retained in the hope of an eventual offer of resettlement. Such discrepancies make target planning very difficult.

Table 3.1 assembles data which have been published over the last two decades on squatters as a proportion of the population of various cities. Most of these broad estimates simply represent totals to which the city authorities have been willing to admit, although in recent years the increased availability of multilateral loans for squatter improvement schemes has in some instances led to more realistic appraisals. In general, however, the static and rounded nature of the figures indicate their imprecision. Frequently no distinction is made between slum and squatter populations so that the totals which subsequently appear are arbitrarily ascribed to one or the other category.

Although many of the published figures must be used warily, there seems little doubt that most squatter populations have been increasing very rapidly. Overall trends are difficult to discern because of extensive variations in definitions between individual countries. Third World cities in general are expanding at annual rates of between five to ten per cent but the World Bank (1972a) and United Nations (1974) have estimated that many squatter settlements are doubling in population every five or six years, which implies annual increases of between 15 and 20 per cent. Where detailed studies have been undertaken, these enormous growth rates have generally been confirmed. Norwood (1972), for example, found that Ndirande, a squatter settlement in Blantyre, Malawi, was expanding at a rate of 22 per cent per annum compared to 12 per cent for the city as a whole.

The broad reasons for urban growth in the Third World have been discussed in Chapter 1. The tremendous pressure which has been put upon existing housing resources has consequently forced many families into illegal occupation of land or shelter. The dwellings which have resulted from this movement, together with their location, are many and varied. Most cities have some squatter communities in their central areas adjacent to the major employment sources such as the central business district. In some, these concentrations are particularly heavy, such as the Tondo and Intramuros settlements in Manila, and pose severe problems for urban development. In other cities, such as Hong Kong or Ankara, the centrally located squatters are on steep-sided hills which hitherto have been regarded as unsuitable for conventional buildings (Plate 2). In general these central squatter pockets are occupied by the older families, more recent arrivals having been forced to establish their houses in the peripheral areas which are much further from the main employment sources. There are, however, some compensations in the outer settlements, such as the availability of larger building space and the freedom from restrictive municipal legislation. These considerations exert a strong attraction for larger households which have less dependence on job proximity, and there is abundant evidence throughout the Third World that movement has taken place from the old, crowded central districts to the more open squatter communities on the edges of the city (MacEwan 1972, Vaughan and Feindt 1973, Davies and Blood 1974, Feldman 1975, Drakakis-Smith and Fisher 1975).

Whilst there are certain spatial features common to the squatting process, individual characteristics can be readily identified in most cities.

Table 3.1: Estimates of Squatters as a Percentage of Total Population in Selected Cities

City				
Blantyre	56 (1970)			
Dakar	60 (1970)	30 (1969)		
Dar-es-Salaam	50 (1970)	34 (1967)		
Kinshasa	60 (1970)			
Lusaka	27 (1967)			
Algiers	33 (1954)			
Amman	12 (1974)			
Ankara	65 (1970)	47 (1965)		
Baghdad	25 (1970)	29 (1965)	25 (1960)	
Casablanca	70 (1970)	16 (1969)		
Istanbul	45 (1970)			
Izmir	65 (1970)	35 (1965)		
Oran	33 (1954)			
Tunis	16 (1960)			
Bangkok	4 (1970)	20 (1970)	23 (1968)	5 (1966)
Calcutta	33 (1970)	33 (1961)		
Colombo	57 (1973)			
Delhi	14 (1968)	9 (1959)		
Hong Kong	10 (1979)	5 (1971)	10 (1970)	
Jakarta	25 (1971)	26 (1969)	80 (1968)	25 (1961)
Kabul	21 (1968)			
Kaohsiung	20 (1970)			
Karachi	23 (1970)	27 (1968)	33 (1961)	
Kuala Lumpur	37 (1971)	25 (1969)	25 (1961)	
Manila	35 (1977)	18 (1973)	35 (1972)	20 (1968)	35 (1968)
Seoul	30 (1970)			
Singapore	34 (1970)	15 (1970)	15 (1966)	
Taipei	25 (1966)			
Saigon	26 (1973)	35 (1970)		
Arequipa	40 (1970)	40 (1968)	40 (1961)	9 (1957)
Brasilia	41 (1970)	41 (1962)		
Buenaventura	80 (1969)	80 (1964)		
Cartagena	50 (1974)			
Caracas	40 (1969)	35 (1964)	21 (1961)	
Guayaquil	49 (1968)			
Lima	40 (1970)	36 (1969)	21 (1961)	9 (1957)
Maracaibo	50 (1969)	50 (1964)		
Mexico	46 (1970)	46 (1966)		
Montego Bay	40 (1971)			
Rio de Janeiro	20 (1975)	30 (1970)	16 (1964)	27 (1961)
Santiago	17 (1973)	25 (1964)		

Sources
The main sources used in the compilation of this table are the World Bank Working Papers on Urbanization (1972) and Housing (1975), Grimes (1976), the United Nations' Housing Surveys of 1973 and 1974, the United Nations' Improvement of Slums and Uncontrolled Settlements (1971), together with various United Nations' regional reports and individual research papers too numerous to cite individually.

Physical site features play an important part in this variation but even in similar topographic situations, social and cultural variations can give rise to quite different settlement forms. Rooftop or boat squatters are less frequent, but attract disproportionate attention because of their 'visibility'. More common and yet less appreciated or acknowledged are the pavement dwellers who appear in the most congested cities such as Calcutta or Jakarta (Suparlan 1974). Although these people do not normally erect dwellings, they illegally occupy ground space and can be regarded as squatters.

As these variations indicate, it is difficult to draw useful generalisations on either the appearance or distribution of urban squatters in the Third World. Perhaps the most that can be said is that almost all settlements are, or have been, physically marginal to the city as a whole, whether on steep hillsides, marshy inlets or in peripheral areas. It is important to note that only in this physical sense can squatters be considered as marginal elements within the city. Nevertheless, the concept of marginality has been widely but erroneously extended to cover squatter participation in economic, social and political activities. In this respect squatter taxonomies based on physical characteristics alone are of dubious value because they explain little of the people themselves, or of the processes by which they settled and are forced to remain in squatter communities.

Formative Processes

Whilst there are many ways in which individual families may become residents of squatter communities, two major systems may be identified. The first and most widely known is the organised squatter 'invasion' by relatively large groups, a phenomenon most frequently found in Latin America. The second is a much slower process of infiltration by individual households or small groups of people and occurs widely throughout the Third World.

As Mangin (1963), Turner (1967) and Ray (1969) have shown, squatter invasions tend to be highly organised operations which have been planned long before the movement itself takes place. This implies that most of those involved have a reasonable amount of experience of urban life and are aware of the precautions which must be taken. In addition, the families who participate have usually progressed to a stable, if still low, income and are less reliant on proximity to employment. As yet the actual process by which invasion organisations emerge is imperfectly understood but prior association through district or employment groupings seems common. The planning involved in the invasion goes far beyond the selection of an organising committee. Careful screening of applicants takes place before they are accepted as part of the group. In addition, some form of tacit approval or backing will have been secured from politicians or political groups interested in the future support of the residents. This support is essential in the immediate post-invasion period when eviction and reprisals are most likely to be effected. Other planning precautions include careful selection of the date of the invasion. In this respect the night before a public holiday is particularly favoured since it allows several days for consolidation and usually means that the police forces are deployed elsewhere in the city.

The actual invasion and establishment process vary according to the political and physical conditions in the city concerned. Where possible the site is quickly demarcated into building plots which are allocated by the organising committee. Occasionally very sophisticated and expensive methods are employed. Turner (1967) has described one such operation at the 'Pampa de Cueva' *barriada* in Lima in which a group of topographers was hired at a cost of US$1,000 to survey and mark out the land. However, most invasions are neither so well co-ordinated nor so financially viable and the immediate objective is simply to settle quickly onto the chosen area and to obtain *de facto* possession by a display of group solidarity.

Successful invasions are usually reinforced by later settlers so that the entire area selected for occupation is covered within a relatively short time. The earliest constructions on individual plots comprise simple matsheds; subsequently brick walls are erected around the plot and, within the privacy which this provides, the construction of the permanent house can then take place. Building is usually undertaken with the assistance of families and friends, although for specialised work, such as concrete roofing to support a second storey, experienced labour may well be hired. The subsequent development of the squatter settlement, in terms of both individual houses and the community as a whole, is a more complex process and is strongly related to the socioeconomic status and motivations of its inhabitants. This process will be analysed a little later in this chapter since the related typologies also apply to some stages in the development of the second type of primary squatter settlement — that of infiltration.

The slower process of squatter infiltration is undoubtedly more typical of Asian or African urbanisation. Several writers have suggested that it is more likely to occur in cities where there is little active official opposition to squatting because this makes it much easier for individual families to move into existing settlements through connections with family or friends (Mangin 1967, Ross 1973). However, infiltration is also found in cities such as Manila where government has often been very vigorous in its reaction to squatting (Keyes and Burcoff 1976). Moreover, migrant families often have to seek formal permission from the recognised leader of a squatter settlement before being allowed to establish residence, so that even slow, accretive growth has its formalities.

Kampong Maxwell, a small squatter settlement in Kuala Lumpur, illustrates this process very clearly (Drakakis-Smith and Johnstone 1977). The population of Kampong Maxwell in 1977 was approximately 1,600 – all illegal squatters on government land with 80 per cent living in homes they built themselves. The settlement, which is located on ill-drained land between a main road and the river Gombok (Figure 3.1), was initially developed in the 1930s by Chinese families. It remained very small until the 1950s when a large number of Malay households moved into the area following the partial demolition of two nearby squatter *kampongs* to make way for road and river improvements. Squatters continued to infiltrate Kampong Maxwell until 1964 when the two *kampongs* were finally demolished.

Over the next ten years Kampong Maxwell continued to grow as more families moved in, but as the site filled up the remaining space became less suitable for building. The rate of growth between 1971 and 1977 was therefore only 3.6 per cent per annum, less than half that for the Kuala Lumpur metropolitan area as a whole. Entry into the settlement is normally through the medium of family or friends who approach the headman and discuss possible building sites. However, this is not an official or formal procedure. As a result of this slow growth the demographic composition of Kampong Maxwell was quite varied despite its small size. One-third of the houshold heads had come directly from rural *kampongs*, another third from towns and one-quarter from city residence, primarily in Kuala Lumpur itself. Families were spread evenly throughout the size and age ranges and there were no single-person households in the settlement.

Whilst mature communities of this nature can be found throughout Asian cities, there are many other types of squatter settlements in which more rapid growth and greater demographic imbalance are characteristic. In addition, not all infiltrating families choose to move into squatter settlements and build their own house. Many newcomers

Figure 3.1: Kampong Maxwell, Kuala Lumpur, 1976

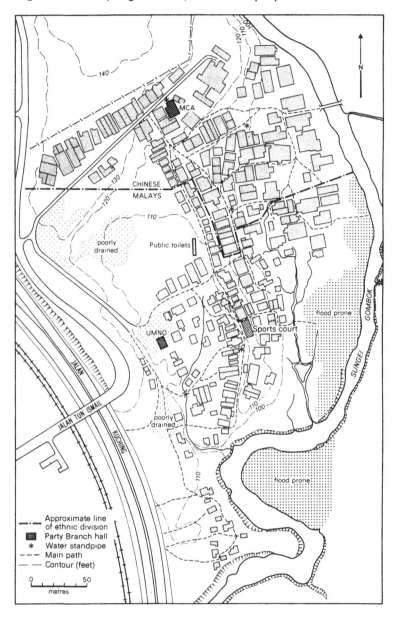

prefer to rent existing structures or rooms in slum tenements until they acquire a more secure niche in the economic life of the city.

Developmental Typologies

Contrasts in the formation of squatter communities, together with the obvious physical variations which occur both in space and time, have led to the adoption of taxonomic classifications as a means to understanding the development processes in operation. One of the earliest and most influential of these classifications was by Charles Stokes (1962) who made a distinction between successful and unsuccessful communities – in Stokes's own terminology those of 'hope' and 'despair'. In some ways the initial novelty of this distinction constrained later inquiry so that over the last two decades many detailed studies of squatter settlements and their development have been made simply on this binary basis (for example Parkes 1971). The specific defects of this approach will become more apparent in the case studies presented later in this chapter, the main emphasis at this point is that such assessments fail to recognise the multitude of mobility incentives existing in all squatter communities whether old or new, peripheral or central, organised or haphazard. The root cause of squatting does not lie in the nature of the squatters themselves but is a response to their lack of access to conventional housing. This is caused not only by insufficient production but by excessive cost in relation to the income level of the urban poor. The lack of synchronisation between housing supply and effective demand is a function of the nature of urban social formation, and not the fault of the individual.

Analytically, it is much more worthwhile to examine squatters in the wider urban framework within which they live and work. In order to understand fully the process of squatter development, therefore, knowledge of physical evolution must be supplemented with information on urban economics, politics and culture. One line of investigation has been to examine the broader priorities of squatters at various stages in their 'development', not only in terms of their housing demands but also in relation to wider ambitions for themselves or their children. This often leads to contradictory situations and poor households are forced to choose between considerations such as employment proximity, cheap rents or access to various amenities. The balance eventually selected will govern the area and type of housing in which they seek to live, although the restrictions imposed by the urban authorities are frequently

as influential as individual preferences in deciding the actual place of
residence. The combination of interests which governs preferences
is rarely static but shifts according to changes in economic circumstances within the household. Once the primary phase of settlement
is over, a wide variety of environmental and social considerations, such
as sewerage and electricity connections, street paving, or police and
postal services, become important. Significantly, most of these involve
closer links between the squatter settlement and the urban community
in general.

John Turner (1969a, 1972) has been particularly prominent in the
development of typologies of this nature, basing his approach on the
premiss that the market value of the squatter house is less important
than its use to the consumer. He has thus classified squatter housing
according to its use value as expressed primarily in terms of tenure,
location and amenities. Turner's argument is that individual households will assess their economic and social status and will either move
to a community which satisfies their particular priorities or will remain
in a settlement which is changing in line with these priorities. He consequently developed a threefold classification of individuals into bridge-
header, consolidator and status-seeker, each of which supposedly
corresponded with successive stages in income growth (Figure 3.2). This
taxonomy assumes that as economic security is attained there is a
revaluation of 'vital needs' which is reflected in housing preferences.

The model is very simple, although it can be made more complex by
the addition of alternative preference criteria such as the availability of
increased space or access to modern amenities. It can also be extended
to cover the developmental stages for squatter communities as a whole.
Not all experience change and, as noted above, individual households
may exhibit upward mobility in socio-economic terms whilst remaining
spatially static. Conversely, the household may move from a stagnant
settlement to an improving one in order to satisfy its changing priorities. Turner has also produced descriptive models to cover each of these
alternatives. Of these, his settlement typology (Turner 1969b) is the
least useful, despite its multiple categories, as it incorporates little
beyond the physical, tenurial emphasis of earlier taxonomies. More
informative is his hypothetical schedule of *barriada* development
through time (Turner 1972) because it encompasses a wider variety of
both personal and community changes. The squatter is attributed
various socio-economic ambitions and also the energy to pursue these
goals. Such a positive evaluation has not always been applied to
squatter settlements and Turner was one of the first to urge a revision

of attitudes and policies along these lines.

Figure 3.2: Economic Improvement and Changing Priorities

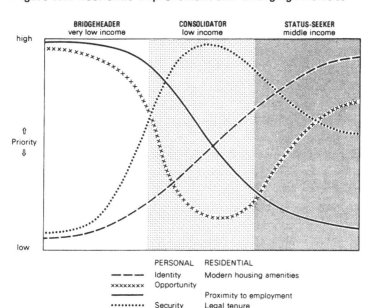

Despite the value of Turner's approach, it is clear that his static and somewhat idealistic typologies explain very little of the squatting process. It is not enough to note that improvements do occur and convert such description into a theory of development, it is essential to discover how and why such changes come about, and why they do not. Burgess (1977) has argued that squatters do not live in an autonomous system and that their building activities are severely circumscribed by the dominant mode of production in the city, whether in the form of private capital or the authorities. As self-help construction operates within such a system, the end product must have a market value or at least a potential market value which is determined by factors other than the occupant's own scale of utilities. Burgess thus concludes that most squatter building is petty capitalist and not autonomous, and that the interaction of individual preferences and circumstances with the dominant mode of production can give rise to considerable variation within and between squatter settlements in the same city. This feature will be evident in the case study of Ankara at the end of this chapter. However, detailed investigation of the dynamics of change are few, although Peter Ward (1976) has shed some light by his work in Mexico City. He distinguishes between the generally consolidating *colonias paracaidistas*

and the usually static and stagnating *cuidades perdidad*. Ward argues
that the factors which inhibit the auto-improvement of the latter settlements are closely related to their position within the capitalist landlord
system. The relatively high rents, the risks of default and eviction, all
act against the accumulation of savings and in favour of the spending of
surpluses on consumer durables. The inferior position of the renters
also mitigates against the development of group cohesion and the emergence of political leaders, in contrast to the relative proliferation of
power brokers in the consolidating *colonias proletarias*.

The existence of such power brokers is extremely important in
determining the pace and direction of change in squatter settlements,
although the extent of their influence is always subordinate to and
dependent upon the prevailing attitudes amongst local and national
government officials (see Rew 1977b, Hollnsteiner 1977). In this respect there appears to have been considerable progress over the last few
years, with many authorities seemingly more responsive to suggestions
for squatter improvement rather than eradication. Closer examination,
however, indicates that these changes are more apparent than real.

Attitudinal Change

Until the last decade it was not fashionable to see squatters as positive elements within the general framework of urban development.
Indeed the early post-war assessments of squatter communities were
largely pejorative despite the general sympathy which the writers had
for their subjects. Thus Matos Mar (1961:171) commented that 'the
common feature of all the *barriadas* is their instability. They are unhealthy and populated by individuals and families who are at the
bottom of the urban social scale'. Others have been more scathingly
inaccurate. Lerner (1967:24), for example, has described squatters as
'the flotsam and jetsam that [have] been displaced from agricultural
life without being incorporated into modern industrial life' who live
in 'tin-can cities that infest the metropolitan centres of every developing country from Cairo to Manila'. Over the last ten years these rather
extreme sentiments have fortunately given way to more positive assessments in which the work of William Mangin and John Turner has
figured prominently. Squatter settlements were shown not to be centres
of political unrest, anomie, disease and crime but instead were recognised as making major contributions to the city as a whole — adding
to its labour resources, consuming some of its production, whilst at

the same time housing themselves at little direct cost to the city government. In addition, squatter settlements were seen to contain an enormous reserve of individual enterprise which had given rise to a myriad of small commercial and industrial units engaged in what Gerry (1977) has termed 'recuperative production' – the recycling of material discarded by the consumption and production processes of the formal sector.

This realisation of the positive attributes of squatting led to a widespread intellectual reaction against 'aberration theory'. It was claimed that squatting was a manifestation of the normal urban growth process in the Third World, and consequently required programmes of assistance and improvement rather than demolition. As Chapter 5 will show, these policies have brought undoubted benefits to some squatter families, but it is surely wrong to assume that widespread inequality in income distribution and lifestyle is normal and thus somehow acceptable. Considered in this light, the apparent efficiency of squatter settlements in satisfying many of their own needs can be seen to benefit the already wealthy urban capitalist sector. The extent and unfairness of this relationship has only recently become fully appreciated despite the sympathetic approach adopted by most investigators. Two conceptual shortcomings have contributed to this situation. One was the overextension of the dualistic type of sectoral model previously discussed in Chapter 1, the other was linked to the popularity of the associated notion of squatter marginality.

Although there is a large body of literature in cultural anthropology which deals with 'marginal man', the concept as it is currently applied to the urban Third World has two more recent origins. The first covers the work of writers such as Charles Stokes (1962) and Oscar Lewis (1966) in the early 1960s, and is linked to their development of theories which suggest that many of the urban poor are locked into a cycle of poverty from which they cannot escape. The associated concepts of 'slums of despair' and 'culture of poverty' will be discussed in some detail in the following chapter; at this point it is sufficient to note that one of their main tenets was that people affected by these situations comprised a culturally separate group living on the physical, social and economic margins. Such opinions were reinforced by the emergence of broader theories on dualism in developing countries, particularly as a result of the adoption of the residual analysis methodology used in initial investigations. This approach took the relatively easy way of defining what was 'formal' and labelling the remainder 'informal', assuming in the process a degree of homogeneity which does not exist. In terms of explanatory potential this was little different from the earlier work of Stokes and Lewis, and marginal populations were simply seen as living in a state of exclusion from the socio-economic heart of the city.

This approach postulates that the 'informal sector' is marginal to, and in transition towards, the modern capitalist economy on which urban development and prosperity ultimately depend. The typologies of Turner outlined earlier in this chapter contain this assumption, and Berry (1973) too has offered support for the idea by arguing that squatter communities are best called 'transitional urban settlements'. With the growing realisation that this process is not occurring in many contemporary Third World countries, the concept of marginality has thus been subject to increasing scrutiny. In particular, it has been recognised that it is not only the degree of exclusion which is important but also the nature of that exclusion. One of the most critical analyses has been that of Janice Perlman (1974) who has examined what she has termed the 'myths of marginality' in the context of Brazil. Perlman divides her analysis into four component parts, social, cultural, economic and political, and in each instance successfully illustrates the considerable integration which exists between the squatters and the 'mainstream of urban life'. Whilst she convincingly disproves the myths of isolationism, traditionalism and anomie which allegedly pervade squatter life, this is not the main value of her work since earlier studies, notably that of Nelson (1969), have been equally effective in this matter. The strength of Perlman's study lies in her analysis of the nature of the integration which exists between squatter communities and urban society as a whole in which she argues that the apparent marginality of the squatter way of life is not so much a function of its segregation as of its exploited integration. Squatters, in her opinion, 'are not economically marginal but exploited, not socially marginal but rejected, not culturally marginal but stigmatized, and not politically marginal but manipulated and repressed' (Perlman 1974:2).

Whilst this type of marginality theory paints a more vivid and accurate picture of the exploitative relationship which exists between the urban elites and the squatter poor, it offers little insight into the processes through which the situation emerged and is maintained. Gerry (1977), in particular, has argued strongly in favour of adopting the more informative approach of analysing marginalisation as a process, rather than marginality as a set of relationships, in order to identify the mechanisms through which exploitation and deprivation take place. These conceptual changes have not yet been satisfactorily incorporated into the broader, related theories on peripheral capitalism, particularly as this relates to housing, and 'marginal' may be substituted for 'peripheral' in much of the literature with little change of meaning. Some writers, for example Obregon (1974) and Rew (1977b), have suggested that many households are so marginal as to be superfluous to the urban economy. This is patently not true. Whilst the emphasis on modes of production has emerged from a reaction to Turner's theories on squatter autonomy, there still persists a chimerical, but unconfirmed, implication that such communities are largely self-built. Recent field studies, on the other hand, have emphasised that there are many links between squatter construction and the 'formal sector' through the purchase of materials, loans or the use of hired labour. In addition, squatter *rentiers* and commercial builders are not uncommon, thus supporting Burgess's (1977:18) observation that the squatter 'has not escaped capitalism . . . he is merely in another part of it'.

There is little doubt that *en masse* squatter construction results in considerable capital accumulation and as such could be said to effect large savings for municipal and state governments, although this presupposes that public funds are to be invested in housing squatters. On the basis of the perceived accumulation of capital, some observers have imputed capitalist motivation to all squatter construction, but this has yet to be convincingly demonstrated and in some of the more recent literature there would seem to be an inherent danger of attributing sophisticated rationale to what is essentially almost a reflex desire for adequate shelter.

Despite many criticisms, the concepts of marginalisation, marginality and peripheral capitalism all offer valuable, if conflicting, information for policy formulation. On the one hand they suggest that, given the likely persistence of an urban informal sector, eradication policies are unwise and programmes of improvement and encouragement are needed. On the other hand, strategies which permit the continued existence of income inequalities would seem to bring more benefit to the capitalist elements of the urban population. Indirect evidence of this statement has already been read into the increased financial support given to aided self-help programmes by the large multinational organisations and the subsequent enthusiasm shown by many Third World governments. These points will be discussed at greater length in Chapter 5.

Case Studies

So far the discussion has primarily focused upon changing attitudes towards squatter settlements, seeking simply to establish their basic character and their relationship with the wider urban societies of which they are part. Many of the issues raised become clearer and more comprehensive when related to real situations, so the final section of this chapter will be given over to two case studies of squatters in Bangkok, Thailand, and Ankara, Turkey. Geographically, neither the countries nor the cities share many points of similarity although both states had populations of about 40 million in 1975. In broad economic terms Turkey is the more developed country having a higher Gross National Product per capita (US$1,110 in 1977), with almost a third of its export earnings coming from non-agricultural products such as textiles. However, cotton and tobacco are still the major revenue earners and in this respect Turkey has more in common with Thailand where the major exports are rice, maize, rubber and tin. Although Thailand has a smaller GNP per capita (US$420 in 1977) than Turkey, it is growing more rapidly and there is a slightly more equal distribution of income in the kingdom.

The wide contrasts which exist at the macro-level are to a certain extent mirrored in the urban squatter settlements. Whilst the case studies stress the fact that such communities can vary enormously, they also illustrate that even within very different circumstances some important common themes can be identified. Each case study has a different emphasis. The first, in Bangkok, examines the nature of the relationship between the squatter community and the city as a whole, showing clearly the gulf between the assumed and real character of such settlements. It also illustrates the extent to which attitudes must change if effective planning responses are to evolve. Although the second case study also stresses the positive attributes of squatters, its main purpose is to show how minimal legal or official encouragement can give rise to strong, viable communities.

Bangkok

In 1975 Thailand's capital district of Krung Thep Maha Nakhon, usually known as Bangkok, had a population of 4.3 million. This makes it one of Asia's largest cities although Thailand itself is amongst the least urbanised nations of the continent with only 14 per cent of its 44 million people living in towns and cities. The capitals of Thailand have traditionally been located in the fertile central plain and have always attained 'primate' status. Bangkok is no exception and although founded only in 1782 it is more than 30 times larger than the second city of Thailand, Chieng Mai, dominating all aspects of the country's political, economic and cultural life and exerting an enormous attraction for migrants. For the 1960-70 period the average annual population growth of metropolitan Bangkok was 6.2 per cent, more than half of which was the result of migration (Sternstein 1976, Nathalang 1978).

Physically, the site of the capital is unsuited to large metropolitan growth. The entire area lies only 1.5 metres above sea level, so that the high precipitation causes severe drainage problems and many areas are flooded during the rainy season. But metropolitan Bangkok has not only outgrown its physical site, it has also outgrown its administrative framework. The city extends into four provinces and contains six separate municipalities, whilst several important services are provided by state enterprises loosely attached to national ministries. This fragmented administrative system, coupled with the traditional Thai antipathy towards governmental control, has produced a chaotic urban sprawl in which property speculation is rife. Much of the land in and around Bangkok is owned by the Crown, the government, religious bodies or the traditional elitist families — few of whom are responsive to pleas for restraint. The result is a *laissez-faire* type of development which has benefited the wealthy and caused tremendous planning problems in the city.

One of the most pressing problems is the shortage of adequate housing. Whilst the severity of the situation is visually apparent to all, its quantitative and qualitative dimensions are poorly documented. No formal definitions of housing fitness or squatting exist so that estimates even of a general 'slum' population have varied from 6 to 30 per cent of the metropolitan total. Most official reports and policy statements thus consist of expressions of concern together with some rather hopeful target figures. Angel *et al.* (1977) have identified a series of components in the low-cost housing system in Bangkok (Figure 3.3). Of these the private sector is the least important although it is fairly productive of new units. The government built very few houses until the present decade and only since 1975 has there been any serious investment in or attention paid to the problems of housing provision in the capital. Given this meagre output of conventional homes most of the massive migrant influx over the last twenty years has been housed in the slum and squatter communities of the city.

Within metropolitan Bangkok there are three main types of squatter or quasi-squatter housing. The most spectacular is the wholesale and

Figure 3.3: Bangkok: The Low-income Housing System

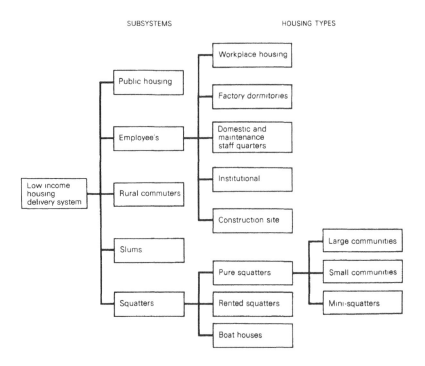

completely illegal settlement on large tracts of land belonging to government agencies such as the Port Authority or Thai Railways. Smaller communities of similar juridical status are more widely distributed throughout the city on parcels of private land held by speculators. These average about 1,000 to 1,500 people per site. The third type of 'squatting' occurs on the small plots rented from a *wat* (temple authority) or the Crown, which have acquired more than the one house stipulated in the original lease. These are known locally as mini-squatters and total approximately 100,000. As the majority of squatters in Bangkok are scattered in numerous small enclaves hidden from view, the most visible squatter communities, and the ones which have attracted most attention, are therefore the very large settlements located on government or quasi-government land. The largest of these communities is Klong Toey, situated in the southern part of the metropolitan area over marshland at the edge of the Chao Phaya river (Figure 3.4). The settlement is locationally marginal in two ways. First, it is on the periphery of the main metropolitan area some 15km from the central business district; second, and probably more important, it has grown up on land which belongs not to the Bangkok municipality but to the semi-independent Port Authority of Thailand, neither of whom will take responsibility for helping the 25,000 people who reside in Klong Toey. In fact, the Port Authority wishes to extend its operations into the areas occupied by the squatter settlement and has been actively campaigning for its removal. The threatened demolition of the dwellings has spawned several social surveys, the largest of which was undertaken in 1970 by the Social Work Department at Thammasat University and forms the basis of this case study (Sakornpan 1971).

Klong Toey is a well-established community, having been in existence for more than twenty years. Almost half of the household heads have lived in the area for over a decade but there is no direct evidence as to whether these people moved directly into Klong Toey on arrival in Bangkok or whether they initially settled elsewhere. Some oblique evidence is available on the number who came to Klong Toey because of eviction from, or the expense of, other houses (22 per cent), the total who have lived in Greater Bangkok for more than ten years (67 per cent) and the proportion who had previously been employed in agriculture (6.3 per cent). The general picture is one of long-term residents of somewhat mixed origin with sizeable proportions coming directly from the rural areas as well as indirectly via other residential districts in Bangkok. Very few people return to their traditional home for employment purposes and the overall situation is one of considerable commitment to urban life.

Living conditions within Klong Toey are not good. The huts stand on stilts over stagnant, sewage-filled marsh water and are connected by rickety, perilous plankways. The area is also crowded, with five or six people to every dwelling and an average of 3.5 persons per room. The mean amount of residential space per person in Klong Toey is five square metres and whilst this is limited it is worth noting that it compares very favourably with some government housing projects in the Third World — for example, low-cost housing in Hong Kong has only three square metres per adult even in the most recently built estates. All city services stop at the edge of the settlement so that only 3 per cent have direct access to a water supply, although 30 per cent use an indirect connection from another house. The rest have to purchase water from vendors. Sewerage connection and rubbish disposal facilities are virtually non-existent, so that almost all waste material accumulates in the marshy swamp over which Klong Toey is built.

These conditions are primarily the fault of the city authorities who refuse to extend infrastructural services to Klong Toey even though the

Figure 3.4: Bangkok: Land Use and Residential Sprawl

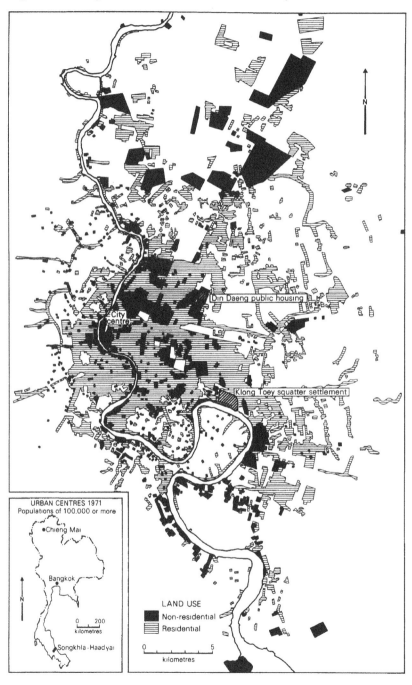

residents themselves show considerable initiative by constructing their own facilities such as toilets and illegal electrical or water connections. Moreover, despite the physical deficiencies there is general satisfaction with living conditions, largely because almost all families live in their own rent-free accommodation. Houses are generally made from wood with galvanised steel roofs and most were built from new materials by the occupants themselves with the assistance of friends or relatives. In terms of welfare facilities the integration of the residents of Klong Toey with the services available in Bangkok is undoubtedly poor. The popular explanation for this is that the squatter residents are 'not interested' in family planning, education or other welfare services. This is not true and the 'marginality' of the squatter settlements in this respect is almost entirely explained through the inadequacies of communication between the authorities and the residents. Educational provision and its utilisation by the squatters provides a clear example.

Approximately 30 per cent of the school-age children of Klong Toey currently do not attend school; of these, half have received some education but the rest are unlikely to receive any formal schooling at all. The educational officers in the area assert that this is because of lack of interest by parents, but the real situation differs widely from this claim. One of the principal reasons proffered by residents is the complicated and potentially disadvantageous procedure for enrolling a child in a school. This required the presentation of both birth and house registration papers, but less than half of the houses in Klong Toey are registered since the people fear that their illegal occupation will be discovered. In fact, a house may be registered easily, provided it is habitable and is not on public property. The Port Authority is not a public body and can therefore only put indirect pressure on the registration authorities not to issue papers.

However, house registration is not the only reason for the low school participation since attendance rates are low for both registered and unregistered houses. The main cause of non-attendance is the poverty of the Klong Toey families and the expense involved in sending a child to school. No fees are charged in government primary schools but books, uniforms, lunch and transportation can all amount to an excessive cost for a poor family. In addition to these direct costs there are the indirect financial sacrifices of losing older children who look after the family whilst both parents work, or who supplement the family income with part-time employment.

The allegation of non-interest in education is not borne out by the actions of the Klong Toey residents themselves, since large numbers of children attend private, unlicensed schools, some within the squatter settlement itself. Other children are sent back to the home village of the parents to be schooled. The real explanation for the educational 'marginality' of the children in Klong Toey thus lies in the basic poverty and in the gap in communication between the residents and officialdom. One of the interviewers in the Thammasat survey made this comment after talking with a district educational officer. 'The supervisor has never been into the slum and therefore tends to think of the people as all alike. The Municipality has no programme to inform the citizens about school enrolment procedures . . . nor any effective plan to follow up cases of non-attendance or drop-outs' (Sakornpan 1971:98).

If social ties with the city as a whole are capricious, in economic terms there is extensive integration. Most of the residents originally came to Bangkok for economic reasons and all but a few are gainfully employed in one form or another. Occupations vary within Klong Toey, the largest category (approximately one-third) being manual labourers, the majority of whom work on construction sites. A quarter are self-employed, mostly as street vendors, whilst the same number work for the Port Authority on whose land they live. The great majority of people in Klong Toey are therefore well integrated into the economic structure of the city although almost half of them work within Klong Toey itself or in the port. The extent of the economic ties between the squatters and the city is further emphasised by the long hours of work since most people worked ten to twelve hours per day, seven days per week.

The rewards for such arduous labour are meagre. Remuneration from peddling and the Port Authority, two of the main sources of employment, is much lower than in other activities. The median monthly earnings for Klong Toey households are around B1,200 (US$60) and two-thirds have incomes below the B1,500 (US$75) frequently used to define 'low-income' families. Despite this remunerative 'marginality' the average household income in Klong Toey is higher than that of the country as a whole; this is a significant factor in the continued growth of Bangkok. Largely as a result of this economic exploitation many squatter families find themselves in debt, not from profligacy but simply to survive. Most of these debts are internal in the sense that they are owed to family or friends within Klong Toey, a feature which illustrates again the self-sufficiency of the community.

To sum up, in the fields of labour and ingenuity the squatters of Klong Toey have made a considerable contribution to the economy of

Bangkok whilst at the same time making few demands for assistance. Despite this situation there is little evidence to show that the squatters receive the co-operation or opportunities necessary to improve their lifestyle. On the contrary it would seem that the city authorities have sought to deny them the economic or social rights which they have earned. Attempts to rehouse squatters in Bangkok have been few, with most of the public housing units being far too expensive for those households affected by clearance schemes. This situation will be analysed in greater detail in Chapter 5 but at this point it is worth noting that it is unlikely to change much either in the near or distant future, particularly as the squatters themselves are not sufficiently politically organised to exert any degree of pressure on the authorities. The importance of such political organisation and its effectiveness in bringing about improvements cannot be overemphasised. Its influence has already been demonstrated in Latin America and will be further illustrated in the second case study.

Ankara

In 1970 approximately one-third of the total population of Turkey lived in officially designated urban settlements, although many of these were still predominantly rural in their occupational character. Unlike Thailand there is no primacy within the urban hierarchy because Istanbul, the principal Ottoman city, was replaced by Ankara in 1923 as the national capital. Since this date the two cities have shared the expansion of primate functions. Initially the capital was a small commercial centre of about 20,000 and the influx of government employees meant that plans for a rapid development of the city were necessary. At the time it was predicted that growth over the next half-century would be nearly 250,000, but this proved to be a gross underestimate which was exceeded within twenty years. The initial planned area of Yenisehir (Figure 3.5) was soon overwhelmed with buildings and speculative developments so that the municipal boundaries had to be extended to a massive 6,550 hectares. However, co-ordinated planning controls were never implemented so that speculators and squatters were allowed virtually free rein. On the other hand, the illegal residential constructions did much to relieve the pressures on accommodation which the continued population growth had brought about. After 1945 the growth in rural population and the effects of increased mechanisation were both severely felt in Anatolia and migration to the urban centres began on a large scale. Although Istanbul has received the bulk of this movement (Srikantan 1973), the impact has been more

marked in the smaller city of Ankara where the population increased
by over 400 per cent from 1950 to 1970, and in 1979 stood at about
1.8 million.

Figure 3.5: Ankara: Land Use, 1975

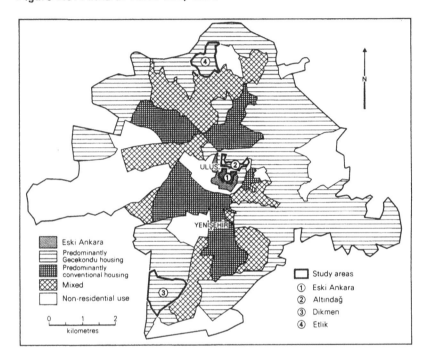

The rapid population growth of the capital has created many problems for its planners. In semi-arid Anatolia the provision of adequate
water and sewerage reticulation systems has proved very difficult
(de Planhol 1973). In addition, the physical bowl of Ankara's site and the
predominance of anticyclonic weather are beginning to create severe
air pollution problems for the expanding metropolis. At present, however, the greatest single problem facing Ankara is its housing shortage.
Two-thirds of the population are classified as 'squatters', distributed
throughout the city from centre to periphery in all directions except in
the west where the military and government zones are located (Figure
3.5). At the same time, increasing congestion has occurred in the old
central houses of Eski Ankara, the original pre-republican settlement.
   Squatter settlements have always been of considerable importance in
housing migrants because Eski Ankara was not large and had relatively
few dwellings which could be subdivided into small, cheap units. With

the planning of the new capital there was a considerable movement of middle- and upper-income groups away from the old central areas to new suburbs in the south and west. Migration into the city was high from the outset, with refugees flooding into Turkey from the ceded areas of the defunct Ottoman empire. In the post-war period this has been replaced by a heavy movement from the rural areas of Anatolia.

In spite of the initial intention to plan the development of Ankara, population growth has been so rapid that no real attempts have been made to control the sprawl of construction until the last ten years. Most newcomers were unable to find or afford housing through the semi-official agencies which existed and so built their own housing on any available land, whether it was private or public. These squatter houses are described in Turkish as *gecekondu*, which literally means 'built overnight', and once established they were legally difficult to remove. The initial *gecekondu* settlements were around the centre of the old town, Eski Ankara, on the steep-sided hills which surround the medieval citadel. As squatter momentum grew, so the *gecekondu* settlements spread to the more open, rolling slopes around the city proper. Many of these outer areas had the additional advantage of being beyond municipal jurisdiction so that no planning controls existed in relation to the location or quality of the building. The first real attempt to control the spread of *gecekondu* settlement came in 1966 during the first Five Year Plan which empowered municipalities throughout Turkey to clear or improve squatter areas, or to prepare special 'prevention sites' in which self-help schemes would be promoted for the benefit of evicted or newly arrived households. In Ankara, however, the cost of pursuing these objectives and the sheer scale of squatter settlement has resulted in little positive action. More than 50,000 new *gecekondu* houses have been built since 1966 although the law expressly forbids such construction.

As a result of the uncontrolled settlement pattern, almost two-thirds of Ankara's population is estimated to live in *gecekondu* housing. It was noted in Chapter 2 that in collated international statistics this is inaccurately assumed to represent the slum or squatter population, but the reality of the situation is very different. None of the *gecekondu* residents live in slums, which are located almost entirely in Eski Ankara and comprise less than 2 per cent of the city's population. Of the remaining *gecekondu* houses few are completely illegal in the sense that they occupy land without permission and fail to meet building regulations. It has been an increasing practice in Ankara to give *de jure* or *de facto* recognition to *gecekondu* areas by granting land rights, imposing taxes or contructing roads. These activities have tended to occur prior to elections, notably during the last ten years when the two major political parties in Turkey became evenly balanced in the national parliament.

Important differences exist in the nature of this recognition, particularly between the old central settlements and the newer peripheral ones. Several of the central *gecekondu* districts around the citadel received their rights as a by-product of an enactment of 1953 relating to general land use. As a result of this law the inhabitants became legal occupants of the land on which their houses were built but were prevented by other legislation from improving the properties themselves. The effect has been to freeze most of the inner *gecekondu* houses in a state of dilapidation. In contrast, there were few laws which affected peripheral squatters and many had legally bought plots in the area in which they settled. Unfortunately the absence of detailed cadastral maps has meant that precise location and therefore complete legality has been difficult to establish. Nevertheless, most of the newer *gecekondu* units in the peripheral areas have been built as near to legal standards as possible and constitute very different housing units from those in the central areas. A more detailed examination of the contrasts which exist in Ankara reveals the wide-ranging problems that 'squatter' settlements can pose for planners in the Third World (Figure 3.6).

Figure 3.6: Ankara: *Gecekondu* Household Characteristics, 1974

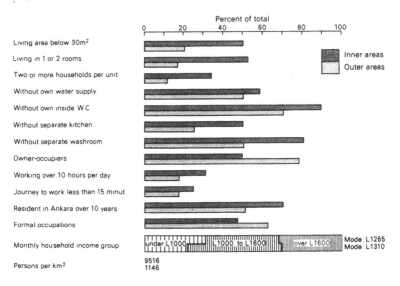

One of the older districts in central Ankara is Altindag, which ironically means 'golden hill', a steep-sided area to the north of the citadel which contains more than 50,000 people, over two-thirds of whom live in wooden *gecekondu* units (Plate 3). Living conditions within the area are very crowded in terms of both ground and housing densities whilst the majority of households lack adequate water supply, toilet, cooking and washing facilities. Although there is a sizeable minority of more recent arrivals, most of the families are long-term residents of Ankara, more than half having lived in Altindag itself for over ten years. The low rents in the area and the proximity to job opportunities in the city centre were the main attractions for the residents. This is borne out by the occupational structure which emphasises employment in petty commerce, such as hawking, and in service activities, such as *dolmus* (shared taxi) driving.

Very different conditions are found in Dikmen and Etlik, two of the extensive peripheral squatter areas. Almost 90 per cent of the accommodation here is solidly constructed from stone or brick and is much more spacious, internally and environmentally, than housing in Altindag (Plate 4). In addition, the great majority of these units are self-contained with regard to washing, toilet and cooking facilities. The deficiencies in the outer districts are mainly infrastructural, a consequence of their relative newness and distance from the city proper. A large number of houses therefore have no electricity, sewerage or water connections and arrangements for rubbish disposal are poor. Despite these defects areas such as Dikmen and Etlik are popular with new migrants. Almost half of the residents had lived in Ankara for less than ten years, most coming directly from villages located outside Ankara province. In contrast, the older migrants of Altindag were more likely to have come from the towns nearer to Ankara. This indicates an important shift in migration patterns over recent years as improved communications have facilitated both the diffusion of news and the movement of people. Although Dikmen and Etlik have only recently been settled, their occupational structures differ markedly from those usually assumed to exist in such areas. Almost all of the households heads are in regular, full-time employment in either factories or offices. Many of these jobs involve considerable travel and almost one-third of the workers face journeys to work of at least two hours each day.

Ankara clearly contains two very different types of *gecekondu* settlement, a feature recognised by the residents themselves. At least ∩ne-quarter of the households in Dikmen and Etlik formerly lived in the central areas and had moved out in order to obtain better accommodation. The socio-economic contrasts between the inner and outer *gecekondu* areas are such as to pose many problems for a government attempting to deal positively with such settlements. If the disorderly sprawl of Ankara is to be curbed, it is evident that the benign indifference which has existed to date in lieu of effective policies must cease. On the other hand, the *laissez-faire* policies have enabled diligent families to create for themselves a reasonably satisfactory living environment, although problems of confused tenure and deficient infrastructure remain to challenge government planning programmes. But it is the older central *gecekondu* communities which pose the most complicated problems since any improvement must involve some property demolition and hence resettlement. Whilst the affected residents of these areas might favour improved credit facilities as a means of obtaining better housing, it is evident that some form of direct government contribution is necessary to help the poorer families. What form this contribution should take is difficult to determine at present because so little information is available on either the character of the squatter populations concerned or the capacity of the various sectors of the building industry.

There is little point in discussing some of the more detailed aspects of *gecekondu* improvement in Ankara when the positive elements of existing legislation have yet to be executed with any great enthusiasm. The current *ad hoc* response by both the government and the squatters has produced a not unsatisfactory situation which both sides seem content to accept. But the urban poor in Ankara, and indeed in Turkey as a whole, have not yet become fully aware of the political power which they hold in the existing evenly balanced parliamentary system. The minimal pre-election improvement manoeuvres which are now used to win votes will soon be recognised for their true worth by a new generation of *gecekondu* residents who are beginning to realise how little the city has given their families over the last two decades. The very names of some of the *gecekondu* districts reflect this new determination — Yigitler (the courageous), Caliskanlar (the hardworking) and Yilmazlar (the undaunted). The present situation thus represents a short breathing space during which new realistic policies must be formulated for the future.

4 SLUMS

Introduction

As there is no straightforward legal definition of a slum, this form of low-income housing is much more difficult to identify than squatter settlements. Most urban authorities do have some operational rules by which houses are classified as substandard but the concept of habitability differs for virtually each individual and makes aggregate comparison of housing standards a somewhat futile exercise (see Fraser 1969). This is true of both international and intranational comparisons involving the Third World. In these circumstances it is perhaps not surprising that the popular image of the slum often relates less to the physical fabric of the dwelling itself and more to the assumed nature of the environment and the associated lifestyle of the inhabitants. This is not altogether undesirable because it does focus attention on the character of slums as well as on the processes involved in their formation and persistence rather than on the traditional, but more restricted, geographical concern with spatial variation in physical features (Peet 1977).

David Ward (1976) has argued persuasively that most contemporary attitudes on the nature and origin of slums are derived from the Victorian era. During this period slum dwellers came to be considered in social and spatial terms as an isolated group whose separation was attributed variously to preferred deviance, the rejection of the work ethic, and other such anti-social values. These views undoubtedly persist today so that even the most 'liberal' approaches still define the spatial characteristics of the slum poor in terms of their distinction from the rest of society, thus implying that slums require 'special' solutions, such as clearance and renewal. Perhaps even worse are the attempts to identify subgroups of 'worthy' or 'organised poor' who, because they are clearly attempting to emulate 'established' values, should receive favoured treatment in both physical and social planning.

The popularity of the view that inner slums comprise areas of permanent poverty rife with structural, social and sanitary disorder, has ensured its rapid transference to developing countries. Thus Portes (1971:239), in a not untypical passage, has described urban slums in Chile as housing 'the poorest of the poor . . . the unemployed, the unskilled, and illiterate, and often the alcoholic, the vagabond and the delinquent . . . the slum and its inhabitants have both reached dead-

end situations . . . a refuge of ultimate destitution'. Whilst there is a
little truth in this observation, it presents a grossly distorted picture of
most slum communities in developing countries – a criticism which
this chapter will substantiate in a detailed examination of both the
evolutionary process and the nature of contemporary 'slums' in the
Third World.

The Evolution of Slums

In developed countries most images of slums are derived from the
recent historical past through the literature of the last century, but
slums have proliferated on many previous occasions whenever intense
population pressure has stretched urban resources. Such conditions
existed in medieval Europe and many historians have described the
subdivision of property and high rents which characterised contemporary cities (Mumford 1961, Smith 1967, Russell 1972). The London
of Chaucer's time was thus redolent of many cities of Asia today:

> The streets were ill-paved and had no side-walks; the crown of the
> causeway sloped down on both sides to the kennels into which
> the filth ran; weaker passengers . . . went to the wall and splashed
> through the mud. Too little checked by municipal authority, house-
> holds and tradesmen threw their garbage, litter and offal into the
> street from doors and windows (Trevelyan 1966:76).

Although similar conditions existed in the centres of most large
cities it was not until the Industrial Revolution that such unhealthy
and congested areas became physically and socially dominant. This
period has exerted considerable attraction for urban historians in
Europe and North America but, whilst a large corpus of informative
literature now exists (see for example Ward 1971, 1976), the most
vivid descriptions of prevailing conditions are still those of contemporary writers.

Although the conditions of nineteenth-century European and
American cities have many parallels in the urban slums of the Third
World, there are substantial differences in the demographic, social and
economic characteristics of the populations involved. In industrialising
Europe and North America, transport innovations such as the urban
railway, the tramcar and the omnibus had precipitated a flight to
suburbia by the middle classes who abandoned their centrally located

houses to unscrupulous landlords and desperately poor families. In contrast, in the cities of the Third World a large proportion of the middle classes, particularly those engaged in commerce, still live adjacent to their workplaces in the city centre. In this respect the contemporary situation in Asia or Latin America has a good deal in common with the pre-industrial cities of medieval Europe.

However, irrespective of the areas from which the imagery of the slum emanates, there was, and still is, implicit in almost all of the literature a sense that the urban poor had brought these conditions upon themselves by ignorance, idleness or choice. The Malthusian view of the poor in the nineteenth century was that they constituted a surplus population which, if it could not be made useful and productive, should be allowed to 'starve to death in the least objectionable way', consequently reducing the number of children born into poverty (Engels 1892:309). The living conditions and poverty of the urban poor were thus symptomatic of the dialectic philosophy of industrial society in Western Europe.

This relationship between housing standards and poverty is one which has persisted to the present, together with the associated view that the socio-spatial segregation of the urban poor is deliberately chosen. Muth (1969), for instance, has noted that when low-income families are forced to curb their expenditure housing is frequently the first component to suffer. Less money spent on accommodation means that a smaller space is obtained, producing overcrowding and excessive demands on communal facilities. Muth has thus claimed that 'low grade occupancy' is part of the preferred expenditure pattern for impoverished families and consequently represents an optimal resource use for slum housing. He fails to appreciate that this 'preference' occurs within a financial framework which is already subject to severe socio-economic constraints, a factor which McGee (1976a) clearly illustrates in his study of expenditure strategies adopted by the urban poor in the Third World. Even in developed countries Muth's view has been refuted by many critics. Rothenberg (1967), for example, argued that slums in the American context represent an inefficient market response which is artificially maintained by landlords, or by questionable activities such as ethnic discrimination; an opinion which has been supported by more recent radical literature on this subject (for example Harvey 1973, Castells 1977).

These contrasting views on the nature of slum poverty have been important factors in the development of urban housing policies in both developed and developing countries. If one accepts the existence of a permanent subculture of poor people, then investment in the direct improvement of slum housing seems to be virtually a waste of money; on the other hand, the argument that the poor are the socio-economic residue of an acquisitive, affluent, capitalist bourgeoisie means that housing investment is less useful than the provision of greater job and educational opportunities. In most developing countries arguments such as these are eagerly accepted by governments already reluctant to invest in 'non-productive' housing schemes, but this eclectic approach makes a gross simplification on the nature of the relationship between poverty and housing in the cities of the Third World. In the same way that Gans (1972) has broadened the base of urban poverty studies by stressing the interaction between poor and non-poor society, so any attempt to understand the real nature of urban slums in developing countries must break away from the assumption that all dilapidated central tenements are inhabited by poor families.

There is, of course, no denying that a strong general relationship exists between slums and poverty. This has emerged very clearly in the relatively few studies of slums which have taken place over the last two decades (for example see Kaye 1960, Yeh and Lee 1968, Drakakis-Smith 1977, Leeming 1977). Nevertheless, as the case studies in this chapter will illustrate, the central districts of most cities contain a wide range of family and income groups. The process of slum formation in developing countries is generally more complex than in the West, one of the most important differences being the role played by chief tenants in the leasing system. The widespread use of rent control in the Third World has meant that the minor landlords, particularly of older buildings, often receive insufficient returns to maintain their property in an adequate state of repair. On the other hand, subletting is usually unaffected by legislation so that the bulk of subtenants are still subject to profiteering despite the deteriorating condition of their accommodation.

This situation has been a notable feature of the chinatowns of Southeast Asia where it has been facilitated by the subdivision of rented property into cubicles. Such arrangements were known as *t'ang-lou* and were particularly characteristic of tenement buildings in which the chief tenants were able to rent entire floors. Leeming (1977) has noted that within the system of subletting the original intention was probably not to make a profit so much as to reduce high outlays on rent and services whilst still retaining the best portion of the leased unit. Rapid population growth and the introduction of rent control by expatriate administrators changed this situation into one where the returns to chief tenants were huge in comparison to expenditure. At the height of demand for accommodation profits are often further increased by requests for premiums, known by various euphemisms, to be paid by prospective occupiers. In addition, tenements particularly close to major sources of employment frequently contain leased bed-spaces occupied in succession by single men working shifts.

Proximity to work is, in fact, the key to the success of this entire system. Minimum space rents for maximum returns in the central areas because of the employment and business opportunities available. Ironic-ally, the rigidities of rent control enable maximum profits to be made in the oldest properties. In some cities, such as Singapore or Hong Kong, the situation has now been eased by controlled immigration, the construction of large amounts of government housing and a gradual easing of rent control. In addition, most of the new multistorey private construction is based on the Western style of separate, self-contained flats sold to individual owners. Of course, this does not prevent sub-letting which still occurs on a wide scale even in relatively new apart-ments, particularly those with provision for the construction of internal partitioning. Indeed, the deliberate construction of new buildings for intensive subdivision and high occupation densities is one way in which 'instant' slums have been created and in parts of Asia this has not been uncommon. Typically, such investment has been popular with capital-ists either when housing has promised rapid returns *vis-à-vis* alternative sources of profit, or during periods of general investment surplus.

The latter conditions have in the past often prevailed in countries dependent on primary production during periods of high prices and profitability. Thus in Colombo, Sri Lanka, tenement housing has been a popular area of investment for local capitalists who have not been able to break into the more lucrative fields of plantation invest-ment (Marga Institute 1976). The euphemistically termed 'tenement gardens' subsequently built in Colombo usually consisted of rows of two-roomed units with communal water and sanitary facilities. The introduction of rent control and recessions in the plantation industries reduced profitability and the propensity for maintenance. This type of housing now constitutes some of the worst slums in the city, accommo-dating over 22 per cent of Colombo's population – almost as many as its squatter settlements.

A similar climate of profitability has developed in cities affected by large influxes of urban refugees, for example in Hong Kong following the Chinese Civil War. During the 1950s when refugee pressure on the colony was at its height and the public housing programme had barely begun, new legislation was enacted to encourage private sector residential construction by permitting increased ground densities and reducing the legal complexities involved. However, little attention was paid to the provision of services and amenities so that the result was a plethora of densely crowded high-rise tenements, shoddily built, intensively subdivided, but much more expensive than the existing accommodation.

In recent years there seems to have been a trend away from such construction, at least in some of the cities characterised by rapid economic growth. Unfortunately this is not the consequence of a capitalist conscience, rather it is the result of changes in residential preferences by the middle-income groups who appear to be placing increasing emphasis on the more 'spacious' Western style of accommodation as an indicator of social status. This tendency has been encouraged in some cities by legislation designed to improve the standard of facilities in new buildings. As a result, central residential developments are increasingly taking the form of relatively large, undivided flats occupied by a single, but not necessarily nuclear, family. The trend does not adversely affect the developers themselves since it is simply an alternative use of internal space. In fact, by discouraging subdivision the process is increasing the overall demand for accommodation, thus pushing up prices and profits. Of course, middle-income families are not a new or recent phenomenon in the central areas of Third World cities. They have long been a feature of such districts but it is only in recent years that residential developments have begun to reflect their presence. Previously these households competed with the poor for minimum standard accommodation, thereby contributing to the relatively high rents.

It is evident, therefore, that slums in developing countries are affected by complex mixes of social, economic and political forces which, in many instances, differ markedly from those operating in the West. It is equally clear that any attempt to understand the situation must proceed through an analysis which abandons many of the precepts of the Western approach. However, as the following sections will show, this change in emphasis has been slow to emerge.

Quantitative and Qualitative Aspects of Slums

One of the major avenues of research on slums in the First World has been the attempt to define substandardness and thus quantify the extent of the slum problem in any location. Since the 1920s, when welfare housing programmes began to emerge in the West, almost all quantitative assessments of housing have been couched in terms of the physical quality of the dwelling and its component parts. The human element has been incorporated into the calculations only as a symbol, for example in numbers per room or per toilet. As assessments of fitness can and do vary within developed countries then the cross-cultural application of selected standards to the cities in the Third World is futile. Whilst this seems fairly obvious it is precisely what has happened, and is happening, throughout Asia, Africa and Latin America. Colonial administrators introduced the standards related to their own metropolitan countries and personal values, and enshrined them in local legislation. Although most colonial regimes have now been politically superseded, the old building and planning regulations are still on the statute books and are strongly upheld by the now indigenous elites who aspire to the standards of the former metropolitan countries in which they are likely to have been educated.

Any serious attempt to assess urban housing standards in the Third World must obviously abandon such unrealistic measures and adopt more flexible criteria which seek to avoid cultural bias. One method is to devise a standardised scale from graded or ranked measurements of individual items of fitness obtained for specific areas, such as census districts or neighbourhoods. This permits a choice of fitness levels appropriate to the particular local situation and makes intra-urban rather than inter-urban comparisons. Such a system has recently been adopted in Hong Kong in order to evaluate the metropolitan housing stock within the colony and identify areas worthy of government attention (Pryor 1975). However, it is difficult for any standardised scaling system to incorporate much more than the measurable elements of the physical quality of the dwelling itself; this raises the question of what constitutes 'habitability' even in the context of one particular city. It has already been noted that the concept must be culturally relative in both space and time in order to possess any validity. But in addition to the instrinsic and environmental factors, consideration must also be given to what Fraser (1969) has referred to as the extrinsic elements which influence their appraisal. Onibokun (1973) has taken this a stage further and identified four subsystems of habitability which all focus on the tenant as the recipient of feedback from the other subsystems. Unfortunately, Onibokun's own model does not illustrate this centripetal emphasis particularly well.

In short, the resident himself is the ultimate arbiter of habitability and in the context of the Third World this arbitration involves a wide range of values. Accommodation may be assessed, for example, in relation to the location of potential employment, to anticipated changes in income or family size, to the ethnic character of a particular district or to personal cultural values. A migrant to Kuala Lumpur, therefore, may well select accommodation in a Chinese tenement neighbourhood more for its proximity to the central business district rather than for its rent, size or amenities. On the other hand, Australian Aborigines often find less privacy in a conventional house than in their traditional bush camps where rigid social *mores* afford such protection. It follows that the statistical evaluation of slums, although providing basic planning data, is insufficient on its own and needs to be supplemented by a more humanistic evaluation if sympathetic and practical policies are to be formulated. The problem is how to structure such a qualitative investigation since individual slums can vary enormously in character even within the same city. Certainly at the international level massive contrasts exist. This can be illustrated by briefly comparing the characteristics of the main types of slum districts in two culturally distinct regions – the *medinas* of the Middle East and the shophouse tenements of Southeast Asia.

The Medinas *of the Middle East*

The long urban history of the Middle East and North Africa has strongly affected the morphology of its cities (Costello 1977, Blake and Lawless 1980). Until the European colonisation of the last century most urban centres were compactly contained within defensive walls with their central districts, themselves the nucleus of earlier settlements, spatially organised on the basis of kinship, ethnicity and occupation rather than socio-economic class. The colonial era saw these old cities, or *medinas*, redesignated as 'native' quarters, often separated by a *cordon sanitaire* from the newer suburbs of the alien elites. Migrational growth was crowded into the *medinas* and soon caused a movement by the more affluent residents to other parts of the city. The families that found it easiest to relocate were those linked to the colonial power structure, such as the Cairene Copts or the Maghrebian Jews. Their places were taken by newer and poorer arrivals to the city so that by the 1920s the 'proletarianisation' of the *medinas* was virtually complete and the process of *taudification*, or slum creation, had begun. At present the *medina* slums of the largest cities in the region are indistinguishable from slums elsewhere in the Third World in terms of densities and overcrowding. In the old city of Tunis, for example, 28,000 households occupy only 15,000 dwellings and the ground densities are four times those of the city as a whole (Ben Mahmoud and Santelli 1974).

It is unwise to generalise too much about the *medinas* of Middle Eastern and North African cities. Although there are certain common features, there is by no means a stereotypical pattern of *medina* deterioration and the nature of physical change has depended largely on the pace of economic growth, together with the cultural and political character of the country as a whole. Thus in parts of the Maghreb and Arabia the old cities have retained their traditional vigour and organisation but in some of the larger cities of the region they have all but disappeared beneath burgeoning commercial redevelopment or intensive residential overcrowding. This latter process is well illustrated in Cairo where the old medieval city still houses almost half a million people (Abu-Lughod 1971). The situation appears to have reached saturation point at present and the population has risen little over the last decade compared to other parts of the capital. The buildings in the old city are generally run-down and dilapidated (Plate 5) and their inhabitants poor even by Egyptian standards. However, whilst it is a very traditional quarter in many respects, the old city is thoroughly urban with thousands of small-scale commercial and industrial activities intermingled with the densely crowded residential units. Although some of the more traditional *suqs*, such as that of the sword-makers, have faded, many still persist and those selling precious metals, carpets and fine cloths have developed into modern tourist attractions. Yet only a few metres away from these newly patronised commercial centres are some of the worst slums in the city.

The physical deterioration of the old central districts in Middle Eastern and North African cities has not been synchronised with the change in residential and commercial functions. On the one hand, these extensive areas of dendritic, narrow lanes are regarded as an obstacle to efficient urban transportation planning; on the other, they usually contain the most valued architectural and cultural heritage of the city. Until recent years 'modernisation' was the dominant force in urban planning with the result that regular networks of broad roads were often forced through the old cities of the region, completely destroying the intricate network of physical and social relationships which existed (Figure 4.1). The emergence of tourism as a major source of income has changed this situation and posed a serious planning dilemma in relation to *medina* redevelopment. The conflict between the desire to modernise and renovate has now to be balanced against both the need to conserve areas of historic and tourist value, as well as the

Figure 4.1: Isfahan: Land Use in the *Medina*

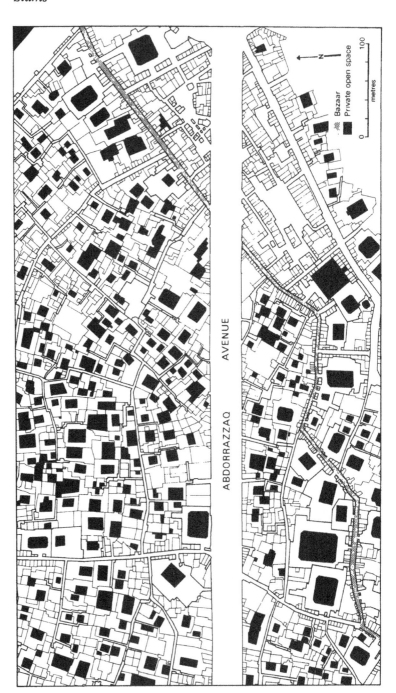

demand for low-cost housing. As yet there have been few attempts to resolve seriously this situation other than to 'modernise' the areas with tourist potential. At its heart the problem is not merely an architectural one of refurbishing old buildings, there are deeper cultural conflicts within the urban societies of the Middle East. At the top are the Westernised, educated elites who regard traditional values and their physical manifestation as obsolescent; below are a mass of urban poor for whom the old way of life, organised around an interior courtyard, is still very important — a clear indication that housing problems and their amelioration cannot be divorced from the wider issues involved in development as a whole.

Shophouse Tenements in Southeast Asia

In contrast to the Middle East and North Africa, many of the largest cities in Southeast Asia have only a short history because they were essentially the creations of the colonial trading system which developed in the eighteenth and nineteenth centuries. Their urban morphologies are less reflective of local historical or cultural traditions, and more a function of practical commercial development. The architecturally distinctive buildings are those of the metropolitan culture. Almost all of the primate cities of Southeast Asia are ports and during their growth they have experienced and benefited from a constant stream of migrants from China anxious to participate in the commercial expansion of the compradore cities. As a result each has its chinatown, a crowded, congested central district bustling with economic and social activity, all of which usually takes place within a crumbling, dilapidated physical setting (Plate 6). In many ways the physical fabric of Southeast Asia's chinatowns is the result of their commercial success which has constantly attracted more migrants into already crowded districts. On the other hand, chinatowns have seldom received much attention or investment from indigenous governments who are anxious not to be seen to be favouring alien populations in urban renewal programmes.

As Figure 4.2 illustrates, there is a remarkable degree of consistency in the construction and utilisation of shophouse tenements in Southeast Asia both through space and time. The long, narrow sites are supposedly the consequence of the size of the original structural timber, the China fir pole, which was usually about four metres long, although it is unclear why this should have spread to areas where other types of timber were used. Within this physical constraint most shophouses had a length to breadth ratio of about 3:1 and were two to four storeys high.

Figure 4.2: Space Utilisation in Tenement Floors

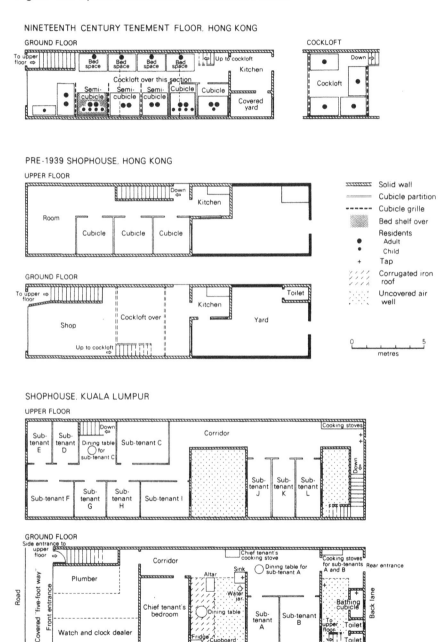

Ground floors were usually given over to commercial use, with the shopowner and his family often living in a specially built 'mezzanine' floor, or cockloft, over the shop. The upper storeys were rented out for residential use, although domestic industries and service activities, such as brothels, were not uncommon. Chief tenants normally rented an entire tenement floor, retaining a reasonable portion of it for themselves and subletting the remainder as cubicles with perhaps a few bed spaces beneath the staircase. Cubicle partitions do not reach the ceiling and although wire mesh was often added for security, there was little privacy between the units.

On average cubicles were only about 2.5m^2 but sometimes housed families of six or seven persons. Jackson (1975) reports that the shophouse tenements in Singapore and Malaysia usually contained three to four families, giving a total population of 20 to 30 people per dwelling. But the figures often rose much higher in the densely populated central streets of the chinatown. Most of the tenements built during the present century had toilet, kitchen and washing facilities on each floor, although in earlier buildings these might have been restricted to one floor only. The facilities did not resemble their Western counterparts very closely, often consisting merely of an open space, sometimes enclosed, with a tap. The kitchen was thus distinguishable from the bathing area only by the presence of stoves rather than tin baths. Few of the cubicles had access to windows, the chief tenants tending to monopolise these, so that ventilation and lighting were poor. Although individual living units were kept neat and clean, communal areas and corridors were not and vermin were common. It was necessary therefore to suspend food and clothing in baskets from the ceiling joists.

Appalling as these conditions appear to Westerners, they comprised the normal, accepted living environment for the great majority of Chinese families throughout Southeast Asia until long after the Second World War. This implies that assessment in terms of physical conditions alone, particularly culturally biased assessment, is inadequate and that in order truly to appreciate the role of the slum in the lives of the urban poor it is necessary to examine its functions *vis-à-vis* the individual and the city as a whole.

The Functions of the Slum

Charles Stokes (1962) wrote that 'the function of the slum at any one moment in city development is to house those classes which do not participate directly in the economic and social life of the city'. This view is closely analogous to the concepts of squatter marginality which were discussed and discredited in the previous chapter. However, the disparaging assessments of slum life have been much more persistent and investigators have seemed reluctant to apply to slums the new ideas and values which evolved from the study of their squatter counterparts.

Perhaps the major influence in the formation and consolidation of this approach has been Oscar Lewis (1966) who popularised the term 'culture of poverty'. Lewis takes great pains to point out that not all poor people are part of the culture of poverty, attributing even to ordinary poverty a relatively high degree of social organisation and an integrated and self-sufficient culture. It is, however, extremely difficult in Lewis's empirical writings to distinguish between those families who fall into the culture of poverty and those who do not; this has formed the basis of many of the criticisms of his work. A large number of the features which Lewis claimed characterise the culture of poverty are denied by examples from real life, even those selected by Lewis himself. Such discrepancies are extremely important in understanding the fuller nature of urban slums in the Third World, for although Lewis does not confine his theories to slums, and in fact uses the term very loosely, most of his case studies were carried out in such areas, in the *vecidades* of Mexico City and the tenement *barrios* of San Juan, Puerto Rico.

Despite its faults, the notion of the culture of poverty has exerted considerable influence over the last decade on conceptual thought relating to slums. Simply by directing attention to the hitherto neglected study of slums within the wider urban context, Lewis had performed an important function, and yet some of the more detailed aspects of his work have given rise to misleading and misinterpreted notions on the nature of slum life. The remainder of this section will critically examine these assertions largely as they relate to a comprehensive but contentious study of Singaporean slums by Iain Buchanan (1972).

One of the main characteristics alleged to be typical of households caught in the culture of poverty is their limited integration with major institutions within the wider urban society. Whether this is through fear, ignorance, apathy or discrimination, the slum poor supposedly have minimal involvement with unions or political parties, and make little use of organisations such as banks, department stores or hospitals. Whilst not denying this isolation, Buchanan claims that in Singapore it has enhanced the sense of unity amongst the poor who look inwards to their own community for help and support. The labour exchange is therefore ignored as a means of finding employment in favour of personal contacts, many of which lead into illegal activities such as unlicensed hawking. In Singapore, however, the self-contained-ness has been translated into political terms since the more radical, left-wing parties reputedly have a strong hold amongst the poor Chinese in the tenement slums. This phenomenon contrasts markedly with the general political apathy attributed to those in the culture of poverty.

The second major trait which Lewis attributes to the slum poor is the economic insignificance of the individual who is alleged to produce little wealth and receive little in return. Unemployment, underemploy-ment and low wages are said to give rise to a situation where savings are small or non-existent, purchases are made daily in small quantities and consequently at higher prices, and indebtedness is common. This condition of shared poverty in which many people exist on tiny incomes is undoubtedly widespread in both slum and squatter communities, but it would be a mistake to assume that because output and remuneration for particular jobs are low, general productivity or earnings must be correspondingly limited. Household incomes are supplemented in a variety of ways with most members of the family engaged in some form of gainful employment. Nor is work necessarily restricted to the informal or traditional sector. Occupations such as domestic service, retailing, domestic manufacturing and transportation all take the participants outside their own slum district and into the wider, urban economic system. This economic contact is also mirrored to a certain extent in the consumer purchasing patterns of the slum poor. Although possessions may be minimal and acquired through expensive hire-purchase schemes, they usually include items such as radios, sewing machines, refrigerators and occasionally televisions – all of which reflect the materialism of Singaporean society as a whole.

At the group level within the culture of poverty there is alleged to be minimal organisational ability outside the nuclear family. In this respect the findings in Singapore, particularly for the Chinese slum communi-ties, vary widely from Lewis's theoretical concepts. Many different types of functional clusters may be identified in Singaporean slums – economic groups, such as guilds and *tontine* (loan) clubs, social organisations such as the secret societies or *tongs*, and various cultural associations bound by ties of clan, dialect or place of origin. Such groupings are not confined to Singapore and feature prominently in slums throughout the Third World particularly amongst single men, those vanguards of more permanent family moves who, in theory, should be the least organised but who, in fact, eagerly seek out regional, economic and religious groups with which they can associate.

The last and perhaps most controversial of Lewis's assertions on the culture of poverty is that the majority of individuals affected by it experience feelings of fatalism, helplessness and inferiority which resign them to their disadvantaged life. Furthermore, Lewis asserts that these attitudes are passed on to the children, implying that such slums are self-perpetuating. This statement, if it is true, brings the argument full circle back to the Malthusian proposition of the poor constituting a surplus population who cannot be helped out of their poverty. Fortunately the evidence collected to date on the motivations, aspirations and ambitions which exist within slum districts belies the case for such widespread anomie. Nelson (1969), in a collation analysis of previous studies in Latin America, has suggested that progress within and movement out of the lowest economic strata indicate that modest occupational mobility and probably other types of progress are fairly widely distributed and that psychologically this progress is extremely important. Moreover, the Latin American evidence indicates that children who are born into the urban slum are even more likely than their parents to move out of the lower echelons of the urban hierarchy because they are aware of their underprivileged position in society and respond aggressively rather than in silent resignation. It is significant that one study in Buenos Aires indicated that 83 per cent of city-born sons of unskilled fathers had managed to move out of this occupational category.

Whilst these criticisms of the culture of poverty may seem a little severe, it must be admitted that many of the traits described by Lewis do exist and his theories draw attention to the fact that the urban poor live a distinctive lifestyle, responding resourcefully to the difficulties which face each family. However, whilst the slum community is a socially and economically distinct entity within the Third World city, it is not as isolated nor as uniformly depressed as the culture of poverty theory would suggest. In many ways this misjudgement is the product of an attitudinal block similar to that which affected squatter assessment for so long, viz. that visible, physical dilapidation is assumed to have parallels in all other aspects of slum life. Buchanan, although openly admiring the resourcefulness and economic vitality of Singaporean squatters, still concludes that they are socially and economically marginal. Gans (1969), in contrast, has suggested that the behavioural traits of even the long-term poor are formulated by their attempt and failure to live up to the moral, legal and economic standards of the affluent society generally.

Perhaps the most important links between slums and wider urban society as a whole are economic. Slums in the Third World tend to be located near to the central business districts where maximum employment opportunities are generated, particularly in the informal or service sectors. These opportunities not only attract the urban poor and the new migrants but strongly influence the residential patterns of almost all persons engaged in commercial enterprises, including the middle-income groups. As the following case studies will illustrate, the slum districts of most cities in developing countries contain a large proportion of non-poor households. For those engaged directly in central area enterprises, this location has specific economic advantages. However, many other middle-income families live in slum housing because no other suitable alternative exists. In cities where the benefits of government housing programmes are restricted to civil or military servants, to the very low-income groups or to squatters, middle-income households frequently face enormous difficulties in finding what they regard as suitable accommodation. Private construction firms usually build for the commercial, industrial or upper-income residential market so that middle-income families find themselves in a barren zone between the public and the private sector.

A great deal of the character of the so-called slums of the Third World is thus derived, not from any inherent culture of poverty nor from the ingenious responses of the underprivileged urban poor in general, but simply from the very range of households and individuals who live within the tenements and the way they interact with the rest of the city. The ensuing case studies have been chosen to illustrate precisely these points. The first describes the old city of Ankara, thus complementing and building upon the analysis of *gecekondu* settlements in the previous chapter. The second examines an inner-city tenement district in Hong Kong and constitutes the first of two case studies from the colony, the second of which will appear in Chapter Five.

Case Studies

Eski Ankara

Eski (old) Ankara is essentially the original town which was selected to be the capital of the new Turkish Republic in 1923 (Figure 4.3). Its focal point is the *kale* or citadel, the steep, surrounding slopes of which were covered with small, predominantly wooden houses built in traditional village style. With the expansion of population in Ankara during

the inter-war period the houses in the old city experienced a process of
subdivision and, in some cases, extension, but the limited size of the old
quarter prevented the emergence of a large slum district. Eski Ankara is
not the only slum district in the capital nor does it consist entirely of
dilapidated housing. To the northwest it is bounded by the old
commercial focus of Ulus and to the south by the even more traditional
Samanpazaar (Haymarket). Both of these commercial centres still
flourish and infuse Eski Ankara with extensive non-residential
buildings. In addition the western boundary is gradually being redeveloped for modern commercial and administrative buildings whilst
in the southeast areas have been cleared during the construction of
Hacettepe University and its associated park, a deliberate *cordon
sanitaire* between the intellectuals and the slum residents.

Figure 4.3: Ankara: Urban Growth, 1923 to 1975

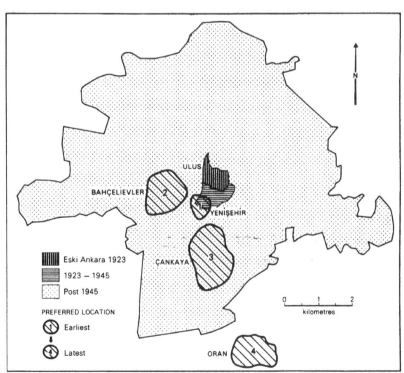

Eski Ankara is not large and in 1965 contained about 58,000 people
or 6.5 per cent of the total city population at that time. Since then the
population has slightly declined as commercial redevelopment has taken
place and its proportion of the total urban population had dropped to

around 4.5 per cent by 1976. In general the buildings are much older than their inhabitants with more than half of the houses erected at least forty-five years ago. The proportion is much higher in the inner residential heart of Eski Ankara around the citadel, where 76 per cent of the houses were built before 1930. Not all of the houses are of traditional construction and at least one-quarter are fully or part *gecekondu*.

Whilst ground densities are reasonably high at 8,400 per square kilometre they are in no way comparable to those which occur in Asian or Latin American slums. Superficially, Eski Ankara would seem overcrowded (Figure 4.4), with about 40 per cent of the dwelling units containing two or more families and over one-third of all households living within one or two rooms, but in comparison with either the old or the new *gecekondu* districts Eski Ankara offers a much better living environment since rooms and houses are generally larger whilst families are smaller. Thus only 49 per cent of the slum households have less than ten square metres per person compared to 65 per cent and 74 per cent in the new and old *gecekondu* districts respectively.

Figure 4.4: Eski Ankara: Household Characteristics, 1974

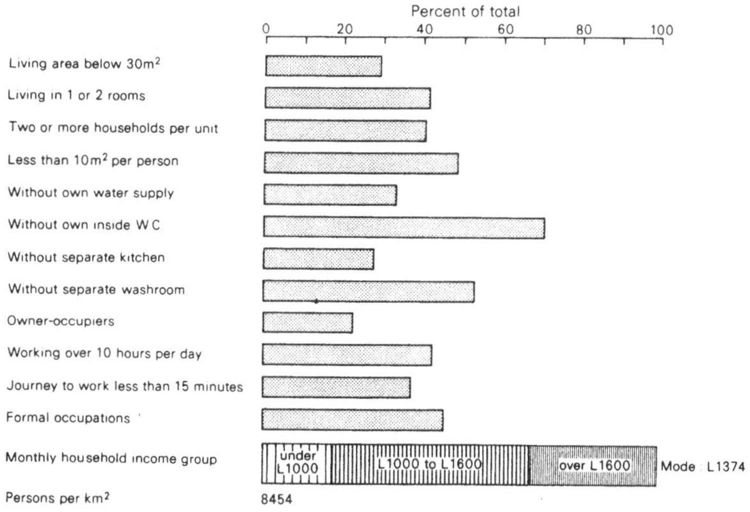

The great majority of the families who live in Eski Ankara rent their accommodation and the proportion of owner-occupiers has been dropping steadily since migration pressures began to increase during the 1950s. Most of the residents initially settled here because of the proximity to work and low rents, but rents are currently cheaper in the squatter areas. Whilst the cost of housing in Eski Ankara is not low in

absolute terms, the proximity of the slum to employment opportunities in both the old and the new commercial districts has made it
acceptably low to the residents. Moreover, the higher proportion of
rentable accommodation in Eski Ankara provides an additional attraction for newcomers to the city. Keles (1971) has shown that considerable movement occurs between houses within the district; this indicates
the range of accommodation which exists both in size and cost,
enabling households to adjust relatively easily to changes in their social
and economic circumstances.

There is a wide range of occupations represented in Eski Ankara
(Figure 4.4) with white-collar administrative jobs being just as important as the more traditional informal sector employment, such as carpen-
try or carpet-making. The single most important source of employment
is in commerce, with relatively wealthy merchants and shopkeepers
being as numerous as those in the more informal occupations such as
street peddling. Because of the nature of employment in Eski Ankara
there is a tendency for its residents to live near their workplace and to
work for much longer hours, even in the formal occupational sectors
such as the public service or manufacturing. The range and the diversity
of occupations found in the old city indicate that slum residence is not
confined to the poorest elements in the capital. The incomes commensurate with these jobs are also wide-ranging and in general are much
higher than those found in the adjacent *gecekondu* district of Altindag.
It is the proximity to remunerative employment that makes Eski
Ankara so attractive for its residents despite the congested environment,
of which most are very much aware.

This is not to say that the residents of Eski Ankara are completely
satisfied with their living conditions or that they have not considered
moving away from the slums. In fact, their awareness of, and attitudes
towards, housing improvement are far more positive than those of the
squatters in Ankara. Almost half have considered moving out of the old
city and a similar number would like to see an extended government
housing programme to help realise their ambitions. However, these
aspirations retain a sense of reality and the great majority feel that the
only sure way to improve their housing situation is to obtain accommodation in the private sector with the help of improved credit facilities.
Attitudes such as these are not consistent with the theoretical constraints of a culture of poverty and whilst the evidence does indicate
the presence of both social and cultural *malaise*, one must concur with
de Planhol (1973) that 'la vieille ville d'Ankara n'est pas une zone de
dégradation'. The diversity of socio-economic character in Eski Ankara

suggests that there is a dynamic living environment with many positive attributes which should be incorporated in any future redevelopment programme.

Tenements in Hong Kong

To a certain extent the previous case study in Ankara can be taken as representative of slum development on a small scale with relatively low densities and population totals. In contrast, Hong Kong provides a much more complex setting in which relatively recent but powerful historical forces have produced extensive, fragmented slums and tenement districts of varied character (Drakakis-Smith 1979b). Much of the government response to this situation will be examined in the next chapter; this case study concentrates on building up a picture of an inner-city tenement area to illustrate some of the general comments made earlier. The following introduction to the housing situation in Hong Kong thus serves as a preface for all subsequent case studies from the colony.

The growth of Hong Kong's population since the Second World War has been phenomenal, with the 5.5 million living in the colony at present representing a ninefold increase on the 1946 total. During the 1950s high natural growth rates were an important factor in this expansion and although the birth rate has fallen considerably, it has not yet stabilised, and the number of women in the fertile 20 to 35 age group is expected to increase by half over the next ten years. But in Hong Kong changes in natural growth rates have been less important than the overall effect of immigration from the Chinese mainland. The steady stream of post-war refugees swelled to tidal wave proportions following the nationalist-communist Civil War and over 1.25 million people moved into Hong Kong before effective border controls were imposed in 1950 (Hambro 1955). Between 1961 and 1971 there were 101,000 legal entries into the colony but during the 1970s the situation fluctuated tremendously. Since 1976 the annual total has risen steadily, not only as a result of the relaxation of controls in China but also because of increased refugee arrivals from Vietnam. In 1978 alone, legal and illegal immigration equalled that for the whole of the 1960s, and this figure was surpassed in just the first quarter of 1979.

The problems of population pressure have been exacerbated by the rugged topography which has severely restricted urban growth. The resultant pattern of development is such that 88 per cent of the population is crowded into the relatively level land on either side of the harbour, land which constitutes only 18 per cent of the total area of

1,045 square kilometres. As a result, densities are extremely high and the colony average of 3,962 persons per square kilometre in 1971 was exceeded only by neighbouring Macao. Within the urban areas densities are much higher than this and at their peak in 1961 reached 238,000 per square kilometre for the central tenement area of Sheung Wan.

Population growth to densities of this magnitude suggest that severe housing problems exist in Hong Kong. The response of low-income groups to the shortages has been to construct squatter settlements or to subdivide existing tenements. Private builders have at times also constructed large numbers of relatively cheap houses. The Hong Kong government has steadily developed a very large low-cost housing programme which in 1979 accounted for 50 per cent of the dwelling units in the colony, but the mix of private, public and popular responses to the housing shortage has varied considerably over the years. Throughout the 1950s self-help solutions were very prominent so that squatter settlements and slum subdivision continued to proliferate. As early as 1951 over one-half of all tenement flats had been converted into cubicles, cocklofts or bed-spaces. Most of these older buildings were rent-controlled so that the owners seldom received any of the increased income from the intensified occupation of the dwelling; this accrued instead to the chief tenants who had no responsibilities for maintenance of the property. The result of this subdivision is difficult to quantify since information on internal arrangements within tenement floors is very scarce. Population densities have undoubtedly worsened since the maxima for the central districts were all recorded in 1961.

Most buildings had been subdivided to the maximum by the mid-1950s but no government rehousing programme existed for tenement dwellers so that as families grew there was a definite movement out to squatter areas. At the same time the demand for housing space from a wide spectrum of economic groups was beginning to attract the interest of private developers. In 1955 the expensive legal procedures related to redevelopment were considerably simplified; the following year a change in building regulations was enacted to permit much higher plot ratios (floor space to ground space) and therefore profits. The result was the intensive development of the multistorey blocks which now epitomise contemporary Hong Kong.

The building boom lasted until 1966 and during this period considerable redevelopment took place in the tenement districts, although most was on a small scale. There was a dearth of capital equipment in the industry during this period so that it was very labour-intensive, a feature which may have been encouraged by the small size of redevelopment sites in the central areas. However, this did not prevent high-density developments, particularly in districts where street widths, which also conditioned building height, were greater. In some of the hitherto undeveloped sites, spot densities reach extraordinary proportions, culminating in the Ba Man complex in Yau Ma Tei where densities soared to almost 13,000 per hectare (Plate 7).

The government reacted to this in 1962 by modifying the building regulations in an effort to lower densities, but in response to lobbying by developers a four-year period of grace was allowed before the new measures were to become effective. The result was a frantic building boom as developers sought to take advantage of the existing legislation. In the rush many tenements were torn down to make way for the new high-rise buildings. This furious construction activity had a tremendous impact on the urban landscape of metropolitan Hong Kong as the 10- or 20-storey residential blocks began to tower above the pre-war tenements in a bizarre mixture of old and new. Superficially, it seemed as if the miserable lot of the tenement dwellers was being improved overnight as the clean, symmetrical lines of the high-rise blocks rose above the city.

The real situation was very different. Many of the new multistorey blocks were poorly built in the haste to recoup quick profits. In 1971 one such building was condemned after only 13 years of active use when it was discovered that salt water had been used in the concrete, causing widespread metal corrosion. The new flats were small and internal subdivision continued, so that it was not unusual for 15 to 20 people to be living in a three-room flat. Although the size and standards of the new units showed little improvement over the old tenements, rents were very different and between 1958 and 1966 they rose by 20 per cent despite the existence of statutory rent controls. The effect was to put the cost of the redeveloped accommodation beyond the reach of the poor who were forced to move out to a squatter settlement or to try to find some space within the tenements unaffected by clearances.

Throughout this period government reaction to the housing problems in Hong Kong largely revolved around the resettlement of squatters, and until 1964 no public housing was available for the overcrowded mass of tenement poor. The subsequent Low Cost Housing programme, as it was officially designated, was always regarded as less important than squatter resettlement and after ten years it still comprised only 10 per cent of all public housing units. Since 1970 private construction has been largely stimulated by increased commercial

activity in Hong Kong so that office, factory and retail buildings have
tended to predominate. However, the private sector continues to build
at least 12,000 new housing units each year. Most of these are still
classed as tenement floors or small flats but in fact their average size
has increased by 30 per cent over the last five years whilst rents have
almost doubled. The average rent for a small tenement floor in 1975
was HK$590 (US$118) per month, which effectively priced out the
poorer families whom redevelopment had displaced.

The situation in the tenement areas of Hong Kong contrasts
markedly with the apparent success of the squatter resettlement programme (which is discussed in the following chapter). Within the seven
years from 1964 to 1971 the metropolitan squatter population in the
colony had been reduced from over 600,000 to less than 190,000. In
contrast the slum tenement population was not even known until
recent years and the small urban renewal project is virtually moribund.
To a large extent the lack of attention paid to the problems of the inner
tenement districts reflects the goals of Hong Kong's housing programme,
which for a long time revolved around the need to acquire land for
redevelopment. Squatters received priority for this reason alone, not
because their housing conditions were any worse than those of the tenements.

Attempts to measure the extent of slum conditions in Hong Kong
did not begin until the present decade. The results indicate that, exclu-
ding squatters, some 1,250,000 people are living in substandard
accommodation in Hong Kong (Pryor 1975). More interesting than the
sheer size of this figure is its composition, since almost 500,000 live in
public housing. These are the residents of the earliest resettlement
estates which were erected almost twenty-five years ago and which are
now being torn down or converted into larger units. The remaining
750,000 are housed in various tenement slums but it would be incorrect
to assume that conditions throughout these districts are uniform. The
variation in the character of slum and tenement districts in Hong Kong
is such that it is virtually impossible to analyse in detail the entire
situation in the colony. The district of Yau Ma Tei (Figure 4.5) has
therefore been selected for examination with a specific purpose in mind
— to illustrate that an old and somewhat dilapidated tenement neighbourhood does not necessarily exhibit the type of socio-economic
conditions often associated with Western slums.

Figure 4.5: Yau Ma Tei: Major Land Uses, 1977

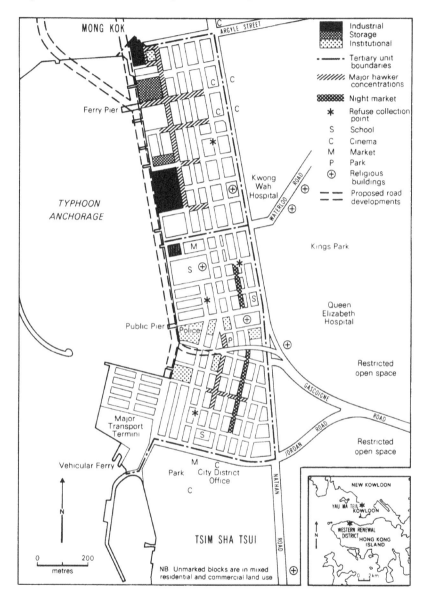

Industrial
Storage
Institutional
– · – Tertiary unit boundaries
/////// Major hawker concentrations
▓▓▓▓ Night market
* Refuse collection point
S School
C Cinema
M Market
P Park
⊕ Religious buildings
– – Proposed road developments

MONG KOK

ARGYLE STREET

Ferry Pier

TYPHOON ANCHORAGE

Kwong Wah Hospital

WATERLOO ROAD

Kings Park

Queen Elizabeth Hospital

Public Pier

Police

Restricted open space

GASCOIGNE ROAD

Major Transport Termini

Vehicular Ferry

JORDAN ROAD

Restricted open space

Park M C City District Office
C

NATHAN ROAD

0   200
metres

N

TSIM SHA TSUI

NB Unmarked blocks are in mixed residential and commercial land use

NEW KOWLOON
YAU MA TEI KOWLOON
WESTERN RENEWAL DISTRICT HONG KONG ISLAND
N
0   2 km

Yau Ma Tei. Yau Ma Tei, located on the western side of the Kowloon peninsula, was first developed in the 1860s soon after the peninsula was ceded to Britain. Early growth centred upon port activities and extensive private reclamation took place along the coast. By the turn of the century a small but densely populated settlement had appeared within a rectilinear street plan. The expansion in trading activity from 1920 to 1940, together with increasing civil unrest in China, saw the population of Yau Ma Tei rise considerably, and the physical con-straints of military land to the south and the attractions of water-front employment led to an intense residential concentration. It was during this inter-war period that the district became densely built over with the three- to four-storey tenements described earlier in this chapter.

The massive refugee influx in the late 1940s caused further sub-division within the old tenements but the government rehousing pro-gramme barely affected Yau Ma Tei until the introduction of Low Cost Housing in 1964. Far more significant in the physical development of the district was the liberalisation of building regulations in the 1950s which resulted in substantial demolition and reconstruction. As noted earlier, the Ba Man complex built in Yau Ma Tei during this period was one of the most intensive residential developments ever experienced in the colony.

The population increase of Yau Ma Tei reached a peak of 163,000 in 1961 when overall densities averaged more than 1,100 per hectare. By the 1970s the situation had eased somewhat because of residential movement to government or private developments in the urban peri-phery, and in 1976 the population had fallen to 132,000. Despite this decline the district still suffered a severe housing shortage and in 1976 there were still 1.8 families for every living quarter whilst government surveys indicated that, in terms of sharing and overcrowding, Yau Ma Tei was the worst area in the colony. The demographic structure of the district also reflected the small size of housing units available, with a large number of one- and two-person households and relatively few children (Figure 4.6).

In addition to being overcrowded, Yau Ma Tei also has some of the worst physical and environmental conditions in metropolitan Hong Kong, although compared with slums in other Asian cities the district is well provided with sewerage, water and electricity connections. How-ever, sewerage drains into the typhoon harbour and, together with the practice of gathering rubbish from a limited number of collection points, causes a high level of environmental pollution. Tenement floors account for 95 per cent of the domestic premises in the district, one-third of these being less than 40m square. In 1976 only 2.7 per cent of the buildings had been built before 1940; this compares with 31.5 per cent recorded in 1971 and indicates the extent of demolition in 1971-6. Not all of these have been replaced by other residential structures but on average 436 new domestic premises have been built each year during the 1970s. This may seem high, and in contrast to other cities it is, but in Yau Ma Tei the reconstruction rate is less than half that for metropolitan Hong Kong as a whole.

Figure 4.6: Yau Ma Tei: Household Characteristics, 1976

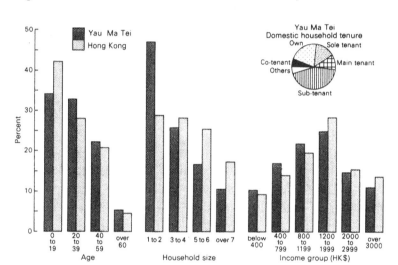

Households tend to rent their accommodation and subletting is still widespread. Most premises built before 1973 are subject to some form of rent control but this has been ineffective in controlling sublet rents which are much higher than tenant rents in terms of cost per square metre. In 1976 the average monthly rent was HK$339 (US$68) which is exactly three times greater than that of 1971. Not surprisingly, much of the residential construction since 1971 has been taken up by middle-income owner-occupiers anxious to avoid the rent inflation.

In view of the high population densities in Yau Ma Tei it is surprising to discover that more than half of the land area is road space — an excessive amount but one that still gives rise to traffic congestion as most streets are very narrow and obstructed with parked vehicles and petty traders. The roads are, in fact, used extensively for outdoor activities, both recreational and commercial. Several streets are noted for their hawker concentrations (Figure 4.5) and in 1970 it was estimated

that some 2,800 daytime hawkers operated in the district. These clusters of petty traders are one of the few forms of socio-spatial clustering
left in Yau Ma Tei, the old clan and regional residential groupings
having long since disappeared under the pressure of housing constraints.
The notable exception to this trend is the junk or boat dwellers in the
Yau Ma Tei typhoon shelter — 11,500 Tanka people who have until
recently strongly resisted all attempts to settle them on land.

Spatial distinctiveness in the rest of Yau Ma Tei has been extensively
eroded by the ubiquity of the mixed residential/commercial block.
Approximately 25 per cent of the total floor area is in commercial
usage, most of which caters for the daily needs of the residents, but
there are industrial concentrations nearer the harbour. In terms of
community facilities, the district is fortunate to be bounded by the
tourist area of Tsim Sha Tsui to the south and by extensive open space
in the south and east, although much of the latter is of restricted access.
The availability of recreational facilities is therefore reasonably good.
This is fortunate since there is less than one hectare of open space
within Yau Ma Tei itself.

So far the physical description of Yau Ma Tei has been somewhat
depressing, and this is the image of the district which is fixed in the
minds of most government administrators. In their eyes, Yau Ma Tei
comprises a typical slum replete with features such as destitute families,
dilapidated buildings, high crime rates, a poor health record and little
community spirit; in short, a culture of poverty. But as the preceding
discussion has indicated, this is very far from the truth and is contra-
dicted markedly by the economic and social characteristics of the
district. Economically, the most important feature of Yau Ma Tei is the
wide range of incomes which exists about a mid-point which is only
slightly below the average monthly income for the colony as a whole.
In 1976 over 25 per cent of the households in the district earned more
than HK$2,000 (US$400) per month which put most of them well
above the upper limit for eligibility for subsidised housing. This has had
a considerable effect on the expenditure patterns of the tenement
households who spend a much larger proportion of their income on
housing than do government tenants.

The larger incomes in Yau Ma Tei tend not to come from the availability of well-paid jobs but simply from the existence of widespread
opportunities in 'service, sales, production or transport', as the unhelp-
ful census categorises them. This means that those who want to work
can usually find employment quite easily in the district itself — even
children are readily recruited to work in the numerous restaurants. A

negligible proportion of the workforce is unemployed and almost half work within Yau Ma Tei. In addition the area provides jobs for a further 25,000 to 30,000 who live in other parts of Kowloon. Economically, therefore, Yau Ma Tei is a very vital and viable district which is strongly linked to the major industrial and commercial enterprises of the colony as a whole and certainly not inward-looking or destitute. The economic strength of the area has long been reflected in the reputation of its traditional community organisations, the Kaifong and trade associations. All of these bodies, whose functions encompass welfare, social, political and administrative activities, have depended for patronage on successful middle- and lower-middle-income merchants and traders who have made their fortunes within the district. Their continued influence is therefore indicative both of the economic status of Yau Ma Tei and its level of community spirit.

This does not imply that the degree of community involvement has always been high in Yau Ma Tei; as in most Chinese societies, welfare has traditionally been a family affair and the concept of community philanthropism was the prerogative of the wealthy. However, informal co-operative activity related to commercial ties has always been considerable in Yau Ma Tei and the government has built an extensive network of new community organisations on this base. These range from district-wide ventures, such as fighting syndicated crime or promoting festivals, to projects related to individual buildings, such as the Mutual Aid Committees which have sought to raise the standard of maintenance, security and cleanliness in the multistorey blocks.

In short, Yau Ma Tei is a complicated rather than a problem area, comprising a flourishing community with little of the anomie associated with Western slums. However, its environment does pose a severe challenge to planners in Hong Kong — one which has not yet been effectively resolved. The only attempt at urban renewal on the colony, in Western District on Hong Kong Island, has not been a success (see following chapter) and this has discouraged comprehensive redevelopment programmes elsewhere. The proposals put forward for Yau Ma Tei in the early 1970s have been successively diluted to the present outline zoning plan which, in effect, merely illustrates the future impact of major transport developments on the district, whilst the physical planning of the area has been reduced to the introduction of a few (much needed) community centres and recreation spaces. Housing improvement will be almost entirely in the hands of the private sector, with some prompting from the government through repair and/or demolition orders. It is also possible that a little redevelopment by the quasi-independent Housing Society may occur.

The elements of positive planning at present thus relate more to community development than to physical improvement. Within this broad field the emphasis is on grass-roots participation — co-ordinated self-help to tackle various social disorders. It must be admitted that this approach has had remarkable success over the last five years and most residents are aware that Yau Ma Tei is a 'better' place in which to live. However, it is essential that this improving community spirit should be supplemented by a more imaginative approach to physical planning in the area. A reduction in the amount of land devoted to road space, if linked to a comprehensive restructuring of the internal traffic systems, would both reduce the environmental conflict between people and cars, and give much needed space for housing. The government should take the lead in this respect by acquiring property, using existing resumption orders or rescinding expired leases, and amalgamating several blocks into land for government housing development.

The construction of public housing in Yau Ma Tei would have several positive values. First, it would enable the restructuring of current street and block systems which is badly needed for more efficient land use. Second, it would allow many families to improve their housing without moving from an area to which they are economically tied. Finally, a competitive element would be introduced into the private redevelopment of the area and might help restrain rents and improve standards. However, even if the government does enter into the housing market in Yau Ma Tei, the bulk of the dwelling units will still be privately owned. Apart from redevelopment *per se* there is also a great need to encourage better maintenance and further improvement of much of the older property in the district. At present this 'encouragement' operates on a punitive basis with repairs being ordered by the Public Works Department and rental increases being permitted after improvements are made. Many owners cannot afford to improve their property because of controlled rents and it would seem appropriate to offer more incentives for improvement — perhaps loans or even grants for specific purposes. Tenants as well as owner-occupiers would benefit from such policies.

Current planning policy for Yau Ma Tei is too timid — the government is using apparent costs as an excuse to opt out of more imaginative and comprehensive programmes. However, *laissez-faire* policies in districts such as Yau Ma Tei will mean the persistence of environmental and residential defects over many years to come. In view of the rapid deterioration in living conditions elsewhere in Hong Kong, this will merely accumulate enormous difficulties for future governments.

CAPTIONS TO ILLUSTRATIONS

1. *Kuantan, Malaysia.* Hybrid housing in Tanjong Api. This *kampung* was originally intended for resettled squatters but until recently very few of the houses were built with legal authorisation or located on tenured land. Over the last few years some land rights and temporary occupation licences have been granted and houses are being built and extended with municipal approval. *Source: Mike Johnstone*

2. *New Kowloon, Hong Kong.* Hillside squatters still exist in large numbers along the Kowloon foothills, despite massive government resettlement programmes. Current building programmes are taking place further away from the main metropolitan areas and fewer squatters are being rehoused in such schemes. *Source: Hong Kong Government Information Services*

3. *Ankara.* *Gecekondu* housing on the slopes of Altindag near the city centre. Although some of the residents have been granted land tenure, they are not allowed to improve their dwellings. *Source: David Drakakis-Smith*

4. *Ankara.* These new *gecekondu* houses are being built on the north-western edge of the city on the land of uncertain tenure. Whilst most are quite substantial in size, being constructed with experienced hired labour, all lack infrastructural services. *Source: David Drakakis-Smith*

5. *Cairo.* Away from the tourist areas of the old city the *taudification* of the buildings continues as increasing numbers of migrants seek cheap accommodation. *Source: Dick Lawless*

6. *Singapore.* These dilapidated tenements in Sago Lane have been demolished but used to function as death houses for old people. The paper objects in front of the house are to be burned in the funeral ceremonies. High-rise flats now stand on this site, but increasing concern is being voiced about the wholesale demolition of such areas. *Source: David Drakakis-Smith*

7. *Hong Kong.* The Ba Man complex of eight multistory blocks shown here comprises the highest spot densities of any comparable area in the world, with 4,000 people per hectare. *Source: David Drakakis-Smith*

8. *Hong Kong.* Hawkers in Shek Kip Mei Resettlement Estate before the improvement programme. Note how they completely filled up the open space within the blocks, making rubbish collection very difficult. However, the hawkers performed an essential retail function for the residents and are gradually being relocated into prepared market sites within the estate. *Source: David Drakakis-Smith*

9. *Hong Kong.* Tsz Wan Shan Resettlement Estate is the largest single agglomeration of public housing in Hong Kong and was amongst the first to be constructed with 16-storey Mark 4 and Mark 5 blocks. *Source: Hong Kong Government Information Services*

10. *Hong Kong.* Overshadowed by the massive high-rise government housing programme in Hong Kong are these terraces of site and service housing. They are intended for squatters who do not qualify for conventional public housing when their huts are cleared for development. Each family rents a serviced space under the fixed roof and constructs its own dwelling. Almost 100,000 are housed this way in the colony. *Source: David Drakakis-Smith*

11. *Malacca, Malaysia.* A joint-venture, low-cost housing project between public and private enterprise which has adhered rigidly to existing building regulations and produced an estate with tiny houses and enormous roads. *Source: David Drakakis-Smith*

1

2

3

4

5

7

9

10

11

5 GOVERNMENT HOUSING

Introduction

The limited size of public investment in low-cost housing provision
has been noted in earlier chapters, but this does not always correspond
with a government's perception of what its role should be. Some would
be quite willing to invest much more in housing if the availability of
capital made this feasible and the eventual policy decision is usually
dependent on weighing a variety of considerations. The rationale behind these investment priorities and its relationship to the general
development process will be explored later in the book; this particular chapter is more concerned with the direct evaluation of the limited
range of public housing programmes which currently exist in the Third
World. The assessment will not be restricted to the fiscal or physical
aspects of the dwellings themselves, for example their design, standards
or rent, but will also examine the way in which they satisfy the needs
of the urban poor and the goals of the government. In this context it
will be useful to group government attitudes to the provision of low-
cost housing into four broad categories: indifferent, reactionary,
Westernised and innovative. This classification is based primarily on
policy motivation rather than the physical characteristics of the programmes themselves, although some of the subcategorisation incorporates both elements.

Indifference

The meagre investment policies of most governments in the Third
World are often dignified by the term *laissez-faire*, implying non-
interference for a deliberate purpose. Dwyer (1975) has more accurately described the situation as one of simple apathy in which urban
authorities adopt a policy of inaction in the hope that the migrants,
whom they consider to be the cause of the housing problem, will
eventually return to the rural areas where they are assumed to originate. Many reasons have been suggested for the widespread government
apathy towards urban housing problems and the arguments are worth
closer scrutiny. One suggestion is that fear of the latent political power
of the squatters has forestalled any reaction to their acquisition of large

tracts of urban land. The realities of this assumption have been discussed in previous chapters but, in general, it would seem that even in Latin America, most of the present generation of squatters are basically conservative. More pragmatic explanations of indifference appear to lie in the administrative difficulties which characterise the great majority of cities in the Third World. A sheer lack of information is one of the most crucial factors, not only of reliable statistics but also of basic cadastral maps.

Typically, planning information appears to be sought more for political than for planning purposes. Thus in Saigon in 1963, President Diem's planners were busy gathering information on the locations from which the palace was vulnerable to snipers or the distance suspects could be chased by vehicle. Some useful planning data were collected along with this general security information but all charts and maps were subsequently destroyed after the 1963 coup. By 1969, at the height of the Vietnam War, the situation was little better and Seltz (1970) described the planning system as being characterised by a total shortage of knowledge in such vital areas as demographic and occupational structure, or land use.

Even when planning information is available, effective use of the material is frequently hindered by political corruption or electoral gimmickry. Nominal improvement of squatter settlements or partial recognition of tenure both figure prominently in the vote-catching tactics of almost every political group in the Third World. Special agencies are set up and disbanded almost overnight as a result of fluctuations in political fortunes, so that the roles and responsibilities of each organisation towards housing provision become increasingly confused. The Philippines is usually considered to display considerable evidence of such bureaucratic chaos and before the establishment of the National Housing Authority in 1975, numerous agencies and departments were involved in the planning and execution of housing programmes. In a single squatter relocation project (which is discussed in more detail below), twelve separate government departments were represented. Each had its own field office as well as staff operating within the central administrative bureau.

But administrative disorder is not confined to the Philippines and is equally rife in many other Third World countries which ostensibly appear more organised. Malaysia is one example. Here, the principal difficulties stem from the federal system of political organisation. Housing *per se* is a state responsibility because of the nature of landownership, but funds, technical expertise and planning assistance have always been available from the federal government through various departments or agencies. This assistance has constantly been subject to political pressures at both national and state levels, so that its overall extent and specific application have varied enormously over the years. Until 1973 the main channel for federal housing funds in Malaysia was the Housing Trust. On the whole its record was unimpressive until the 'crash programme' launched in 1968 in conjunction with the Federal Department of Town and Country Planning. The aim of the programme was to impress the voters before the 1969 elections and, in order to reach as large a number of people as possible, it took the form of dispersed schemes of low-cost houses in the smaller towns which had not hitherto felt much impact from the public housing programmes. During the pre-election period the Trust completed almost 10,000 units but this failed to improve the low standing of the Alliance Party which, although remaining in office, lost heavily in the elections. Widespread racial riots followed in the wake of these losses. The government subsequently became very disenchanted with the political utility of housing investment and this has been reflected in the low levels of investment in development planning since 1969.

Most public housing programmes in Malaysia now originate with State Economic Development Corporations (SEDC), although a miscellany of other organisations still exists at both state and federal levels with various responsibilities in this field. This situation has been exacerbated by the fluctuations in federal responsibility for housing policy. After adverse criticism of the Ministry of Local Government and Housing during the First Malaysia Plan period of 1965-70, public housing was reallocated to the Ministry of Home Affairs. The separation of the housing portfolio from Town Planning weakened the administration and affected the speed of technical work, and in 1973 the housing portfolio reverted to a restyled Ministry of Local Government and Housing which also took over the Federal Department of Town and Country Planning (Alithambi 1975). By 1977 responsibilities had again been transferred, this time to the Ministry for Housing and Village Development, but during the current Third Malaysia Plan (1976-80) it is hoped to co-ordinate all policy decisions with a new Department for Housing. Fluctuations such as these at the federal level have made the establishment of national objectives very difficult and have affected the pursuit of even the modest targets contained within the various development plans so that achievement levels have been low.

Operational confusion, such as exists within the Malaysian administrative system, is frequently compounded elsewhere in the Third World by a lack of spatial synchronisation between the real and officially designated extent of many urban areas since 'the boundaries of local government and planning authorities have been slow to respond to fundamental changes in urban configuration' (World Bank 1972a:49). India is replete with such confusion. The Indian capital Delhi, for example, sprawls over Union Territory into the neighbouring states of Uttar Pradesh and Haryana, each of which has a separate planning authority (Ewing 1969). The Master Plan for Delhi covers all three districts and also involves two additional planning and administrative organisations, the Delhi Development Authority and the Delhi Muni-cipal Corporation. The corollary of involving so many powerful agencies in the Master Plan is that none has a clearly defined role in its implementation. Many other instances of sectoral and spatial inefficiency can be identified in the Third World and their cumulative hindrance to effective planning has been considerable. The lack of data, administrative conflict and delays, the isolation of planners from policy-makers, all combine to convert enthusiasm, efficiency and pragmatism into the apathetic indifference characteristic of too many developing countries.

Reactionary Attitudes

Although it is true to say that administrative indifference towards housing problems has been characteristic of many cities in the Third World, several urban authorities have implemented more vigorous policies. The most prevalent, but least useful, of these policies can be described as reactionist or as Mangin (1967:69) has more colourfully termed it, 'the festering sore [hard-nosed] view'. This approach seeks to eradicate the housing problem for cosmetic reasons and pays little attention to the real plight of the people actually involved. The reactionary measures employed vary enormously but may be usefully grouped into those which are 'preventative' or 'remedial' in nature.

Preventative Measures

Most preventative policies involve migration controls aimed at stemming or deflecting the steady movement of people into the large metropolises. One early attempt at such control on a national scale occurred in Turkey during the 1950s. At that time 80 per cent of the Turkish population was rural, working within an agricultural system that was inefficient, overreliant on climatic conditions and characterised by considerable seasonal unemployment and disguised underemployment.

The deluge of Marshall Aid tractors which descended upon the country in the immediate post-war period also increased the amount of surplus labour in the countryside. The resultant drift from the rural areas produced serious economic problems in Turkey because the towns and cities had not yet commenced substantial commercial or industrial growth. Employment opportunities were so limited that the first Five Year Development Plan (1962-8) actively encouraged direct out-migration to Western Europe as a palliative measure. This policy was short-sighted and had little chance of success. Its immediate effect was the loss of many young and skilled workers, whilst in the long term the returning migrants, whatever their original birthplace, usually settled into the tertiary sector of Turkey's two main cities, Istanbul and Ankara.

Few attempts to deflect urban migrants have been as formally structured as that of the Turkish government, although external migration *per se* has been encouraged in many other developing countries in an attempt to reduce the pressure on large cities. This tendency has been particularly marked in certain ex-colonial territories with out-migration directed mainly towards the former colonial power. Internal controls on urban migrational growth are much more direct and primarily consist of restricting access to the cities to those who have a guaranteed job and/or a residence. South Africa and various West African nations have all used this system, with little success (Hance 1970). Administratively it is very difficult to enforce and creates numerous opportunities for corruption. Two brief examples will illustrate some of the features of the restricted access policy.

Port Moresby is the capital of newly independent Papua New Guinea. In 1977 the city's population was estimated to be about 105,000 with an average annual growth rate of 12 per cent (Bryant 1977). Although it has over one-quarter of the total urban population of the country and is twice the size of the second city, Lae, Port Moresby is by no means the fastest growing urban centre. Nevertheless, it is estimated that the population of the capital will reach 200,000 by 1986 (Papua New Guinea Housing Commission 1975) and the substantial in-migration over the last decade has imposed severe strains on the housing resources of the city.

The housing situation in Port Moresby is, at present, very confused, largely due to the complexities of local land tenure systems. Much of the land in and around the city is still classed as customary, or tribal, with ownership vested in the members of the group. Migrants to Port Moresby have settled on these lands, in both existing and new villages

(Figure 5.1); others have established themselves on government land. Although the latter are illegal squatters, the extension of this description to people on customary land would be incorrect because most have received permission to settle from one or more of the traditional owners, by means of either an exchange or cash arrangement. The movement of rural migrants to Port Moresby has caused concern to the administrative authorities since 1945. The colonial links and close physical proximity to Australia have limited the growth of jobs in both the formal and informal sectors (Jackson 1978). At the same time, the government has been unable to build houses the migrants can afford, although it has heavily subsidised the accommodation of its own employees (Stretton 1979). In order to forestall the feared accumulation of unemployed squatters in the capital, preventative legislation was enacted in several different fields.

Figure 5.1: Port Moresby: Settlement Patterns, 1975

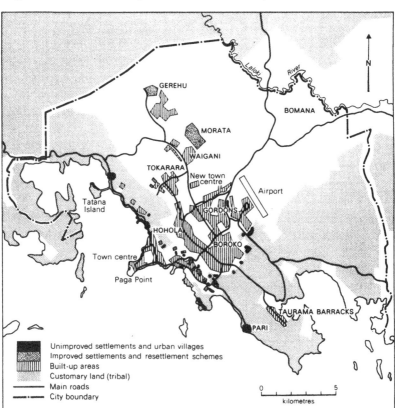

In the immediate post-war years various Native Labour Ordinances provided the principal means of migration control. The restrictions aimed at preventing long-term urban settlement by the migrants and in order to achieve this a variety of health controls, residential obligations and permits was employed. Throughout the 1960s the House of Assembly debated the adverse effects of rural-urban migration and several proposals for pass systems were put forward. Fortunately none were adopted because all would have proved almost impossible to operate. However, the failure to implement a pass system did not mean that the Port Moresby authorities had resigned themselves to uncontrolled migration – the emphasis was merely switched to physical eviction from the city.

In contrast to Port Moresby, the Indonesian capital of Jakarta is a city of more than five million people, 80 per cent of whom are migrants (Papanek 1975). Although the population of Jakarta is growing at an average of 7 per cent per annum, the urbanisation process in Indonesia has barely begun and over 80 per cent of the population still live in the countryside. Partly as a consequence of this, Jakarta is one of the poorest and most chaotic cities in Asia. Over the years it has grown hugely but haphazardly in a series of interlinked *kampongs*, and may accurately be described as the largest village in the world. To prevent the situation from deteriorating further, Governor Ali Sadikin imposed stringent migration controls in 1970. The system requires all migrants to Jakarta to obtain a residence card in order to remain in the city. To qualify for a *kartu* each migrant has to prove that he has a job, accommodation and permission from his previous neighbourhood council to leave, as well as making a deposit equal to the return fare to his point of origin.

In operation the system has spawned widespread corruption. Papanek (1975:10) has reported that the price of a residence card and related documents ranges between Rp3,000 (US$7.14) and Rp6,000 (US$14.28), and the market is so well organised that credit terms stretching over several months may even be arranged. Whilst these prices might seem high for low-income migrants, their increased earning power in the city soon enables debts to be paid off. In many cases the risk of being caught without a card is not great, particularly for the lowest-income groups, such as shoe-shiners and cigarette-butt collectors. In contrast, most of those with more stable jobs do have cards, particularly those employed in occupations which involve more frequent contact with government officials, for example in obtaining trading or *becak* (trishaw) licences. One notable effect on housing has been to encourage migrants to seek the sponsorship of known persons

who offer both job and accommodation prospects. This has given rise
to clusters of fellow-villagers in lodging houses, or *pondoks*, oriented
around particular trades (Jellinek 1978). Although the operation of the
pass system is inefficient, migration to Jakarta has slowed perceptibly
during the present decade. But this is more the result of increased
economic uncertainties within certain types of informal-sector employment than the direct consequence of restricted migration *per se.*

Remedial Measures

In cities where migration controls have not been enforced or have failed
to reduce migration flows, the most common reactionary response has
been the forcible relocation of 'surplus' urban population to the rural
areas. The authorities concerned will usually claim that the squatters
or pavement dwellers removed in this way disfigure the city and act as
a drag on the urban economy, but in most instances the main reason for
the operation is the desire to obtain more land for 'progressive' and
profitable development projects. The mechanics of eviction and relocation vary considerably, with one of the most simple measures being the
implementation of vagrancy laws. This system, under which individuals
without formal employment may be ousted from the city, has been
used in both Port Moresby and Jakarta. In the former it operates as a
substitute for immigration controls but in the latter acts as a comple-
ment to the *kartu* system. At its peak in 1970-1, vagrancy violations
constituted more than a quarter of the cases heard in Port Moresby
courts. Although welfare officials arranged for transport back to home
villages, the majority of those convicted quickly returned to the city
(Oram 1976).

In Jakarta the vagrancy component of the pass system has been
strongly enforced since 1972, but it has been the associated restriction
on certain occupations in the city which has had most effect. Hawkers
and *becaks* have been excluded from certain areas, notably the
Westernised central district. The result has been to lower incomes in
two of the most important employment sections. When coupled with
the increased cost of residence permits, this has effectively discouraged migrants who hoped to enter these occupations. Whether it has
actually caused an outflow of people is another matter, although the
circular migration noted by Hugo (1975) must be closely tied to the
limitations on urban employment in the Indonesian capital.

Not all 'remedial' measures relate to individuals. The most frequent
response of this nature is the wholesale demolition of squatter settlements and the eviction of their residents *en masse* beyond the city

boundaries with no provision for rehousing or employment. This process is usually undertaken to acquire building land, but on some occasions it is done simply to improve the 'image' of the city concerned. In Jakarta, for example, it has been alleged that prior to the arrival of eminent foreign dignitaries, the *gelandangan*, or pavement dwellers, are 'seized by the police, dumped into trucks, and taken to places outside [the city] where they are left on streets or roads' (Suparlan 1974:51).

Few eviction schemes have had a long-term effect on population movement to the city. Most families eventually return and resume squatting, frequently in the place from which they were originally cleared. In Ankara, for example, one squatter is known to have rebuilt his house four times on the same site. Ostensibly more reasonable in comparison with straightforward eviction is the practice of relocation to prepared reception sites in rural areas. Whilst more humane in character, such schemes are nevertheless reactionary because they are based on the mistaken premiss that the migrants can be returned to, and resettled in, an agrarian lifestyle. Great care is usually taken over the selection and preparation of the site and the resettled squatter is given as much help as possible. However, even with careful organisation there has been little success in counteracting the economic lure of the city, and wholesale abandonment has been characteristic of such schemes.

On the whole there has been little documentation of these projects and the reasons for their frequent failure. Few governments wish to be embarrassed in this way. Perhaps the most celebrated Asian example of a well-meant but disastrous relocation project is that of Sapang Palay in the Philippines (Juppenlatz 1970, Poethig 1972). In 1963 the Slum Clearance Committee in the Philippines recommended that a large group of squatters be transferred from Intramuros, Tondo and North Harbour in central Manila to a relocation site at Sapang Palay. The new scheme was, in essence, an agricultural co-operative with core housing provided on demarcated lots. For the first few years remuneration was to take the form of food handouts from United Nations donations, a policy which was not likely to appeal to the independent, self-reliant families involved. In this instance, not only were objectives misplaced but the administrative machinery to fulfil these goals was non-existent. In particular, there was no provision for funding the project, so it was eventually decided that each government department would make a budgetary allocation for its own role in the relocation scheme. A separate Squatter Resettlement Agency was then set up within the Office of the President to co-ordinate the work. The result of this *ad hoc* administrative organisation was the cumbersome combination of departments and the overlapping of functions previously outlined.

In the relocation exercise itself, the well-intentioned but inadequate planning by the government was placed under intense pressure by the precipitous action of the Manila city authorities, who rushed through the operation in order to take advantage of a brief period in which they could legally obliterate squatter communities. The destruction of homes and eviction of the squatters proved to be the more important aspect of the project as far as the city authorities were concerned. Some 15,000 families, approximately 90,000 people, were affected by the operation but only about one-quarter moved to Sapang Palay; the remainder drifted into other squatter areas within metropolitan Manila.

In total almost 6,000 families, or 30,000 people, were registered for the Sapang Palay relocation project between 1960 and 1964. A large number of international and domestic agencies, both governmental and private, were involved in the preparation of the site and the supervision of resettlement. Many individuals worked long hours to cope with the immediate problems of housing, health and food provision posed by the rapid transfer of such large numbers of people from Manila. Nevertheless, the overall co-ordination left a great deal to be desired and the long-term plans for community centres and on-site employment failed to materialise. In fact, the whole concept was ill conceived since the majority of those involved were deeply committed to urban life and had neither the inclination nor the skills for employment in agriculture. The failure to provide social and economic roots within the Sapang Palay community served to accentuate the isolation of the site which was 37km from Manila, over an hour away by bus on a road which ended four kilometres short of Sapang Palay itself. Many people had sensibly retained their jobs in Manila but were forced into the expense of lengthy commuting. Inevitably, men began to stay in Manila during the week and, as few families enjoy such separation, eventually entire households resettled in Manila, usually in existing squatter communities. In 1970 the Central Institute for the Training and Relocation of Urban Squatters (CITRUS) discovered that since 1964 the Sapang Palay settlement had diminished by an average of 3,000 people per year – a sad testimony to poorly defined objectives and administrative ineptitude.

Westernised Reponses

Whilst it is generally true that government investment in urban low-cost housing is limited, there have been many instances in various parts of the Third World of well-meant and well-financed attempts to rehouse the urban poor. The extent and success of these schemes have varied considerably, but until the present decade they have usually followed established Western concepts of planning and design. In most Third World countries this is a direct legacy of colonialism which has affected the residential construction industry in numerous ways. The most direct is the accumulation of supply links with the former colonial power which means that most building materials are imported. In addition to being expensive this also ensures that the Western designs which predominated in the colonial era are retained after 'independence'. In many countries the Western style of house is enshrined in local legislation relating to building standards, a factor which has considerably inhibited the production of low-cost units by the private sector (see Chapter 6).

Not only do the legislative and economic legacies of colonialism contribute to the conventionality of current planning practices; elitist attitudes also persist in relation to housing design. This is partly due to Western-style housing being regarded as a symbol of success during the colonial period. However, in most contemporary developing countries it is more related to the type of professional training which planners and architects receive. It is rare for these countries to be able to afford the luxury of a technical or professional training establishment and where they do exist it is often difficult to staff them with instructors familiar with the local environment. Most personnel are consequently trained by overseas 'experts' either at home or abroad so that most of those who eventually work in their home country are inculcated with inappropriate planning concepts. As a result of all these factors, most public housing tends to be of conventional Western design. This usually makes it very expensive to construct and therefore to rent. In general, such characteristics are the unfortunate consequence of a genuine attempt to help the urban poor, but in some cases the housing is built with other, less philanthropic, objectives in mind. When this difference in motivation is added to variations in investment scale, it gives rise to a wide range of public housing programmes. The most important of these will be examined below, together with brief descriptive examples.

Tokenism

Token housing programmes are those which are intended to be visible symbols of governmental concern for the poor. Rather than meeting the real needs of the low-income groups, such schemes are designed to win approval and votes, or to impress overseas visitors. For this reason the buildings tend to dominate the urban landscape, usually taking the form of high-rise blocks irrespective of their fiscal or cultural suitability. The real goals are thus political rather than social, and these affect the design and planning of the programmes. In Havana, for example, the first major project of the National Housing Agency following the revolution was the Havana del Este scheme. Despite the poverty of the country the standards were grandiose and dependent on imported fixtures, particularly elevators. Unit costs were as high as US$10,000 but Kessler (1977:206) has argued that this was of secondary importance as 'the product orientation of the housing programs satisfied the government's need for visibility just as the standard unit orientation worked for administrative efficiency'. As such programmes are not primarily intended to alleviate the housing conditions of the poor, allocation of both the estates and the individual units is usually biased. Thus Lamb (1976) reported that one-quarter of the public housing in Trinidad was located in east Port of Spain, the constituency of the then Prime Minister, Eric Williams. Similarly in Manila, the mayor insisted that in the Bagong Barangay housing scheme, allocation priority be given to employees from City Hall (Laquian 1969). However, the displacement of low-income families is not usually so direct. Instead, a slower infiltration of middle-income households occurs as the poor find the regular rental demands increasingly difficult to meet and eventually succumb to lump-sum offers for their leasing rights.

A reasonably typical example of tokenism is the Din Daeng government housing project in Bangkok. The present scheme took the form of a high-rise development of some dilapidated single-storey public housing and squatter huts previously on the site. By the mid-1970s it consisted of 39 walk-up blocks each of five or six storeys, with either 56 or 80 units in each block. The 50m-square units comprise one large room with separate kitchen, tap and toilet, and a small porch for storage. Most are subdivided by screens and have cockloft platforms to provide additional sleeping space, usually for children. The units were intended for households with monthly incomes of less than B2,650 (US$129), allocated according to a priority list which covered disasters, demolition and eviction by landlord or government. In practice most of the original occupants were resettled squatters with a large proportion dependent on irregular incomes derived from informal-sector activity. Din Daeng itself is in the outer suburbs of Bangkok in a prominent position on the airport highway, but far away from major sources of employment (Figure 3.4).

The very visible position of the project is significant since it has always been envisaged as a showpiece estate. The areas between the blocks are well kept and litter free, and to ensure they remain this way no buying or selling is permitted in or around the building, except in a few expensive licensed areas. The effect of these controls has been to remove an important source of supplementary household income, and whilst rents are reasonably low at B100 (US$5) to B125 (US$6.10) per month (electricity, water and rubbish disposal are extra), the regular payments impose severe pressures on families already burdened with commuting expenses. As a result there have been conflicting reports on the popularity of Din Daeng with prospective tenants. Several squatter surveys have indicated that only about 1 per cent of the inhabitants would like to live in such high-rise blocks (Morell and Morell 1972); on the other hand, government sources suggest that the number of applicants far exceeds the number of flats available (Noranitipadungkarn 1975). However, perhaps the most indicative information is provided by the original occupants themselves. The great majority have already sold their residential rights, usually for sums range from B7,000 (US$342) to B10,000 (US$488), to middle-income groups for whom Din Daeng offers acceptable accommodation at relatively low cost.

Misplaced Philanthropism

Whilst a great deal of the low-cost housing investment in the Third World can be classed as tokenism, there are many other projects with more generous motivations. However, the majority of such schemes fail to provide any real help to the urban poor because of inappropriate or inefficient approaches. In most cases the housing is simply too expensive as a result of the slavish imitation of Western standards and techniques without consideration of local circumstances or needs. Large subsidies are needed before much of the public housing in the Third World falls within the financial capabilities of the poor, and few governments are prepared to supply these. Instead, most prefer to restrict access to public housing units to those families able to pay a 'fair' rent on a regular basis. Some governments go as far as to redefine the poor according to criteria which substantially reduce the amount of subsidy required. This has occurred in Trinidad where Lamb (1976) has reported that the National Housing Authority defines low-income occupiers as those with monthly household incomes of between T$500 (US$250) and T$700 (US$350), despite the fact that the median household income of the occupied labour force is T$350 (US$175) and that of the occupiable labour force is T$160 (US$80) to T$180 (US$90) per month.

In most instances the reasons why administrative authorities are forced into such positions relate to the high cost of construction, which in turn is caused by the adherence to inappropriate Western values. The inadequacies of this situation have been noted by many observers. Rapoport (1973) considered it to be the consequence of the high status attached to new forms and materials, in contrast to the low value accorded traditional cultures and lifestyle. But this is by no means the only reason for 'modern', but expensive, building projects. Many socialists or nationalists in developing countries would argue, perhaps with some justification, that as the construction industry itself is pre-dominantly capitalistic and geared towards profit maximisation, low-cost housing cannot be produced. Whilst there is some truth in both of these generalisations, they do not apply in all circumstances and the fol-lowing chapter will discuss in detail the whole question of private-sector participation in low-cost housing production.

Whatever the reasons behind the Westernised planning policies, the general effect is to make public housing units too expensive for the urban poor for whom they are theoretically, and sometimes genuinely, intended. Reliable statistical evidence confirming this assertion has been difficult to obtain until recently, although inferences could be made from reports on the middle-income invasion of low-cost housing. Under these circumstances the full character of misplaced enthusiasm empha-sised in this section is best illustrated by reference to a specific example, in this instance the Rifle Range project in Georgetown, Penang, in Malaysia.

The estate which forms the basis of this discussion is located at Ayer Itam on the outskirts of Georgetown. It is a state housing project which originated in 1968 with the financial assistance of the federal government in a pre-election attempt to preserve support for the ruling Alliance Party. From the outset it was decided that the Rifle Range flats should be constructed using a prefabricated system. The reasons for this choice were never made clear; it could have been due to interests within the administration or a simple desire to be as technologically modern as Singapore. Whatever the rationale, the choice of site was governed by the space demands of the factory producing the prefabri-cated materials. Transport costs consequently dictated that the housing estate should be adjacent to the factory. The site was thus peripheral to the main urban area, away from the major sources of employment and services. In addition it was adjacent to an extensive Chinese cemetery, a further discouragement to the traditional Chinese households which formed the bulk of Georgetown's population.

The estate itself consists of nine blocks, each of 17 or 18 storeys, comprising a total of some 3,700 flats. Whilst the blocks are reasonably well maintained, the estate itself was provided with few communal facilities. Private initiative, however, has led to the development of retail and service facilities in ground-floor flats and on adjacent open spaces. The area around the buildings is further congested by the many public and private vehicles needed to cope with the heavy commuting into the city centre. Not surprisingly, the densities and congestion were high on the list of complaints made by the residents when the area was surveyed in the early 1970s. Originally the Rifle Range flats were intended for families with monthly incomes of less than M$200 (US$80), but in view of the poor initial response this ceiling was raised to M$300 (US$120). Rents range from M$32 (US$13) to M$47 (US$19) per month depending on the size of the flat, but to this must be added charges for water, electricity and maintenance, so that monthly expenditure can easily exceed M$70 (US$28) or M$80 (US$32). Regular payments to this extent have imposed severe financial burdens on many residents, despite the fact that rents are heavily subsidised in order to attract families away from the very cheap tenement accommodation in Georgetown. When added to commuting costs, the fiscal demands of living in the Rifle Range flats caused many families to fall into rental arrears.

The overall result of the Rifle Range development is a project which, although intended to assist the urban poor, has satisfied few of their needs. The basic cause of this situation was the choice of building system which adversely affected the design, cost and location of the finished estate. Prefabrication systems are only cheap when employed on an extensive spatial and temporal scale. Georgetown did not have sufficient demand to sustain the prefabricated building programme beyond the Rifle Range estate. As a result the construction plant was dismantled after the housing estate was finished, and the high production costs had to be absorbed with the state subsidy.

By the mid-1970s the government appeared to have accepted the scheme's failure as a low-cost housing project and raised the income ceiling to M$500 (US$202). This resulted in an influx of middle-income families for whom the flats provide cheap, adequate but temporary accommodation whilst savings are amassed for a more suitable house on the private market. As Abrahams (1975) has noted, the end product is not low-cost housing. At present, only about 25 per cent of the households could be considered as low-income and half of these are in such rental arrears that they are likely to be evicted to make way for more affluent families.

Large-scale Public Housing

Conventional housing programmes on a very large scale are rare in the Third World and for this reason alone it is as necessary to examine the circumstances within which they have evolved as it is to assess the achievements of the programmes themselves. Whilst many of the evolutionary factors will become readily apparent in the case studies of Hong Kong which conclude this chapter, it is worthwhile to indicate at the outset the range of determinants which stimulate massive public housing schemes. Only if the definition of the Third World is extended to include the poorest of the Eastern European countries, such as Yugoslavia, could social objectives be said to be a principal motivation of government housing programmes (see Simic 1973). However, welfare policies of this nature are exceptional and in most instances large-scale government housing programmes are the result of a combination of political and economic factors. Perlman (1974), for example, has argued that the *favela* resettlement programmes in Brazil have been pursued, not for the *favela* residents themselves, but for the profit of the private sector which benefits from the valuable contracts offered and the clearance of land for general development.

Economic justification for large-scale public housing is, in fact, inextricably linked to political manoeuvring, and throughout the cities where such programmes exist they are invariably considered to act as a placebo to the aspirations of the urban poor. However, the degree of political sophistication behind mass housing ventures varies considerably. In Caracas, Venezuela, the erection of the *superbloques* during the 1950s could be regarded simply as an extension of the previously noted desire of most governments to construct visual evidence of their 'concern' for the people. In Venezuela, at that time, the highly centralised political system, together with vast oil revenues, elevated the scale of such construction to monumental proportions. In Singapore, on the other hand, the political role of the housing programmes has been considered much more carefully and the spread of home-ownership throughout the middle echelons of society has played a crucial role in their political castration.

The importance of the political and economic rationale behind mass public housing programmes will be constantly emphasised throughout the remainder of this chapter, but in order to facilitate further analysis it will be helpful to examine the different types of large-scale government housing projects which exist. Contrary to popular assumptions, there is considerable variation, in terms of evolution, aims, design and achievements, even within the limited number of mass housing programmes which exist in the Third World. Three major types of government commitment may be identified at present: large-scale estates, separate 'new town' developments, and urban renewal projects. Although it is not always possible to separate completely activity on this simple basis, the typology will enable some distinctive features to be identified.

Estates. Large-scale estate construction can be examined at three distinct levels – its location within the city, the layout and planning of estates as a whole, and the design of individual blocks and units. The most influential factor in the first of these, estate location, is undoubtedly the availability of land. This encompasses both its physical freedom from existing development and the legal problem of acquisition. With regard to the latter, few cities are as fortunate as Hong Kong and Singapore which have extensive government ownership of land. In most instances, urban land is in complicated systems of private ownership which, together with weak resumption legislation, make the acquisition of suitable development sites very expensive and time-consuming. In some cities, the authorities resort to large-scale squatter demolition in order to acquire land; this happened in Caracas prior to the launching of the *superbloque* programme. However, the central location of most squatter communities in the Third World usually ensures that commercial rather than residential redevelopment takes priority after clearance schemes.

The most viable alternative in the face of high land costs in the central city is for large-scale housing to be constructed on the urban periphery where land is undeveloped, less expensive and relatively easy for the government to acquire. However, such locations frequently · lead to severe economic problems for the intended residents, most of whom have close economic and family ties to the inner city. For various reasons, relocation to the urban fringes usually results in a reduction in household income so that estates are often slow to fill and are characterised by families in rental difficulties. Janice Perlman (1974), in particular, has written a vivid description of the economic problems faced by relocated *favela* residents in Rio de Janeiro.

At meso and micro planning levels, too, there is little evidence that serious research or investment has gone into estate design. The main concern seems to be to house as many people as cheaply as possible and this inevitably means high-rise buildings. Support facilities are rarely considered and this is particularly true of retail marketing services. Many large-scale housing estates in the Third World are consequently characterised by chaotic patchworks of illegal vendors (Plate 8). Educational and welfare facilities are similarly limited, frequently being left for religious or charitable organisations to provide.

The high-rise blocks themselves are culturally difficult for many residents to accept, particularly if they are recent arrivals in the city, and there is little evidence to show that such estates promote community interaction or neighbourliness (Walter 1978). However, there has been very little research carried out in the Third World on the social effects of high-rise development. Most investigations, in Southeast Asia at least, have examined high-density, rather than high-rise, developments (Mitchell 1972, Hassan 1975). However, there are indications that even amongst the tolerant Chinese communities in Southeast Asia, definite preferences exist for medium-rise apartments of four to eight storeys (Yeung 1976, Hassan 1977). Nevertheless, as the following chapter will show, it is the economic rather than the cultural argument that is likely to lead to more low-rise, medium-density developments in the future. Within the buildings themselves conditions are usually very basic, with communal washing, cooking and toilet facilities being the norm rather than the exception. For medium-rise blocks of seven or eight storeys, lifts are seldom provided; when they are, they frequently break down due to poor maintenance. The problem of maintenance is, in fact, very important because this is one of the few ongoing expenses of a public housing project and is therefore liable to be curtailed once rental defaults begin. This is something of a vicious circle since rental defaults most frequently occur when supplementary payments for water, electricity and maintenance are demanded by the government landlord.

Perhaps the most infamous example of an ill-planned mass housing programme occurred in Caracas, the capital of Venezuela. The rapid population growth of this city began during the inter-war period following the development of the country's oil resources. By 1970 the population of Caracas had reached 2.2 million, some 30 per cent of the total urban population of Venezuela, and has continued to expand at a rate of 5.5 per cent per annum. One obvious consequence of such rapid growth has been the inability of the conventional housing market to provide shelter for the migrants who have streamed into the capital.

Extensive squatter *ranchos* have long existed in all of Venezuela's state capitals and in 1964 over one-third of the population in Caracas was housed in this way, despite the massive construction of high-rise public housing over the previous decade. In total, 85 *superbloques* were erected between 1954 and 1958 during a 'crash programme' launched by Jiminez, then dictator, in order to display to the city's population the extent of both his power and concern for their welfare by ridding Caracas of its *ranchos*.

The 'crash' nature of the programme led to serious deficiencies in both the social and physical planning of the estates. *Rancho* communities were simply bulldozed out of existence and the residents transferred to flats in the *superbloques* without any screening or preparation. This situation was exacerbated in 1958 following the downfall of the Jiminez regime when thousands of families invaded the estates and *rancho* settlements sprang up in and around the blocks themselves. The entire situation was beyond the administrative capabilities of the supervisory body, the Banco Obrero, and enormous rental defaults built up. As a result, the programme was suspended in 1959 and a comprehensive evaluation study undertaken (Carlson 1960). The ensuing report severely criticised both the architecture of the blocks and the layout of the estates for discouraging community interaction. Social facilities, such as health and welfare provision, were said to be particularly inadequate and this had contributed substantially to the general aura of unhealthiness and delinquency which characterised the *superbloques*. In this context, educational deficiencies were seen as being particularly important since facilities had been constructed for only half the estimated school population. Some of the specific suggestions of the evaluation report were incorporated into a set of longer-term proposals, crucial to which was the creation of a centralised housing authority specifically concerned with the co-ordination of national and urban housing programmes. Although many of these recommendations have not been implemented, Dwyer (1975) has claimed that within the *superbloques* considerable progress has been made in improving both the social and physical aspects of daily life.

New Towns. The British concept of new town development has had wide repercussions throughout the Third World, although in most instances its primary function has been seen as a catalyst for regional development. In this sense it has fused with the wider concept of growth pole theory and has become a major force in regional planning, occasionally peaking in new capital city development projects as in Brazil and Pakistan. The suitability of these concepts and their practical achievements within the Third World is a separate issue which is not discussed in this book. However, it would be true to state that in general one of the major motivations in British new town planning – decongestion from overcrowded and overconcentrated urban centres – has not received the same attention from planners in developing countries. This is not to say that no new towns have attempted to fulfil such a role, but in general it has been less important than the growth pole function and far less successful.

As later case studies will illustrate, most new towns in the Third World have tended to be located far too close to the original city to act as a counter-attraction for both migrant and existing populations. The effect is to reduce the settlements to mere dormitory suburbs for middle-income populations. This has occurred in both Kebajoran Baru, Jakarta, and Petaling Jaya, Kuala Lumpur, and it is perhaps worthwhile to examine the development of the latter in some detail to discover how and why the change in function came about. A comprehensive study of Petaling Jaya by McGee and McTaggart (1967) provides the basis for this examination.

The initial proposals for Petaling Jaya intended the settlement to be a satellite town of some 70,000 people. The site chosen was about 10km southwest of Kuala Lumpur (Figure 5.2), and whilst a small portion of the land belonged to the state, most was under private rubber cultivation. The primary phase of development in Petaling Jaya was related to squatter resettlement largely from the Jalan Pekililing area in central Kuala Lumpur which was being cleared for high-rise housing construction. Each family was allocated a plot of about 420 square metres for a M$200 (US$80) premium, and given assistance to build its own home. This phase lasted from 1952 to 1954 when the Petaling Jaya Authority was set up. This body was empowered to raise loans for developmental purposes and over the next few years proceeded to acquire a considerable amount of land in the area. The land was cleared, prepared and demarcated by the Authority and subsequently leased or sold to individuals, contractors or developers. An industrial zone was also developed and on the eve of independence in 1957 there were already 28 factories in operation.

Several important changes occurred in 1957 which drastically affected the direction of development in Petaling Jaya. The most obvious related to national independence which in Kuala Lumpur led to a large

Figure 5.2: Petaling Jaya: Land Use in 1971

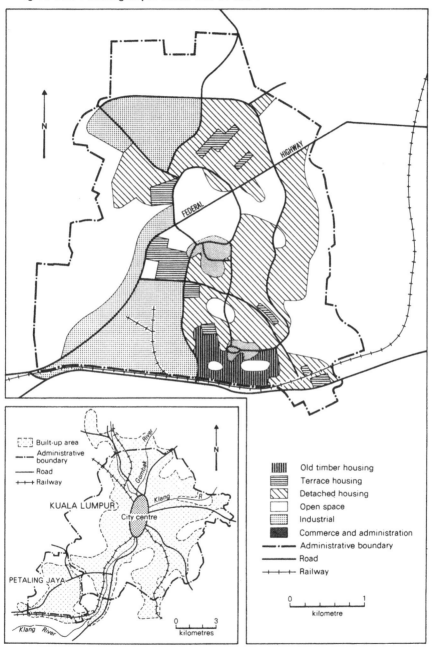

Built-up area
Administrative boundary
Road
Railway

KUALA LUMPUR
City centre

PETALING JAYA

Klang River

Gombak

Klang R

River

0   3
kilometres

Old timber housing
Terrace housing
Detached housing
Open space
Industrial
Commerce and administration
Administrative boundary
Road
Railway

0   1
kilometre

increase in the numbers of administrative and diplomatic personnel. As McGee and McTaggart (1967:36) have noted, 'for such people, the chance to obtain good residential land as near to Kuala Lumpur as Petaling Jaya was too good to miss'. This tendency was increased by the opening of the federal highway linking the new town with Kuala Lumpur. The improved accessibility led to an enormous increase in demand for residential sites on the part of Kuala Lumpur's middle- and upper-income groups. This in turn encouraged large-scale speculative developments by private firms who were encouraged in this by the Malay-Borneo Building Society (MBBS), a quasi-governmental body which was primarily intended to finance low-cost housing projects.

These trends have continued to the present day and Petaling Jaya is now an overwhelmingly middle-class settlement. In 1979 its population was over 100,000 with almost all living in 'bungalow'-type accommodation and commuting to white-collar jobs in Kuala Lumpur. In contrast, the industrial employment in Petaling Jaya itself has been taken up by residents of Kuala Lumpur so that the federal highway is heavily used each day by reverse flows of commuters – a complete negation of the self-sufficiency which is supposed to characterise new towns. The initial squatter resettlement function of Petaling Jaya appears to have been abandoned at an early stage in the town's development. Almost certainly this coincided with the creation of the Petaling Jaya Authority, for although the administrative organisation became more formalised, little advice was given to the new Authority as to the principles which were to guide future growth. As will always happen in such a situation, the Authority decided to opt for commercial development rather than continue to meet the resettlement needs of Kuala Lumpur's congested slum and squatter areas. In short, therefore, proximity and profit have turned Petaling Jaya from a new town giving new opportunities to the urban poor, into the middle-class dormitory suburb that it is today.

Urban Renewal. Few cities in the Third World are in a position to undertake urban renewal, the problems of coping with general housing shortages being sufficient to discourage any further reduction in stock by slum clearance. The adoption of urban renewal policies is therefore restricted to relatively wealthy cities, such as Hong Kong or Singapore. The commitment to urban renewal might also seem to imply a shift in basic policies to incorporate wider welfare goals; a movement away from mere economic growth into economic development. However, welfare objectives do not figure prominently in the few urban renewal schemes in operation in the Third World. Once again this can be attributed to the predominance of alien attitudes derived from renewal experiences in developed countries where the social benefits of clearance and renewal have been seriously questioned. The thrust of the argument is that poverty, not the physical environment, is the basic reason for the existence of slums and as such should receive priority attention. On the other hand, the broad community benefits following commercial re-development of renewal districts have also been well appreciated in the West.

The previous chapter has shown that central city districts in the Third World are very different from those in the West and this must raise doubts as to the validity of Western notions relating to slum clearance and renewal. In developing countries, dense populations exist in and around the main commercial areas, most of whom are heavily reliant on adjacent businesses for direct or indirect employment. In addition, because of the lack of new low-cost housing near the city centre, slums invariably offer the cheapest accommodation on the private market, not only for the poor but for many of the middle-income families as well. The individuals who reside in the central areas of cities in the Third World and who must form the focal point of any urban renewal programme, thus comprise a very heterogeneous group. Whilst most families undoubtedly need improved housing, they are often reluctant to break their established economic and social ties in order to relocate in a peripheral estate or new town. In these circumstances it would seem sensible to make provision for rehousing some portion of the affected slum populations within the renewal districts themselves. Unfortunately, this approach has not received much support so that most urban renewal schemes in the Third World have commercial redevelopment as their prime objective for the cleared areas.

This can be clearly seen in Georgetown, Malaysia, where plans have been in existence for several years to clear and reconstruct a small blighted area to the south of the present business district. The intention of the scheme is to replace some of the present large-scale land uses, such as schools, transportation termini and a hawker market, with multistorey commercial and office space. There are many ramifications from this project other than the expected economic uplift for the city, the most important of which concern the families in the surrounding residential district. The physical fabric of this area is perhaps the worst in Georgetown but, despite the nature of the area, the inhabitants like the low rents and the central location. As a result, traditional values, such as spatial segregation by clan groups, still exist on a marked scale.

The situation is unusual in comparison to Hong Kong and Singapore because the peripheral public housing in Georgetown does not offer the inducement of lower rents to attract families away from the centre. However, the new renewal project will inevitably increase the demand for commercial development in the nearby areas so that land values are certain to rise. Landlords, who at present receive very low rents, are likely to sell their property to developers quite quickly. In addition, the main Chinese school for the neighbourhood will be removed as will the heavily used hawker market, so that the total social effects of the renewal project will be considerable. Despite these considerations, no development plan has been commissioned for the adjacent residential areas and the project is indicative of the way in which economic factors predominate over social considerations in urban renewal schemes in the Third World. In the particular case of Georgetown, the desire to resuscitate the stagnating economy of the city has induced a premature renewal programme, even before the general housing shortage has been met.

Whilst examination of current urban renewal projects in developing countries inevitably leads to their condemnation from both fiscal and welfare standpoints, there is an alternative approach which offers a method of improving slum districts at reasonable cost for the benefit of the residents themselves, viz. rehabilitation – the physical improvement of existing properties capable of useful life for a reasonable period. Programmes of this nature have become very popular in developed countries over the last two decades and provide one instance of Western planning practice which might prove useful if reapplied in the Third World. First, rehabilitation is far cheaper than renewal and involves less demolition of existing property. Second, it offers the opportunity to retain areas of particular cultural, economic and architectural character which might conceivably prove attractive to tourists. Third, it enables improvements to be made to areas which may be suitable for renewal but which the city cannot yet afford to treat on that scale. However, rehabilitation does involve a direct subsidy to property-owners and this may not be politically or financially feasible. Perhaps eventual success will depend on a restructured rent control system where benefits revert to the property-owner for maintenance rather than to the chief tenant.

Innovative Responses

Innovative approaches to the housing shortages of the Third World broadly encompass government-subsidised programmes which involve, in varying degrees, co-operation between the conventional and non-conventional sectors. There may also be a case for including joint venture projects between the public and private components of the conventional sector, but this is a more contentious issue and will be discussed separately in the following two chapters. At present, almost all of the innovative responses revolve around various squatter improvement schemes, taking as a basic premiss the notion that the squatters will be able to improve their own homes if some government assistance is made available.

Previous discussion has indicated that most squatters are responsible and resourceful members of the urban community and that current public housing programmes have been ineffective in improving the living conditions of most of the urban poor. During the 1960s it became increasingly clear that the energies of the squatters themselves could be used to offset some of the more exorbitant costs of government housing, particularly that of labour. In short, the self-help which already existed within certain squatter settlements was transformed into aided self-help. Various programmes, distinguished by the size and nature of the government involvement, have developed from the original co-operative concept. Some have subsidies which cover initial land costs, others finance only site preparation and/or infrastructural installations, so it will be useful at this point to describe some of the distinguishing characteristics of the major types of aided self-help project.

Upgrading

The simplest, and probably the most effective, form of aided self-help is the upgrading of squatter settlements. This can involve the improvement of the dwellings themselves but usually consists of the insertion of basic infrastructural services, such as sewerage connections or water standpipes. In theory, the principal objectives of upgrading are to reduce the costs of housing improvement for the squatter and to avoid the residential dislocation which is involved in clearances to peripheral resettlement schemes. In practice, the benefits vary enormously according to the way the government promotes the upgrading project. Although squatter upgrading appears to be a relatively straightforward operation, it seldom works out this way in practice because the welfare of squatters is not the only, or even the main, goal (see Mathey 1978). The struggle for the improvement of the Tondo foreshore in Manila provides a good illustration of this situation. The Tondo foreshore is reclaimed land originally intended for industrial and port development.

The long delays in promoting these projects and the area's proximity to downtown employment in Manila soon encouraged squatter settlement. By 1968 the number of people living in the area was about 44,000, but this rose rapidly over the following years and in 1977 stood at over 200,000. Prior to 1972 the Tondo was left much to its own devices. Various clearance and relocation schemes had been attempted but the most successful were the very localised infrastructural improvements negotiated through various pressure groups which originated from amongst the squatters themselves. Mutual aid was widespread in the Tondo and the community was well organised around traditional *barrios* (Laquian 1969, Hollnsteiner 1972, 1977).

Since the declaration of Martial Law and the advent of the New Society in 1972, the government has made determined attempts to deal with the Tondo 'problem'. A determination which is not unconnected with the current availability of international finance for long-planned industrial development of the site. In an effort to avoid the mistakes of previous squatter schemes, it has been decided to relocate those immediately affected by the redevelopment in a nearby reclaimed area and to incorporate most of the remainder into *in situ* improvement schemes. The formal government agencies overseeing this activity are the Tondo Foreshore Development Authority (TFDA) and the Tondo Inter-Agency Action Centre (TIAAC). These are supplemented by a series of hierarchical community organisations called *barangays*, made up of 500 to 700 families, which are closely integrated into the system of local government. The *barangays* are artificial 'neighbourhood units' with nominated officials and are clearly designed to replace the existing traditional *barrio* system which is at the heart of community solidarity (Kendall 1976).

Throughout the improvement programme the government has shown little appreciation of the real needs of the Tondo. Physical considerations have dominated the planning programme and the residents themselves have been given little opportunity to participate in the redevelopment process (see Lakha and Pinches 1977, Pinches 1977). This reached extreme proportions when an international competition was held to design the new resettlement plan for nearby Dagat-Dagatan. Entrant firms were supplied with a dossier of facts and maps but no visits to the community were expected and no consultation with the residents was undertaken. Self-help to the Manila authorities obviously means little more than the cheap employment of local residents in construction work. This clearly indicates the elitist approach adopted by the government in its attempts to improve the Tondo squatter area. *Barangay*

officials are consistently given preference in all discussions and open
hostility has been shown to all other representatives, even extending
to imprisonment. Fortunately the community has been well organised
for many years, initially into the Zone One Tondo Organization
(ZOTO) and later into a broader co-ordinating committee, the
Ugnayan, representing several squatter organisations in Manila. Over
the last decade these groups have built up considerable experience in
dealing with the bureaucracy and have been able to take the initiative
in obtaining various concessions and improvements. In no way can this
communication be considered a dialogue since the government is constantly subjecting the squatter leaders to harassment. Moreover, the
interminable political wrangling has considerably delayed the implementation of any improvements to the area and there is the underlying threat that the authorities will eventually lose patience and resort
to alternative measures to obtain the land.

The question of land tenure is very important in squatter improvement schemes as, by definition, most squatters are illegal occupants
of the land on which their house is built and consider that improvement schemes contain implicit recognition of tenure rights. But this
is often much further than many authorities are prepared to go. In
some cities, such as Port Moresby or Lusaka, the granting of land
rights forms an integral part of the improvement package (Figure 5.3);
but in most settlements squatters gain only limited rights to the land or
buildings they occupy. More often than not the authorities only grant
land rights within a purchasing arrangement, knowing that the squatters
are only too willing to legalise their rights in this way. Sometimes the
prices are reasonable, but frequently they are not. In the Bago Bantay
scheme in Manila the selling prices of building plots averaged P7 (US$1)
per square metre but adjacent land of similar configuration was sold to
two corporate bodies at less than half this price (Rew 1977a).

Another important feature of improvement programmes is the distinction between improvements to the dwelling itself and those to the
infrastructure of the squatter community as a whole. Rosser (1972),
in his examination of Calcutta *bustees,* has forcefully argued in favour
of the latter, claiming that the cheapest acceptable form of shelter
already exists in the huts themselves and that government attention
must be directed towards those basic environmental standards, such as
adequate sewerage and water supplies, which promote community well-
being. Whilst it must be conceded that this emphasis is undoubtedly
correct, infrastructural and social improvements are much more costly
than upgrading individual dwellings, largely because specialist labour

Figure 5.3: Port Moresby: Renewal Programme

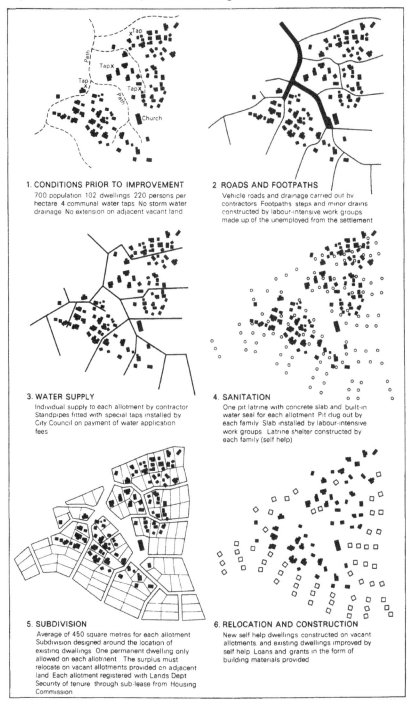

1. CONDITIONS PRIOR TO IMPROVEMENT

700 population 102 dwellings 220 persons per hectare 4 communal water taps No storm water drainage No extension on adjacent vacant land

2 ROADS AND FOOTPATHS

Vehicle roads and drainage carried out by contractors Footpaths steps and minor drains constructed by labour-intensive work groups made up of the unemployed from the settlement

3. WATER SUPPLY

Individual supply to each allotment by contractor Standpipes fitted with special taps installed by City Council on payment of water application fees

4. SANITATION

One pit latrine with concrete slab and built-in water seal for each allotment Pit dug out by each family Slab installed by labour-intensive work groups Latrine shelter constructed by each family (self help)

5. SUBDIVISION

Average of 450 square metres for each allotment Subdivision designed around the location of existing dwellings One permanent dwelling only allowed on each allotment The surplus must relocate on vacant allotments provided on adjacent land Each allotment registered with Lands Dept Security of tenure through sub-lease from Housing Commission

6. RELOCATION AND CONSTRUCTION

New self help dwellings constructed on vacant allotments, and existing dwellings improved by self help Loans and grants in the form of building materials provided must be employed. On average in the Third World, site preparation and infrastructure provision amount to 46 per cent of the total cost of each new site and service project. Moreover, these schemes are normally developed on vacant land; infrastructure improvement within older, irregular and densely populated squatter settlements is even more expensive.

Site and Services

In many cases squatter improvement programmes cannot be undertaken without complementary site and service projects to absorb those families unavoidably displaced. Site and service schemes differ fundamentally from upgrading and often involve entirely new developments, usually on vacant land in the urban periphery. The land is prepared and a service infrastructure added. Lots are then sold or leased and the new residents either build the house themselves or contract out. Government subsidies may also extend to building materials and/or cash loans. In theory, the site and service approach enables the separation of the land, utilities and shelter components within housing provision, thus giving considerable operational flexibility. However, there is still a strong element of government control both in the planning and construction of such projects, particularly in the choice of site, the size of the lots and in house design.

From the resident's point of view the primary attraction of site and service housing is undoubtedly the security of tenure it offers, together with adequate infrastructure and the freedom to build at one's own pace. On the other hand, the peripheral location of most site and service schemes often results in their being some distance from major sources of employment. In this context Modavo and Haldane (1974) have noted that too often public authorities prefer to reserve more central locations for higher-income groups who are actually much better able and equipped to travel the greater distances involved in commuting.

In both upgrading and site and service schemes there is a tendency for middle-income families to put pressure on the affected households to sell either their tenure rights or their lease. As Atman (1975) has discovered in Jakarta, this has promoted speculation in many improvement schemes and the high rate of response to such temptations on the part of low-income families is indicative of the very real financial difficulties which can be experienced, particularly in relocation to a site and service project where the regularity of payment demands are often beyond the capabilities of household heads who are not in regular em-

ployment. In addition, the pressure to construct a basic core house
within a specified period frequently demands resources which the
family may not possess.

The question of payment defaulting raises other important but
seldom considered issues involved in site and service housing. One of
the most complicated relates to the fact that as the residents themselves are heavily involved in the construction programme they are both
loath to meet burdensome payments and even more reluctant to move
since no compensation is made for their previous work. It is unfortunate that one of the ways suggested to overcome this problem is to
screen the resettled families in favour of those with regular employment. Families in real need of help will therefore be ignored. The existence of such attitudes leads on to another important problem – the
availability of suitably qualified and sensitive local personnel to plan
and manage self-help programmes. As Modavo and Haldane (1974)
have pointed out, the acute shortages of experienced staff in specialist
areas such as this have resulted in two-stage projects. The preparatory
planning is usually dominated by expatriates with little understanding
of the real and complex problems of the urban poor; the execution
stage is left to indigenous officials, many of whom, aware of the
scheme's defects, procrastinate and avoid responsibilities as much as
possible.

Core Housing

Despite these administrative and organisational problems, site and
service schemes do offer some definite advantages, one of which is that
there is an opportunity to fuse technological development with self-
help. This has led to some useful research, particularly in the field of
core housing. A 'core' house is a minimum-shelter unit which can be
occupied almost immediately and extended when the occupier can
afford the time or money. Certain prerequisites are necessary for such
schemes to be successful. First, ownership by the occupier is essential
to stimulate investment of personal savings. Second, loans must be
readily available because most of the later construction will be contracted out to trained builders. Third, local industries have to be promoted
to meet the anticipated demand for building materials. Most core
housing projects are linked to site and service schemes, so that the early
technology closely followed that pioneered in Latin America. More
recently there have been attempts to reproduce the advantages of prefabrication at lower cost. Zielinski (1969), in particular, has evolved a
construction system which employs intermediate, on-site technology to

produce standardised concrete panels (UCOPAN) which are easily assembled by unskilled workers into a variety of house designs. Pilot projects at Siliguri in North Bengal have reduced building costs by over 30 per cent compared to conventional methods (Banerji 1972). Whether such a modular system is usable in a core housing project is debatable since it involves considerable effort and therefore expense in the early stages of construction. Most core housing takes up to twenty years for complete development and it must be doubted whether on-site production facilities will last this long. Few core housing projects have been in existence long enough to examine the way in which residential development occurs. The example discussed below is not located in an urban environment but is near enough for the city to have affected settlement patterns.

Teluk Bahang is a small Malaysian fishing community of about 2,700 people situated some 25km west of Georgetown. In 1965 a modular housing project was completed as one of a series of improvement programmes for Malaysian fishing villages. Khoo *et al.* (1974) have examined the social and physical changes which have occurred since then. Although the resettlement plans for Teluk Bahang were initially proposed in 1954, it was not until 1963 that reclamation of the muddy foreshore to the west of the existing village began. It was originally intended that materials be given to the fishermen to construct their own houses. However, in order to ensure that the new structures were sturdy enough to withstand the strong winds characteristic of the area, the state government contracted out the work. A total of 144 units was built at an average cost of M\$2,136 (US\$861) each. This compared very favourably with subsidised housing costs elsewhere in the state. The $31m^2$ units comprised a first floor of two rooms, each about ten metres square, with a bathroom, kitchen and toilet on the ground floor connected by an external staircase. The ground floor amenities covered only half the available space (Figure 5.4). Rents were M\$15.50 (US\$6.25) per month, the cheapest public housing in the state, and house titles were not transferable until fifteen years after the initial agreement.

The core houses in Teluk Behang were obviously intended to be enlarged when the need and opportunity arose, but by 1972 only half had been modified, most by the simple enclosure of the open ground space. Investment in building modifications correlated with two factors. The first was the need for extra space to accommodate an expanding family, the second was the capability to pay. As Teluk Bahang is a poor community, the latter consideration was obviously dominant, so that most modifications were made by the more affluent households. This feature was consistent irrespective of the occupation of the household head. However, within the general trend it was also apparent that Chinese families were more prone than the other ethnic groups to make improvements to their house. In Teluk Bahang, modification of the basic core house has been a function of gradually changing socio-economic circumstances and as such has given rise to a wide range of physical types. The households most likely to have improved their homes are those in which the family head has moved upwards on the occupational ladder into employment which is regular, reliable and provides a stable income. Within this general process family size and ethnic group play subordinate roles.

Figure 5.4: Teluk Bahang: Core House Design

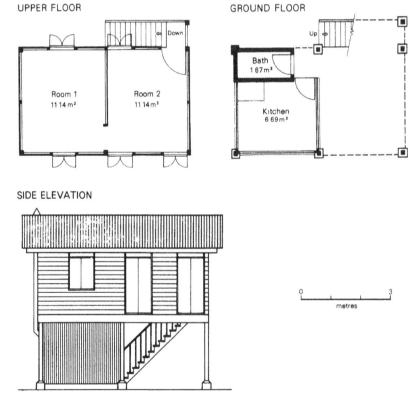

An Evaluation of Aided Self-help Programmes

The various types of aided self-help described above have received increasing emphasis in developing countries during the past decade.

This is largely due to the funds which are now being made available by multinational organisations, such as the World Bank, specifically for such projects. The trend is certainly not the result of a philanthropic transformation on the part of Third World governments. Indeed, as it will be pointed out below, the emphasis on aided self-help has served to reinforce the dominant position of the authorities *vis-à-vis* the urban poor. Some of the early proponents of aided self-help have become increasingly dogmatic about its ability to solve the urban housing problems of the Third World. This is particularly true of John Turner (1969a, 1969b, 1972). But many of the specific planning notions related to aided self-help were derived in the very particular context of Lima, Peru. The low densities and high degree of squatter co-operation which have accordingly become incorporated into site and service projects have very limited application in cities where sites are confined, densities are high and the extent of community integration is low. Dwyer (1975) has pointed out that Turner's ideas on popular systems of housing development are seldom put into the framework of overall urban development. As a result, some of the attempts to put aided self-help into practice without investigation of the wider problems involved have been conspicuously unsuccessful. Several of the more common administrative difficulties have already been discussed and it is clear that one of the major failings of the system has been the inability to prevent a middle-income takeover of the improved and improvable dwellings.

Such conclusions must force a reappraisal of the premisses on which aided self-help is based. As far as Turner is concerned, the question of tenure security has been the central issue on which the improvement potential of squatter households is based. In several different taxonomies (see Chapter 3), he has defined a stage of development in which families place highest priority on tenure or ownership. Turner has given a varied nomenclature to these families, such as 'low income consolidators' or 'incipient squatters'. In each instance they comprise low-income but stable households beyond the first, difficult stages of integration into the city, in which most of the heads are in regular employment. On the other hand, Turner has also argued that aided self-help is most appropriate for communities where unemployment is high and a tradition of home-building exists. This paradoxically implies that such schemes are more appropriate for 'provisional' rather than 'incipient' squatters.

Many of the inconsistencies in the application of aided self-help arise, not from any inherent conceptual weakness, but simply from the attempt to extend its applicability on a universal scale as a panacea to all the housing problems of the urban poor. Turner himself has indicated that the importance of tenure to each family varies with its socio-economic development. Alternative priorities and aspirations therefore characterise households at other stages of development. Even within Lima itself, Andrews and Phillips (1971) have shown that *barriada* residents are concerned about a wide range of interests, and whilst tenure availability does generate intense feelings, this intensity is not particularly widespread. Universal application of aided self-help programmes to all urban squatters thus denies households with alternative aspirations the opportunity to realise them. To use Turner's own terminology, there are many stable low-income households which are 'status-seekers' — unfortunately Turner restricts this description to middle-income families.

Criticisms of this nature, serious as they are, nevertheless are confined to the overenthusiastic application of what is usually accepted as a basically sound concept, viz. government supplementation of squatter energies and skills to improve living conditions. Recently, however, more fundamental criticisms have been made of the concept itself. It has been noted, for example, that as the capitalist, or conventional, building industry within most Third World cities is theoretically capable of housing the low-income groups at standards higher than those of aided self-help schemes, the current overemphasis on the role of aided self-help is therefore denying the urban poor their right to an equal share in the building resources of the city. Instead, it is argued, the energies of the squatters are being exploited in order to provide minimal shelter at low cost to the capitalist sector (McGee 1977, Burgess 1977).

In this context it is possible to interpret the increased availability of World Bank funds for self-help projects, and their eager acceptance by many Third World governments, as a concerted effort by the capitalist sector to short-circuit the aspirations of the urban poor, thereby averting a possible threat to the present unequal economic system. It is significant in this respect that Grimes (1976), in a research publication of the World Bank, has argued that site and service areas should provide a spectrum of plots within which the 'middle income families can outbid the poor for the choice sites and finish their houses faster by subcontracting large portions of the work'. Perhaps even more incisive is Correa's (1976:33) observation that site and service schemes 'often tend to become ghettos of cheap labour, at the mercy of one or two local employers'.

Obviously, aided self-help programmes do have an important role to play in an integrated housing system but, as in the case of conventional public housing or even for squatter and slum dwellings, their function must be geared to the capabilities and resources of the people in question. As Peter Ward (1976) has shown in Mexico City, the improvement of squatter housing is dependent on an investment surplus. Residence *per se* in a squatter settlement does not produce such a surplus; the upward mobility to which it is related is a response to opportunities in the wider urban society as a whole. Situations which produce such opportunities do not occur continuously in either space or time, so that any indiscriminate attempt to extend aided self-help schemes at the expense of more appropriate programmes might justifiably provoke political criticism of the kind described above. Part of the problem stems from the pace at which aided self-help programmes have expanded in the Third World and the difficulty which formal bureaucratic organisations have had in 'coordinating the developmental anarchy of autonomous activities with centralized development projects' (Kessler 1977:204). In contrast to communal self-help schemes, institutionalised self-help has a dual loyalty. The first is to low-income families, whilst the second, and usually the stronger, is to the government through a miscellany of goals concerned with values such as building standards or the national image. In this respect it is crucial that communication be improved between policy-makers, administrators and the urban poor. Mutual misunderstanding has been a frequent cause of project failure. In some developed countries trade unions perform this liaison function, but in the Third World such organisations tend to be too closely tied to the established political system to be effective. The urban poor are already well organised into small mutual assistance groups and it would seem sensible to capitalise on this by extending the system into units of neighbourhood representation. However, as events in Manila have shown, such approaches can be abused, and until these channels of communication are improved in both directions the errors which have plagued public housing programmes of all kinds will continue to occur.

Case Studies

The two case studies discussed below are set in Hong Kong. The first examines government housing policies in general; the second investigates the fate of the urban renewal programme in Hong Kong and in a sense can be considered as a continuation of the case study of Yau Ma Tei described in Chapter 4.

Government Housing Policy in Hong Kong

1954 to 1963. In Hong Kong the mix of private, public and popular responses to the housing shortage has varied considerably, but three phases can be clearly identified in the evolution of policy patterns since the commencement of the public housing programme in 1954 (for full discussion see Drakakis-Smith 1979b). Prior to this date the traditional entrepôt functions of the colony had been severely disrupted both by the conflict in China and by the Korean War with its associated trade embargo. Under such circumstances the government felt unable to help the refugees find accommodation, apart from extending a benign indifference towards both the illegal dwellings which sprang up around the colony and the intensive subdivision of existing tenements. It was hoped that after conditions on the mainland returned to normal the refugees would return to China. However, this did not happen and it became clear that such an exodus was neither likely nor desirable as Hong Kong prospered from the switch to manufacturing based on the exploitation of cheap labour. In 1954 the government's hand was forced by a massive fire in Shek Kip Mei, Kowloon, which made more than 50,000 squatters homeless. Following this incident it was decided to embark on a large-scale programme of high-rise resettlement housing. The initial standards were undoubtedly low and the government admitted that the density, ventilation and amenities of the new blocks were not satisfactory, although it was hoped that the design would permit later improvements along these lines. Given the economic uncertainties of the time, this approach was perhaps understandable. The retention of such low standards for a further ten years whilst the colony prospered is more difficult to justify.

The Mark I and Mark II estates built during this period still house almost half a million people. Their design is very basic, usually consisting of a series of six- to eight-storey H-shaped blocks (Figure 5.5). There are no lifts and all facilities are communal, being located on the central crosspiece of the block. The only water taps are also found there together with the open cubicles of the bathrooms and toilets. Rooms average 11.2 square metres and originally housed people at a theoretical space allocation of 2.2 square metres per adult with children under ten counting as half an adult. In practice, the actual space per person is often less than this allowance. Rooms were completely bare on allocation, with unplastered walls and raw concrete floors;

the resident therefore had to finish and furnish the room with his own money. No electricity was provided in the early blocks and the illegal tapping of mains outside led to networks of wire some of which have only recently been replaced and enclosed.

Figure 5.5: Hong Kong: Mark 1 Resettlement Block

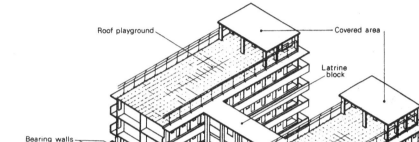

The persistence of these abysmal standards for over ten years reflects the priorities of the Hong Kong government in its resettlement programme. The overriding objective was to acquire valuable building land for redevelopment, not to resettle squatter families on philanthropic grounds. Not until 1970 did the Housing Board recommend that consideration should be given to resettlement of squatters living in the worst housing conditions, in addition to those cleared for redevelopment. Support for this somewhat cynical appraisal of the motives of the Hong Kong government can be seen in the fate of other needy households. Initially, no public housing was made available to the crowded slum dwellers because the land in the central areas was already intensively developed. The only chance of improved accommodation for these families was provided by the semi-independent Housing

Authority and Housing Society which restricted their homes to households with monthly incomes of between HK$500 and HK$1,200
(US$107-257). The mass of tenement poor with incomes below the
minimum level was neither considered nor catered for. Between 1954
and 1964 the number of squatters in the colony increased to 603,000
in spite of the resettlement programme. Some of the new squatters
were recent immigrants; some had voluntarily moved out of their legal
accommodation to take advantage of inflated rents; but most had been
displaced from the old central tenements by private redevelopment
schemes.

1964 to 1973. The second phase of housing development in Hong
Kong began in 1964 when the government reassessed the situation and
decided that its housing programme was too limited. Two government
working parties were set up to advise on the problems of squatting and
slum tenements, and a Housing Board was established to advise on
policy changes. As a result of the Board's recommendations the
building programme was both extended and upgraded. Individual flats
were improved by the gradual incorporation into new units of a toilet,
water tap and kitchen, whilst the space allocation was increased to 3.3
square metres per adult. The new blocks themselves were now at least
16 storeys and, with the overall increase in the size of the estates,
several developments housed well over 100,000 residents (Plate 9). A
more radical change in housing policy was the decision to commence a
Low Cost Housing programme for families with monthly incomes of
under HK$500 (US$107) living in overcrowded or substandard
accommodation of any kind. Allocation was from a waiting list com-
piled according to a set of priorities relating to urgency of need. The
new Low Cost Housing was of superior design to resettlement units
and was long overdue, but remained of relatively minor importance in
the overall housing programme.

One of the major problems which affected all public housing during
this second phase from 1964 to 1973 was the increasing tendency for
new estates to be located on the urban periphery, some distance from
the main employment centres (Figure 5.6). For a time this resulted in
long delays in filling the estates, but steady improvement in both
employment opportunities and transport have eased the difficulties.
The problems encountered in developing these peripheral estates
encouraged a change in policy during the 1960s in favour of new towns.
Throughout this period the two new towns of Tsuen Wan and Kwun
Tong (Figure 5.6) received heavy investment in both residential and

industrial construction. Tsuen Wan was already experiencing a limited but uncontrolled growth prior to the new town development. As a result, its central areas are still rather chaotic in organisation (Hayes 1978). Kwun Tong, on the other hand, was constructed on an area of land reclaimed from Hong Kong harbour and has had a relatively orderly and planned history of development.

Figure 5.6: Hong Kong: Distribution of Government Housing Estates since 1954

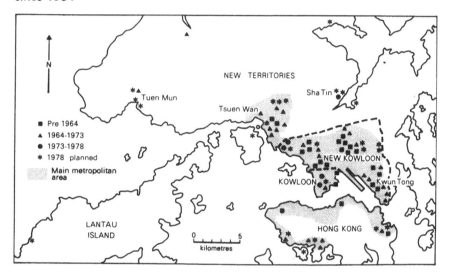

Two features distinguish the new towns in Hong Kong from their predecessors in Britain. The first is the amount of government low-cost housing which has been constructed within the development pro-gramme; approximately 70 per cent of the residential units in each of the settlements were built by the government. The second is the proximity of Kwun Tong and Tsuen Wan to the existing metropolitan core. Neither is more than 10km away from the Kowloon peninsula to which they are connected by dense public and private developments; the new mass transit system will confirm and strengthen these links. Under the circumstances the term 'new town' as applied to Kwun Tong and Tsuen Wan is a definite misnomer.

In terms of quantity there is no doubt that between 1964 and 1973 the government housing programme was a great success. The numbers living in public and quasi-public accommodation rose from 0.8 million in 1964 to 2.2 million by 1973, surpassing for the first time the pro-portion housed in the conventional private sector. But despite this activity the fact remained that in 1973 large numbers of people lived in the most appalling conditions. Despite the number of development clearances and the vigorous demolition of new illegal structures, there were still 272,000 squatters not including the unenumerated people who arrived after 1964. Part of the reason for this was the shift in the building programme to larger sites in peripheral areas where there were fewer squatters to be cleared; but there had also been a notable reluctance to resettle squatters simply because their housing was substandard, even though this was now part of official policy. An increasing proportion of new government housing was thus being taken up by the rehousing of existing tenants rather than the accommodation of families from slum or squatter districts. The sharp downturn in private sector construction in the late 1960s had also resulted in a continued deterioration of housing conditions in tenement areas. By 1974 Pryor (1975) had estimated that some 750,000 were living in substandard accommodation. If this figure is added to the squatter population and the 400,000 living below the original 2.2 square metres per capita space allowance in the older resettlement estates, it produces a grand total of 1.42 million poorly housed in metropolitan Hong Kong: over 40 per cent of the population.

1973 Onwards. The current phase of Hong Kong's housing programme began in 1973 when the governor outlined a ten-year housing programme for the colony which entailed the accommodation of 1.8 million people by 1983. Laudable as the general social aims of this proposal undoubtedly were, its specific goals reflected the uninformed *ad hoc* planning which had characterised public housing policy since 1954. The old emphasis on squatter resettlement was retained as the principal target of the ten-year programme despite the fact that many more people were badly housed in tenement slums and the older resettlement blocks. Fortunately, the programme has been considerably amended over the last few years and more realistic goals now exist. These improvements are themselves a function of the first and most important change which was initiated, viz. the amalgamation of all housing agencies and departments into one co-ordinated Housing Authority responsible for planning, clearance, construction and management of all public housing.

The reconstituted Housing Authority is a two-tiered organisation with the Authority itself comprising the Secretary for Housing together with representatives of the Urban Council and the heads of various related departments such as Social Welfare and Public Works. The exe-

cutive arm of the Authority is the Housing Department which trans-
lates into specific programmes the broad goals established by the
Authority. The main features of government housing programmes since
1974 can be divided into two broad groups. First, there are the principal supply characteristics: the emphasis on new town and New Territory developments; the continued conversion programme in the old
estates; the improvements in flat and estate design; and the recent
introduction of a home-ownership scheme. The second area of activity
has been the specific management changes within existing and planned
estates: the incursion into commercial development; the revised allocation system; and the general improvement of management and maintenance systems.

One of the major projects inherited by the Housing Authority from
the now-defunct Housing Board was the improvement of the early
resettlement estates. In 1975 there were over 400,000 people in the
original Mark I and Mark II resettlement blocks living in conditions
below the original space allowance of 2.2 square metres per adult. A
major policy decision was made to exploit the supposed flexibility of
the early resettlement units' design by refurbishing them to more
acceptable standards. After assessing the reports of a pilot scheme, the
Housing Authority decided on a policy of part-conversion, part-redeve-
lopment of Shek Kip Mei, the oldest resettlement estate in the colony
with over 62,000 residents (Figure 5.7). The operation initially proved
a great disappointment to the Authority since it was expensive in terms
of time and money, gave rise to complicated problems of relocation for
the myriad of small businesses, and provided accommodation for fewer
people than before. For a time it seemed as if the conversion programme might suffer the same fate as urban renewal and be slowly
phased out. However, this has not occurred and it is the government's
intention to proceed with the improvement of all of the Mark I and II
resettlement estates. This volte-face has been brought about by a
reconsideration of the role of conversion in relation to some of the
broader problems affecting the government housing programme.

The first of these relates to the relative affluence of the families in
the older estates, few of whom pay more than 6 or 7 per cent of their
income in rent, even for improved flats. The second problem is the
increasing number of small families entering the housing market, a
situation which has been exacerbated by the Housing Authority's
continued construction of large flats, in the hope that households
would continue to share accommodation as happily and conveniently
as they have done in the past. This has not been the case, however, and

Figure 5.7: Hong Kong: Estate Conversion Plans

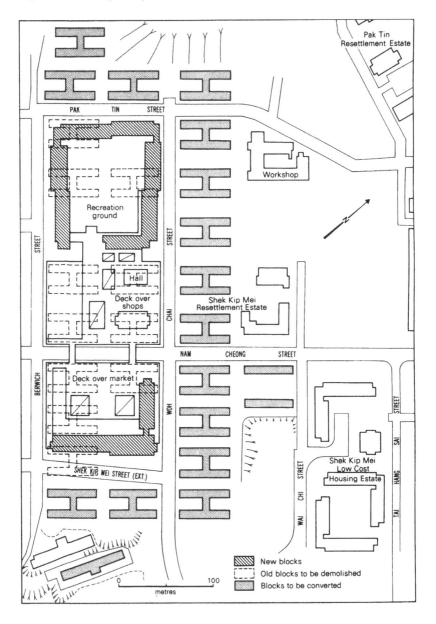

there has been an increasing demand for smaller flats from the growing proportion of newly married couples. Estate conversion has proved to be very valuable in solving this dilemma, largely because the conversion process itself displaces most families into more expensive public accommodation, either in the new towns or new central estates. The crucial point about such displacement is that it is not obviously forced upon the heavily subsidised household, but is subsumed in an overall welfare project. Affected families are thus more inclined to accept such a move than if it were suggested directly. Increased revenues are also obtained from the improvement of the small, vacated flats and from the reorganisation of service components, such as hawker stands and shops, within the estates. The enthusiasm of the Housing Authority for the conversion scheme has thus fluctuated more with its perceived economic or political value rather than its welfare potential.

A major policy change made by the Housing Authority since 1973 has been to give increased emphasis to comprehensive planning. At the macro level this has involved a review of the new towns programme and its extension to sites much further from the metropolitan core (Figure 5.6). In 1974 it was estimated that the existing metropolitan area of Kowloon, New Kowloon and Hong Kong Island could accommodate only another quarter of a million people in new government housing (Pryor 1975). This meant that 86 per cent of the ten-year plan target of 1.8 million new government tenants would have to be housed in the New Territories, and to this end the government has planned to develop two major new towns — one at Sha Tin and the other at Tuen Mun. Both are still in relatively early stages of development but it is anticipated that by 1984 each will have about three-quarters of its projected population of half a million. About two-thirds of these people will be housed by the government and it is intended that the private sector will accommodate the remainder. Ultimately the enthusiasm of private investors will be determined by the likely returns, and these in turn will depend upon the popularity of the new towns as places of residence because relocation will involve considerable changes in family lifestyles. In this respect, the ability of government housing to attract tenants is a crucial factor and many inducements have been offered, including reduced rents for an initial period, more generous space standards per capita, higher income eligibility criteria and subsidised transport.

In contrast to the new towns programme and resettlement improvement schemes, both of which have been inherited from previous housing organisations, the new Authority has brought its own initiatives to meso and micro planning within the estates themselves. Since 1973 there has been particular concern to improve the design of both estates and flats. Apart from the benefits this brings to the individual family, there are considerable returns to the government itself, and not only in the proportional increase in rents which is made possible. This is particularly true of the commercial facilities in government estates which in the past have been underprovided and underpriced. As a result, the private sector has moved in and made considerable capital from the government's spatial concentration of potential customers. To avoid this the Housing Department now constructs large retail shopping centres which are leased off at near current market rents.

Not all new estate design is linked to financial motives. Many of the most important improvements are related to the provision of recreational facilities and the construction of educational and welfare premises, all of which have expanded considerably. In addition, all individual flats will be self-contained and a revised minimum space allocation of 4.6 square metres per adult has been set as a future target. At the moment this latter goal seems rather optimistic, but the overall standard of living has undoubtedly improved remarkably in the new estates.

Most of the changes were evident in the first major estate to be constructed under the auspices of the new Housing Authority. This was at Oi Man in Ho Man Tin, an estate that was something of a showpiece during the first half of the ten-year plan. The project was built on the site of a former low-density cottage resettlement area and comprises twelve blocks which vary in height from 7 to 24 storeys. The site covers nine hectares and houses 46,500 people at an average residential density of almost 5,200 per hectare (Figure 5.8). Particular attention was paid to the provision of commercial facilities and it was intended that the three-storey air-conditioned shopping complex should develop as a retail focus for the entire Ho Man Tin district in which Oi Man is located. In addition to the shopping complex there is a covered fresh fruit and vegetable market, the stalls of which were initially leased to hawkers 'of long-standing operation' from other housing estates. Cooked-food stalls on the Singaporean model are also provided in a covered complex. Other amenities on the estate include five kindergartens and several playgrounds. All flats within Oi Man have a living/dining room with a kitchen, toilet and private balcony (Figure 5.8). Total floor areas range from 33 to 55 square metres with the larger units having two separate bedrooms, a notable innovation in Hong Kong's public housing. Oi Man is also the first estate with a piped gas supply and a communal television antenna — all very different from life in the Mark I resettlement blocks. However, as bitter experience has shown, even well-designed buildings need good maintenance and management if their benefits are to be long term, and the Housing Department has paid very careful attention to these aspects in its current work programme. Considerable effort has thus been made to establish a well-trained staff with a strong morale. As this occurs, an increasing number of the more responsible tasks, such as maintenance surveying, are being transferred from consultants to the permanent management staff.

Eligibility for government housing is based on family size and income, but the actual allocation is made in relation to comparative need. Priority is given to those made homeless by emergencies, then to eligible families affected by clearance schemes and to those living in unsatisfactory dwellings who apply for rehousing. Within this straight-forward list of priorities, however, are many subcategories based on secondary eligibility criteria. For example, residents of squatter huts affected by redevelopment schemes only qualify for government flats if their dwelling was built before 1964 and is registered as such. More-over, the number of flats made available to waiting list applicants is being increasingly reduced by quota allocations to lower-paid govern-ment employees and by internal transfers of existing tenants who are either living in overcrowded conditions, affected by conversion schemes or anxious to move to more spacious accommodation. In 1978 such internal allocations accounted for 22 per cent of new lettings. This is proportionally more than the number of units allocated to squatters or slum dwellers and indicates that the Housing Authority is beginning to cater increasingly for the lower-middle- and middle-income market. This trend became very clear in 1976 when the Hong Kong government set up a working party to inquire into the planning and legislative requirements of a home-ownership scheme which was to be developed, marketed and managed by the Housing Authority. Initially, 42,000 flats are planned for construction in the years up to 1987. Flats range in size from approximately 37 to 60 square metres and are intended for families with monthly incomes ranging up to HK$3,500 (US$700). However, no income limit is applied in the case of existing Housing Authority tenants willing to give up their tenancies.

As yet, it is too early to assess the impact of this venture but cer-tainly it is long overdue. The middle-income groups have been caught between the restrictions of the public and private sectors for at least ten years. Both the direct involvement by the government and the accompanying incentives given to the private sector to shift down-market must be welcomed. The enthusiastic response from the public

Figure 5.8: Hong Kong: Oi Man Estate

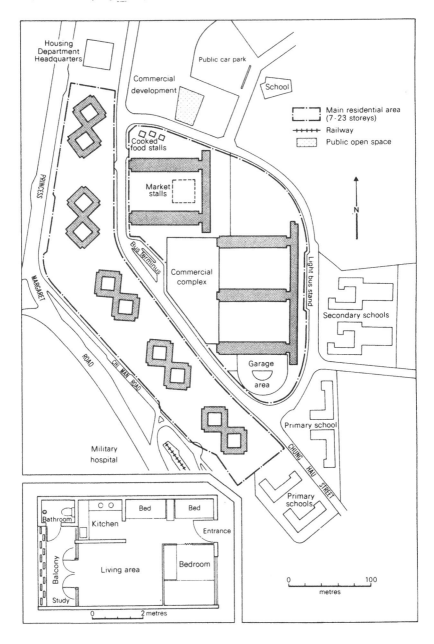

indicates that these measures could and should have been introduced long ago. Although the home-ownership schemes *per se* represent a definite advance in the Housing Authority programme, this achievement should not be at the expense of the poorer strata in the population. Unfortunately, as the second case study will show, this is precisely what has happened.

In addition to the increased care given to the planning of government housing estates since 1973, there has also been a radical change in attitudes towards squatters in Hong Kong. The intent and effect of past policies have been to restrict both settlements and huts to their pre-1964 dimensions. Prior to the implementation of the current ten-year plan, the inhabitants of squatter huts cleared for redevelopment were dealt with in two different ways. Those living in registered, pre-1964 structures were given a government flat; the remainder were offered places in 'licensed areas' where they could build their own shelter but used communal water standpipes and dry latrines. Since 1973 this situation has improved tremendously and the new Temporary Housing Areas (THA) comprise rows of asbestos-roofed wooden frames within which the household can build its home (Plate 10). Each is serviced with water and electricity although toilets are still communal. Rents are HK$5.40 (US$1) per square metre, with the area to be determined by the size of the household.

Most of the old licensed areas have now given way to the new accommodation and it is intended that more than 100,000 will eventually live in Temporary Housing Areas. This aided self-help system is very popular because densities are much lower than in the high-rise estates, whilst placement in one of the Temporary Housing Areas is a transitional step to government recognition. In terms of their standard of accommodation, degree of self-help and efficient management, the Temporary Housing Areas are an undoubted success and offer a useful model for low-cost squatter relocation to other Asian cities. Unfortunately, this aspect of Hong Kong's housing programme tends to be overshadowed by the scale of the high-rise estates and, to be honest, does represent only a minor success in relation to a group from which the government is becoming slowly but increasingly remote; a situation which is closely mirrored in the tenement areas of the colony.

Evaluation of the Public Housing Programme. In Hong Kong, economic and political objectives have dominated government decisions on housing investment. Political stability, low costs of living, and land were all urgently needed for organised industrial and urban growth. The construction of large-scale, low-cost, high-rise housing was one of the most important contributions to the realisation of these goals, and this has remained a crucial element in developmental planning within the colony. Whilst the objectives have stayed constant, the methods used in their attainment have changed considerably with the emphasis switching, for example, from inner to outer districts, or from blue- to white-collar workers. But even within this fluid programme, economic and political influences are readily apparent. Welfare considerations *per se* did not really emerge as a noticeable feature of policy formulation until the present decade when consideration of the individual family became a more prominent element in the planning process. However, it would be unwise to overemphasise these trends because welfare goals are still subordinate to other policy objectives.

Since 1954 the Hong Kong government has financed the construction of over 400,000 domestic units. These now accommodate more than two million people or 44.5 per cent of the population. Not only are the dimensions of the programme impressive but it would also be true to say that most of the units are low-cost. However, as this analysis of current trends in the construction and allocation of government housing has shown, access to such units is becoming both increasingly restricted and oriented away from the urban poor towards the middle-income groups. Those with the most favoured access to the public housing system are families already living within it, and lower-middle- and middle-income households who can afford the rents of the large, well-appointed units now being built. This discrimination will undoubtedly be extended by the decision to construct flats for sale, half of which will be made available to sitting government tenants; and also by any decision to differentiate rents by location so as to encourage movement to the new towns in the New Territories.

The current benefits to the government are the same as those which have been sought since the housing programme began — the release of land for development, tight control of metropolitan expansion insofar as it affects economic growth, and a politically stable population. The clearance of squatters and their replacement by areas of low-cost housing and multiple-use factory buildings has thus dominated the last twenty-five years of urban planning in Hong Kong. It is evident from current trends that as far as the government is concerned, the next phase of development will focus upon the commercial middle classes and the orderly settlement of the New Territories. The urban poor in the old tenement districts and the remaining squatter areas clearly have little to contribute to this plan and are unlikely to feature prominently in new housing developments, unless they can raise their financial status.

It is, of course, one thing to criticise and another to offer pragmatic suggestions for improvement, although it must be emphasised that amendments to programmes *per se* can only bring about limited benefits for the urban poor. Not until basic attitudes change within the Housing Authority and the government in general will any radical reorientation of Hong Kong's housing programme occur. It is unfortunate, in this respect, that in 1979 immigration has once again reached massive proportions. If this continues, the emergency housing shortage it will create is likely to perpetuate the status quo for a long time to come.

It must not be deduced from this critical cadenza that there are no praiseworthy features to government housing policies in Hong Kong. Given the dimensions of the programme, it would be surprising if many families had not received substantial benefits. But the overall impression remains that these welfare gains are largely incidental to the achievement of other goals. But whatever the internal circumstances, there are many useful lessons which can be drawn from experiences in Hong Kong for the benefit of other cities in Asia faced with mounting housing shortages.

Many sceptics would argue that the highly individual and fortunate economic, political and demographic features which characterise Hong Kong have been decisive factors in permitting its extensive building programmes, and that poorer or more populous cities cannot hope for similar success. Whilst there is much truth in this statement, many countries have striven to emulate the apparent success of the colony by following what they consider to be similar methods, viz. the construction of high-rise, high-density housing. Unfortunately, the least transferable elements in Hong Kong's housing programme are the design and technological aspects of the buildings themselves. Massive high-rise estates are economically feasible only when cheap labour or low-cost technology is available, and in contrast to popular opinion Hong Kong relies primarily on the former to keep construction costs down. Other governments have turned to prefabrication but this is totally unsuitable for the relatively small, isolated and discontinuous projects which characterise most Third World countries. The lesson from Hong Kong in this respect is to use local labour resources to the full, even on large-scale high-rise projects.

Administrative co-ordination is another important area where useful lessons can be learned from Hong Kong. Until 1973 there were four separately financed bodies competing for land, money and staff, and with their organisation into a single authority considerable savings have been effected. Not only has this led to a more productive use of resources but it has also enabled a comprehensive planning approach to be adopted throughout the administrative hierarchy, from a colony-wide level down to estates and individual units. Of course, greater administrative efficiency does not necessarily bring great benefit to the urban poor, which is still dependent on overall policy goals, but it does cut down on the waste of scarce resources.

The success or failure of any housing programme must also be measured in terms of the satisfaction of its residents. To a great degree this satisfaction depends on the 'after-sales service' as evidenced in maintenance and management. Following the reorganisation of the Housing Authority, the Hong Kong government put great stress on suitable training and job incentives, and has been rewarded with an improvement not only in tenant-landlord relationships but also in the protection of the environmental fabric of the estates themselves. Without such management changes the Housing Authority would have been prone to the sort of social and physical deterioration which plagued the early resettlement estates and which, indeed, continues to characterise government housing in other parts of Asia.

Within this broad organisational background two individual features can be said to have played particularly important roles in holding down the cost of public housing in Hong Kong. The first involves the government decision to subsidise public housing agencies until they can become at least partially self-financing. Whilst not all governments can afford to do this to the extent practised in Hong Kong, it is nevertheless of vital importance in holding down costs to levels which are within reach of the urban poor. It must be clearly understood, therefore, that without such subsidies conventional housing is unlikely to be low-cost. The second factor involved in holding down housing costs is land. In Hong Kong all land belongs to the Crown and can only be leased. This has not only enabled the government to subsidise public housing projects by allocating sites at reduced prices, but has also permitted funds to be raised by auctioning off portions of cleared land to private developers at considerable profit. The leasing system also makes it theoretically possible to control private redevelopment by planning block renewals in certain areas. However, as the following case study will show, this opportunity has not been acted upon.

Urban Renewal in Hong Kong

Chapter 4 described the conditions characteristic of the widespread tenement areas in Hong Kong; this present chapter has shown that in spite of their extent very little attention was paid to the plight of the tenement residents until the early 1960s. In 1964, shortly after the commencement of the Low Cost Housing programme, the governor appointed a working party to investigate and report on the problems of slum clearance. The terms of reference were vague and it is doubtful whether the statistical information provided at the time was really representative of the situation that existed. One small area was thus isolated as being far worse than any other district on the basis of unrevealed statistics and a vague notion of what 'bad conditions' actually meant. The area was subsequently recommended to be Hong Kong's first Renewal District, but the emphasis it was given at the time has surely been an important factor in the subsequent lack of interest in additional renewal programmes.

Western Renewal District is one of the oldest areas in metropolitan Hong Kong. Prior to the current demolition programme, two-thirds of the buildings were over twenty-five years old, compared to only 9 per cent for the colony as a whole, and only 38 per cent were in 'sound or good' condition (Pryor 1971). Living conditions were correspondingly poor with almost one-third of the households being crammed into cubicles, bed-spaces or cocklofts and having only limited access to basic amenities (Table 5.1). Environmentally, Western District was also heavily disadvantaged with outdoor recreation facilities limited to only 0.85 hectares of dilapidated basketball courts. In addition, the commercial and industrial activities, which together occupy almost 30 per cent of the total floor area, intrude into residential space and generate enormous traffic flows which impede pedestrian movement and create considerable noise and air pollution.

Western District undoubtedly comprises a very poor living environment and one might expect to find it populated by depressed families unable to break away and raise their standard of living. There is no denying that many of the inhabitants are poor, even by Hong Kong standards, but the overall distribution of incomes shows little difference from the range found in the colony as a whole. The major income sources are, first, from manual employment within the slum district itself, particularly in the port activities along the sea-front; and second, from service and clerical occupations located in the adjacent central business district. Over 80 per cent of the population work within these two districts with 70 per cent working either at home or within a 15-minute radius. For the residents of this area the economic opportunities obviously outweigh the disadvantages of the poor physical environment and also compensate for the relatively high rents which the inhabitants of the tenements are obliged to pay. Although rent control does influence the amounts paid, existing legislation is easily circumvented by practices such as key-money, rented furniture or simply subletting.

Table 5.1: Hong Kong: Comparative Characteristics of Western District, 1971

	Western	Hung Hom	North Point	Colony
Percentage number of households:				
living in a single cubicle, bed-space or cockloft	27.3	28.1	1.3	21.8
with less than $3.3m^2$ per person	36.9	44.6	19.3	34.2
without internal washing facilities	40.6	4.8	Nil	15.5
without a flush toilet	43.4	4.2	2.0	16.2
Percentage of children aged 5-14 not at school	9.3	9.4	9.1	15.0
Number of prison inmates per 1,000	4.0	2.0	1.0	–
Number of TB cases per 1,000	2.9	2.7	1.1	2.5
Median monthly income (HK$)	707	754	878	733

Western is here taken as representative of the urban renewal zone although the data sometimes refer to a slightly different census or planning district. Hung Hom is an area of rapidly deteriorating post-war tenements. North Point is a fairly representative middle-income district.
Source: fieldwork, Pryor (1971), Hong Kong Census (1972).

The residents of the district have many incentives to stay despite their living conditions, and the proportion who have seriously considered moving to government housing is much lower than in other tenement areas which are less centrally located. The vitality of Western District and the rich complexity of its economic ties with the central business district of Hong Kong Island belie the stereotyped culture of poverty which might be expected of such a physically dilapidated area. These characteristics are, of course, crucially important for any proposed urban renewal programme and yet they received scant attention in the working party's report. This was partly through ignorance, partly due to inflexibility, but primarily the result of the priority given to economic rather than social objectives.

Initially, the working party considered the possibility of simply paying cash compensation, leaving the displaced families to find their own homes within the private sector. This idea was rejected and it was recommended that direct rehousing should be offered as an alternative to cash compensation; at the same time, the working party turned down a proposal to use part of the cleared area for public housing estates. The reason for this apparent contradiction was the complexity of the leaseholdings in the district, since the government felt that acquisition from the myriad of small owners would be a long and expensive process. The eventual decision not to build public housing within the Renewal District was unfortunate since most of the available statistics showed that the great majority of the present families would have preferred to stay within the area, and in fact almost half the population had incomes which qualified them for the better type of Housing Authority flats. Given the complementary desire of the large number of expanding families for more space, the potential for public housing in the area seemed considerable.

Thus, fiscal considerations on a broad scale, particularly the apparent cost to the government, emerged as one of the principal planning guidelines for urban renewal. If the financial potential of the population in the area had been fully realised, the decision may have been different. It appears, however, that the working party gained little insight into the families for whom it was making plans and all decisions were taken at a macro level. The report assumed, for example, that 80 per cent of the dispossessed households would move into Low Cost Housing units despite the fact that half the families had total incomes in excess of the permitted maxima. As most of the Low Cost Housing accommodation available at the time was in the unpopular peripheral urban areas, the assumption was even more unrealistic. Yet it was precisely this unrealistic choice that was offered to the 13,000 residents of the pilot scheme area when demolition commenced in 1971. Families who refused the offer of Low Cost Housing and accepted cash compensation could either seek expensive accommodation on the open market or move into adjacent tenements unaffected by the renewal project. Given such restrictions, it is not surprising that 75 per cent of the families displaced by the pilot scheme opted for public housing (Wong 1972).

The refusal to construct public housing within the cleared areas negated one of the main social objectives of a renewal scheme, which is to improve the living conditions of the tenement families. Any physical improvements offered by removal to a peripheral estate are more than offset by the disruption to economic and social life. What makes the decision more incomprehensible is that the government was aware that public housing in the Renewal District would provide a better residential environment for the community, but was unwilling to forgo the substantial revenue which would eventually be obtained from land sales. This concern with the financial aspects of renewal has strongly influenced the progress of the scheme to date and it was not until cost-benefit estimates showed a profit that action began on any scale. Even so, progress is slow and, although large areas have been cleared, protracted negotiations between private developers and leaseholders have been allowed to drag on interminably.

By 1979 most of the tenements in the pilot scheme had been demolished, but their former residents had not received special consideration from the Housing Department. The statistical forecasts for the ten-year plan do not include specific estimates for demolitions within the urban renewal project and, as noted in the previous case study, allocations from the pilot scheme to Housing Authority estates have comprised only a tiny proportion of total public housing disbursements. Unfortunately, detailed studies of the actual movements of former pilot scheme residents have not been made.

Despite the concern that was displayed in 1965 when the initial working party report was submitted, the government has found it increasingly difficult to raise any enthusiasm for the urban renewal project. The direct corollary of this lack of interest is the absence of any plans for public housing construction in the cleared pilot scheme area. Government is restricting its input to road improvements and the provision of recreational space. The overwhelming portion of the re-development will be by private investment in combined commercial/residential projects which will be too expensive for most of the former residents. The only government housing investment occurs very indirectly through the loans made available to the Housing Society which is undertaking a relatively small Urban Improvement Scheme on the edge of the pilot area.

The efforts being made by the Housing Society to improve the situation in the tenement slums of Western District are highly commendable, both in motivation and effort. It contrasts starkly with the dismal record of the Housing Authority in this field and makes the government's attitude towards the Urban Improvement Scheme even less understandable. Having transferred the very difficult task of providing housing within the urban renewal project onto the shoulders of the Housing Society, and despite the responsible attitude shown by the Society, government co-operation in both a resource and financial sense is extremely poor. The seeds of success are undoubtedly there, the Housing Society has shown a degree of motivation and effort lamentably lacking in the government's own incursions into urban renewal, and yet little encouragement is given. This is one of the fields where the government's record in housing improvement is bad and getting worse.

It is evident even from this brief examination of Western District that there is abundant scope for urban renewal in Hong Kong, through which a variety of planning goals could be achieved if the work was vigorously and imaginatively pursued. At present this is not the case, and for over fifteen years the renewal scheme has languished for want of enthusiastic support. Furthermore, there seems little prospect of any additional renewal programmes elsewhere in the colony, despite the widespread and rapid deterioration of living conditions occurring in many tenement districts. Neglect of such a large proportion of the population could eventually bring about the political confrontation which the Hong Kong government has been trying so hard to avoid for the past twenty years.

6 THE ROLE OF THE PRIVATE SECTOR

Introduction

The previous chapter has illustrated that there is a polarisation in current government programmes for housing the urban poor. On the one hand, there is the minimum investment of aided self-help, and on the other, the expense of mass housing. The relationship of these approaches to the development process is still imperfectly understood but it would appear that there is a transitional stage during which neither operates to full effect. When real growth is taking place the tendency has been for countries in this transitional phase to initiate mass housing programmes before they are economically or culturally feasible. A paradoxical situation thus exists in which some governments are willing to increase their housing investment but lack the physical organisation to ensure its efficient deployment. In this chapter it is suggested that during the transitional phase the private sector offers a suitable vehicle for increased investment in construction by both national and local governments.

At present the private sector is widely assumed to make a negligible contribution to housing the urban poor since profits are more readily available from building shops, offices, factories or luxury housing. However, commercial builders are involved in low-cost housing construction in several ways. First, the private sector often undertakes the actual construction of government-financed low-cost housing schemes. This activity will not be directly considered in this chapter because the private sector contribution is subordinate to public housing policy. A second form of low-cost housing construction by the private sector is accommodation provided by commercial or industrial firms for their own employees. There are numerous examples of such housing throughout the First and Third Worlds, much of it linked to the iniquitous exploitation of migrant labour, but company housing makes a notable contribution on a national scale only in the cities of Japan where it reached 10 per cent of the total housing stock by the mid-1970s. Although several countries have sought to encourage this type of construction, its alleviation of overall housing shortages is minimal since a great deal of the accommodation is intended only for single men. In addition, outside the formal sector it would impose a heavy financial burden on the labour-intensive industries which are usually those less able to bear it.

Another type of low-cost commercial housing can be found in squatter settlements. It is generally assumed, particularly by Marxists, that all squatter housing is self-built. As noted in Chapter 2, this is not always the case and considerable empirical evidence exists to suggest that a sizeable proportion of squatter housing is either partially or wholly built by informal commercial elements operating from within the squatter settlements themselves. Few detailed investigations have yet been carried out in this field, but it would appear that the agents of production vary widely in size from the skilled individual building for friends or relatives, to highly organised syndicates. In addition, the extent of activity varies considerably with both the character of the squatters themselves and the economic well-being of the city as a whole, since there must be an investment surplus in order to stimulate commercial activity.

In addition to these three 'specialist' types of production, there is also the low-cost housing which appears on the open market. There are many small firms prepared to accept the low profit margins involved in this type of construction, but collectively their output is limited and many operate on an individual contract basis. By and large, most units on the open market are constructed by large-scale developers and are far beyond the reach of the urban poor. However, on certain occasions, when the economic and legislative circumstances have been right, the demand from low-income groups has been sufficient to induce a large-scale response from private developers. For example, in Cairo the large refugee influx resulting from the various Arab-Israeli conflicts has stimulated building activity in the private sector which now builds twice as many low-cost houses as the municipal government, significantly at much lower unit costs (Waterbury 1973).

Some observers, such as Honjo (1967), have condemned all low-income housing by the private sector as deliberately exploitative, offering meagre living standards at relatively high cost. There is no doubt much truth in this assertion but, as this chapter will show, such pessimism is based largely on inadequate knowledge of the private sector, particularly its structural composition. On the other hand, possible exaggerations on the role of the private sector must also be tempered by identifying, with far more precision than has previously been the case, the target population which cheaper private housing could be expected to assist. Although the discussion which follows draws much of its illustrative material from Southeast Asia, there has been little direct investigation of the potential of the private sector for low-cost housing construction. In lieu of a case study, therefore, the chapter will conclude with an examination of the situation in Malaysia which is one of the few countries where the government has tried various ways of involving commercial firms in housing the urban poor.

The Structure of the Private Sector and Identification of a Target Population

The organisational structure of the private sector may vary considerably between countries and this strongly affects the character of the residential construction industry. Perhaps the key factor is the presence of commercial housing developers – companies concerned with initiating and speculating in housing development. Theoretically separate, although with substantial overlap in interests, are the construction firms that actually prepare the land and build the houses. These firms do not normally initiate development projects but work under contract. If housing developers are present within a country, then much of the residential construction by the private sector tends to be large-scale. In contrast, when housing developers are not a notable force in residential construction, most private-sector activity is in small-scale contracts between prospective owners and individual architects or construction firms which in turn recruit labour for specific projects. The presence of developers also has an important influence on the ways governments seek to encourage cheaper residential construction. Thus in Malaysia joint projects with, or assistance to, the larger developers are strongly emphasised by the government because of anticipated economies of scale. The numerous small construction firms are virtually ignored as potential sources of low-cost housing.

In addition to this broad distinction in the structure of the private building industry, there are more subtle differences in the nature of the construction firms themselves which have an important bearing both on the potential and the use made of the private sector for low-cost housing construction. These differences may be identified by using two simple criteria. The first is the internal organisation which may range from a large, formal firm under some form of management or proprietorship, to a more informal group of workers associated with an individual and employed directly by the architect or intending purchaser. The second criterion is the operational legality, or the degree of compliance with official permit requirements for construction and/ or occupation. The resultant matrix (Figure 6.1) is undoubtedly more structured than reality but it does serve to illustrate the complexities of what has hitherto been regarded as a uniform sector with little to offer the urban poor. At one extreme are the registered, permit-abiding contract firms for which documented records exist. These firms are usually associated with large-scale projects sponsored and financed by developers or governments. At the other end of the scale are the illegal, small-scale operators, many of whom are based in squatter settlements.

Figure 6.1: Malaysia: A Typology of Private Building Firms

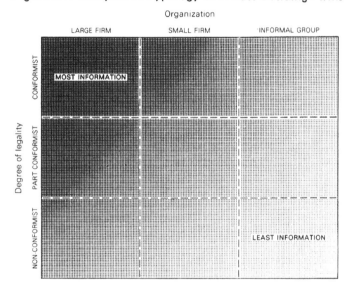

At present there is little knowledge about any component in the private construction sector other than that of formal, registered firms. Even within this group the range in size is enormous and because the small firms account for such a minor proportion of total construction their potential role in residential provision is assumed to be unimportant. This assumption is intensified by the unreliability of such firms in supplying information on their operations. When all the unrecorded, illegal and unaccounted activities of small firms are considered, it becomes evident that both the present and the potential role of the private sector in housing the urban poor have been greatly underestimated. Only occasionally have these been recognised and in even fewer instances utilised.

It is clear that most of the increased activity of the private sector in the field of low-cost housing should be aimed at the families caught between the present areas of production, that is those too poor to afford current private-sector prices but ineligible for public housing. Other than in cities like Hong Kong or Singapore, where government schemes house between 40 and 50 per cent of the population, there is usually a wide gap between households served by current private- and public-sector activity. This 'grey zone', as Filio (1974/5) has termed it, is very difficult to identify in most countries because the inflation which has affected the construction industry since 1972 has made current material, labour and land costs incompatible with the income parameters and groupings identified in the 1970/1 round of censuses. This poses severe problems for accurate calculation of either individual or group potential *vis-à-vis* housing costs.

Despite this general caveat, the identification of the grey zone in some countries seems relatively straightforward. In Malaysia, for example, the 20 per cent of urban households with monthly incomes under M$300 (US$121) are theoretically catered for by government projects, even though the cost of such accommodation is beyond the means of most. Families with incomes in excess of M$500 (US$202) per month, which comprise 57 per cent of the total, can usually find accommodation in the private market, although more favourable credit terms than normal are required by the lower-income households within this group. The remaining intermediate group, with monthly incomes between M$300 and M$500, thus comprise the principal target population at which cheaper private-sector accommodation must be aimed.

In the Philippines, detection of an equivalent group is much more difficult since there is no easily identifiable population theoretically served by government programmes. In 1971 the average cost of a house on the open market was P28,000 (US$3,544). At the prevailing credit rates such accommodation was limited to households with incomes above P1,500 (US$190) per month, about 8 per cent of the population (de Vera 1974/5). At the same time the average cost of housing units built by the People's Homesite and Housing Corporation (PHHC), the main government agency, was around P25,000 (US$3,165). Even at subsidised loan rates such houses were restricted to families with monthly incomes above P500 (US$63), less than 16 per cent of the population. Indeed, a minimum income of P500 has become a virtual prerequisite for a government loan. Ironically, many of these loans are used to purchase houses from the private sector.

The situation in Malaysia and the Philippines illustrates the wide range of circumstances which can affect the identification of target populations in just one region. The temptation is to assume, on the basis of countries where such identification seems clear cut, that cheaper private-sector housing is more likely to assist families in the lower-middle-income range than the urban poor *per se*, but the benefits from a reorganised private sector could be spread much further down the socio-economic scale depending upon the measures taken. Increased access by the lower-income groups to the private housing market depends on two main factors — lower house prices through reduced costs and improved credit facilities. However, it will be evident from the arguments presented below that such changes will not come about, nor will the benefits be passed on to the poor, without some form of government intervention and control. In most cities large-scale production of cheaper housing is unlikely to materialise without very positive inducements from the public sector in the form of joint venture schemes with commercial developers.

The following sections will examine these three elements, viz. the general constraints on construction costs, the improvement of credit facilities, and the nature of government controls, to see if there are any particularly fruitful areas for action. Many of the benefits resultant from such changes, particularly cost reduction, will not be restricted to the private sector and should in theory benefit the residential construction industry as a whole, but for simplicity the discussion will be primarily restricted to the former.

Synoptic Constraints on Construction Costs

Land

Land is a major item in housing costs. In some cities, in situations as varied as those of Hong Kong, Mexico City and Kabul, it is the single most expensive component. The basic reason for high land costs is expanding demand against a relatively inelastic supply, but many other factors also contribute. Some are commercial in origin, ranging from overconcentrated ownership, spatial preferences and development alternatives, to the entrepreneurial skills of the realtors or estate agents; other factors are related to administrative influences, such as urban planning goals, taxation policies and political stability. Despite this range of potential causes, speculation by a relatively limited number of landowners is commonly held to be the principal reason for high urban land prices throughout most of the developing world. To a large extent this is true, and government legislative powers are usually too feeble to oppose this legacy of colonialism. In the Philippines, which may be taken as an example of the situation existing in many countries, the owership patterns were largely established during the Spanish period and subsequently legalised during the American occupation. Land-based wealth was, and still is, the main source of economic and political power in the Philippines. Recently, President Marcos has attempted to introduce measures which have been successful in other countries in curbing land prices. Most public land is now leased rather than sold, governments at various levels are empowered to make compulsory purchases, taxes are levied on idle land and land values are being related to tax scales (Casanova 1974/5, Santiago 1976).

However, punitive taxation is not always the most appropriate response because unless it is linked to a system of general price controls the increased taxes are usually passed on to the consumer. Vested interests in landownership and speculation among the governing elites also prevents effective operation of revised legislation. In fact, much of what is considered to be speculation is often the consequence of other faults in the administrative system, such as the lack of adequate land markets with established, efficient channels for registration of owner-ship, or inadequate facilities for credit mobilisation. Both are a severe handicap to the small private developer and the long delays associated with these deficiencies often provide an excuse for extended, specula-tive holding of land. To a certain extent these administrative short-comings are intensified by the lack of adequate physical development plans for most cities in the Third World. A clearer indication of intended future land use could reduce delays, stabilise land values and thus circumvent speculation. However, even where zoning plans are in existence, their enforcement may be far from satisfactory, particularly in cities where private landowners are influential. It is not uncommon for government officials themselves to be major landowners.

Most of the positive measures that can be taken to reduce land costs involve major policy changes on the part of national and urban govern-ments. Direct appropriation and alienation of land, in particular, seem to be essential if price spirals are to be brought under control. This means increased public ownership, and the success of the government housing programmes in Hong Kong and Singapore has largely been based upon this principle (Yeh and Laquian 1979). However, in many Third World countries resumption is quite difficult, not only because of entrenched elitist interests but also because of extensive land holdings by powerful conservative institutions. Often these institutions are religious in nature, ranging from the very influential *waqf* organisations in Muslim cities to the Chinese clan temples of Southeast Asia, and constitute a substantial impediment to changes in land use policy.

Government ownership of land does not necessarily result in low land prices; all of the other factors noted above may still operate. Land prices in metropolitan Hong Kong, for example, are amongst the highest in the world despite the fact that land can only be leased from the Crown. In this particular case the sheer physical shortage of building land, together with a commercial and industrial boom, have been the main reasons for price inflation and, indeed, the Hong Kong government has itself indulged in speculation to push up the purchase price of its leaseholds. However, the important fact about government control of land is that it enables subsidies to be passed on to the consumer. In most cities this is done within public housing programmes themselves, but it is equally possible for subsidised land to be allocated to private contractors for specified projects. The effect on costs can be further enhanced by subsidised preparation and infrastructuring of such land. It is unlikely that government acquisition and conversion of land could take place within central urban areas where resumption costs are high, but it is feasible for large, peripheral holdings to be acquired at reasonable cost and made conditionally available to private developers in conjunction with proximate employment opportunities.

Building Materials

The materials used in housing construction comprise the largest building cost component, usually accounting for 60 to 70 per cent of the total. Since 1972 costs have risen markedly during a period of general world inflation and this has had severe effects on the price of the finished house. The rise in house prices has been proportionally greater than that for materials since many builders have introduced a 'risk' component into selling prices to cover themselves against the inflation of material costs during construction. These do not always occur so that increased profit-taking has characterised the industry in recent years. Given the importance of material components within total costs, an expansion in low-cost housing construction will depend strongly on an adequate supply of cheap raw materials. Any attempt to reduce overall construction costs must therefore make a close scrutiny of this particular factor.

The effects of world inflation on material costs in developing countries have been aggravated by the heavy reliance of some nations on imports. In addition to the immediate depletion of limited foreign exchange reserves and increase in construction costs, such imports also discourage the development of local raw material sources and related processing industries. This considerably reduces the substantial multiplier effect that the building industry can have on the whole urban economy. The reliance on overseas materials is primarily the result of long-established colonial and neo-colonial links with metropolitan countries which not only affect sources of supply but strongly influence basic housing designs, standards and building techniques throughout the Third World. In turn, these reinforce the external orientation of the construction industry. There is little doubt that many developing countries possess sufficient raw materials substantially to reduce their import costs, particularly in the use of timber and in the production of cement or cement-substitutes. At present, however, most of these resources are only fitfully or inefficiently exploited.

On the other hand, material suppliers would argue that it is the erratic demands of the construction industry which lead to inefficient production schedules and force prices up. This situation is intensified in countries with a pronounced wet season which compels most building programmes to cease operations. The answer here would seem to lie in the establishment of some intermediary, such as a building materials agency, which could not only absorb fluctuations in both supply and demand but also extend credit facilities to contractors. If this intermediary role was assumed by the government, profits could be kept to a minimum. One of the most encouraging developments in this field occurred in Chile during the Allende government when a building materials co-operative was established. At its peak it supplied 20 per cent of the materials used in the entire country, manufacturing some 15 per cent of its own supplies. In this way, the co-operative was able to reduce the price of its raw materials by 20 to 30 per cent (United Nations 1976). The present fate of this venture is unknown.

There would undoubtedly be a great deal of opposition to reorganisation from both contractors and suppliers because there are many links, such as overlapping directorships, between building firms and material sources. In addition, several firms have built up near monopoly conditions for basic materials, such as sand, which may be produced only at a limited number of places. To a certain extent these monopolistic situations have arisen because of the limited production and/or use of indigenous materials. One of the most ubiquitous of these resources is timber which is abundant throughout the tropics yet does not figure prominently in urban domestic construction. Part of the explanation is psychological because in many countries timber is associated with rural or squatter housing and is thus abjured by urban dwellers. But the most influential factor is probably the export revenues which hardwood timbers can earn. Thus, when world prices are high the domestic market suffers shortages, as did the Philippine construction industry between 1965 and 1970 (Makanas 1974/5).

Considerations such as these have discouraged more extensive use of local timber in construction, so much so that very little is known about its suitability as a major material for urban housing. Its resistance after treatment to various forms of pollution and to fire are almost unknown quantities, and there is a great need for co-ordinated research on various timbers before this fairly cheap resource can play a more important role in construction. With the erratic prices of timber in the export market, governments are paying more attention to its potential domestic use so that the near future may well see substantial advances in this field.

Labour

Another important component in construction costs is labour. In most developing countries this constitutes about one-third of the overall total whereas in Europe labour costs are nearer to one-half. In general, labour is abundant in the cities of the Third World and wages are low. However, some countries have recently experienced serious shortages of skilled manual workers, as well as technical and professional staff, which have resulted in a very rapid rise in wage levels. Most of the shortages in the skilled and professional fields are due to inadequate training facilities within the developing countries themselves, at both vocational and professional levels. Potential manpower thus tends to drift overseas for education and the limited number who actually return are inculcated with alien values. Faced with the shortage of skilled workers and escalating labour costs, many developers, both public and private, have begun to consider the use of semi-industrial construction methods. These schemes evolved in the European and American context where labour constitutes a very high proportion of total costs. The application of prefabricated techniques in the Third World is thus of more dubious value unless substantial savings are also made on the cost of materials, since this still constitutes the most important input in developing countries.

In addition to the direct cost of labour, consideration must also be given to the multiplier effect which employment in the construction industry can have on the economy as a whole. Cockburn (1971) has calculated that direct employment in construction, together with associated jobs in extraction, manufacturing and distribution, could involve up to 10 per cent of the total labour force, although in reality it seldom reaches this level. Nevertheless, the potential for construction employment in the cities remains high since they are the focus for most building investment. One widespread assumption about the construction industry is that it furnishes an important source of unskilled employment for new migrants to Third World cities. As it was noted in Chapter 2, there is increasing evidence that this is not the case and that much of the labour is recruited from rural settlements through the personal contacts of the labour foremen (see Lomnitz 1977, Stretton 1978). Whilst the construction industry may not have the absorbent capacity anticipated in urban centres, its role in labour turnover within a circulatory migration system constitutes an equally important part of the process of change. Bettelheim (1972) claims that the maintenance of village ties has been deliberately fostered by capitalism in order to provide a social and economic cushion in times of recession. As a result, this gives the labour recruiters themselves a crucial position as brokers on the interface between the formal and informal sectors.

The far-reaching importance of labour-intensive development in the Third World mitigates against any substantial reduction of labour costs in the construction industry, particularly as improved efficiency will still depend upon advances in intermediate or on-site technologies. Such changes will demand more skilled labour, and the subsequent need for expanded training programmes and increased wages will undoubtedly affect overall costs. The implication for the private sector is that labour costs *per se* are unlikely to be reduced in the near future, although a shift of some of the more costly and intensive labour activities to the public sector could help to reduce overall costs for the private developer. The most suitable form of assistance in this respect would be in site preparation and servicing, fields which have already been noted as offering considerable potential for reduction in general land costs. Government support in these areas could therefore effect substantial savings in two of the principal cost factors, land and labour.

Housing Design and Building Standards

Closely connected with both the land and labour problems outlined above are the regulations governing site development and individual buildings. These cover such elements as building heights, plot ratios, quality of materials and general infrastructure provision. In the great majority of cities the existing standards and regulations are both out of date and out of context, relating more to the Western countries from which they were originally adopted than to the realities of the contemporary Third World. The building code in Delhi, for example, dates from 1911. At the broadest level, the existing zoning regulations often tend to discourage the admixture of industrial or commercial land uses with residential areas. Whilst this may be desirable in a Western context, it does not take into account the necessity for close proximity between residence and employment which occurs in the Third World city. Similarly, the building codes themselves are geared to higher income levels of acceptability and are frequently maintained at these unrealistic levels by many of the overseas advisers to developing countries. Thus in Honduras, one foreign consultancy firm seriously recommended that newly constructed dwellings should have at least four bedrooms and be technically sound enough to last for fifty years (Solow 1967). All this in a country where 70 per cent of urban households earn less than US$90 per month!

Inappropriate standards such as these are the result of basic misconceptions concerning house design — a legacy of colonialism which has enshrined the Western style of residence, irrespective of its lack of cultural or architectural suitability, as the ultimate goal for most urban households. The recent movement towards industrialised methods has taken residential design even further away from indigenous and traditional values into high-rise fantasies. This has been most marked in government projects where the desire to exhibit concern for the poor outweighs the need for appropriate technology. Unfortunately, in many cities the aspirations of the urban poor themselves revolve around Western concepts of habitability with traditional values being rejected as old-fashioned and therefore undesirable. In certain respects, particularly sanitation, traditional housing is inferior to its modern counterpart, but in relation to cost, maintenance and cultural validity, it is often far superior. This would seem to suggest that some sort of compromise in design and standards is needed, with smaller rooms, cheaper materials or communal toilet facilities. Obviously, the actual measures taken will require careful consideration of all the cultural, social and economic factors involved, but all too often only token attention is paid to traditional values — often with farcical results. In the Sudan, for example, one low-cost housing scheme has merely reproduced the round native house with its conical roof, but in concrete and brick instead of mud and thatch; the resultant units are completely unsuited to either the pockets of the poor or the hot climate (Cain *et al.* 1976).

In some countries, incorporation of traditional values also needs to be extended to the layout of settlements as well as the design of the house. This is particularly true for cities where the migrant poor have originated from tribally organised hinterlands. Complicated social and cultural relationships govern the spatial patterning of the residences and related domestic activities of such folk and should be considered in the planning of low-cost housing estates. Failure to do this can sometimes result in the abandoning of the new units. This has occurred frequently in Aboriginal resettlement schemes in Australia (Heppell 1979), forcing a radical reconsideration of planning approaches (Figure 6.2).

Figure 6.2: Mowanjum: Planning a New Australian Aboriginal Settlement

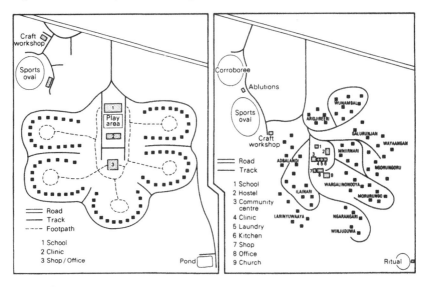

Whilst greater sensitivity and respect for traditional values must rely on a process of re-education, the easing of inappropriate and unrealistic building regulations should in theory be a much more straightforward process. However, even with the best of intentions it is not easy to introduce so many new measures over a short period of time, and much more difficult to ensure that they are followed. Lamb (1976) has noted that in Trinidad the checking of both plans and related construction is cursory because of staffing limitations and conflicting interpretations over roles. Real progress in the field of standards and regulations may thus be dependent on considerations other than legislative change. The centralisation of all bureaucratic functions relating to housing construction is one such step. This might even permit the co-ordination of welfare and economic goals since, all too often, encouragement of the use of traditional designs is tempered by the shortage or expense of appropriate local materials because of their importance as export-earners.

Improving Credit Systems

The credit schemes discussed in this section are those which would enable low-income households to enter more readily into the open market. Two assumptions therefore apply: first, that general housing costs will be sufficiently lowered to bring more units within the reach of this group, and second, that the discussion will relate only to those low-income families in a position to consider investment in the private housing market. Within these parameters it would be true to state that the savings of individual households constitute one of the least utilised sources of finance for housing investment. Throughout most of the Third World such funds, where they exist, are usually channelled into less fixed assets such as jewellery, gold or the non-tangible securities of children's education. The responsibility for mobilising these resources, and thus stimulating private development, falls largely on the shoulders of national and municipal governments.

Family savings may be divided into two basic categories – personal and institutional. The latter encompasses the various social security and/ or superannuation funds to which employers contribute on behalf of their employees, thus restricting its availability to those in 'formal' employment. When fully operational, these schemes provide substantial sources of funds from which sums may be borrowed for various purposes and paid back at little extra financial burden to the borrower. Singapore probably furnishes the most efficient example of such operations since home-ownership, particularly of government flats, has been an integral part of the programme of political stabilisation in the republic. In other countries the theoretical benefits of government security schemes have not been as well realised. Often the accumulated funds tend to be directed towards more immediately profitable or urgent investments other than housing. Moreover, the amounts made available to individuals are restricted to those considered to be good credit risks.

The mobilisation of individual savings and their supplementation by credit facilities for house purchase is an even more complex problem. The principal drawback at present is that in most developing countries the availability of credit is very restricted. The lack of government guarantees for commercial lending institutions means that credit facilities tend to be short-term, expensive and require large equity deposits to be made by the borrower. Typical commercial terms advance 80 per cent of the total house price at an annual interest of 10 per cent over ten to twelve years. It is unfortunate that as the greatest default risks occur in the poorest cities, the most needy urban populations suffer the most stringent loan conditions. Thus in Jakarta, it is not uncommon to find repayment periods of only three years at interest rates of 2 per cent per month. These conditions automatically exclude the urban poor from the system and restrict loans to the relatively wealthy or to those employed in government or quasi-government occupations which operate their own schemes. A more equitable credit system should operate a sliding scale of loans and repayments in which the low-income groups receive loans on more favourable terms – smaller equities, lower interest rates and, above all, a longer repayment period related to the full working life of the borrower.

To most governments, innovations of this nature imply a heavy increase in expenses and if direct subvention is not possible action is easily discouraged. However, private funds alone are often sufficient to stimulate the credit market provided government backing for the changes is forthcoming. The most important change needed to encourage greater investment in housing and a fair distribution of loans is an extension in the number of institutions offering credit facilities, particularly those specialising in housing finance. The increased competition should at least induce more favourable borrowing rates. However, one prerequisite for such improvements is the establishment of a secondary banking system. This will make loans to, and encourage investment from, the primary organisations which deal with the public, thus permitting far more liquidity in dealings with borrowers.

Latin American countries have taken the lead in institutional reforms of this nature, several having established a National Housing Bank specifically to promote development in this sphere. One of the earliest and most publicised occurred in Brazil and it is worthwhile examining its operations in a little detail to assess its effect on the provision of low-cost housing (see Bell 1974, Batley 1977). The Brazilian National Housing Bank (BNH) was established in 1964. Its major resources consist of monthly deposits amounting to 8 per cent of the salary made by employers on behalf of each employee. The employee may draw upon this fund not only when unemployed but also for home purchase or other important needs. The second major source of funds is the Brazilian Savings and Loan System which draws savings primarily from the middle class. The BNH does not deal directly with clients but sets policies which are implemented by associated first-line banks and agencies. Amongst these policies are differential interest rates and repayment periods related to the income of the borrower. However, most of the direct loans to assist house purchase have been made to middle- and upper-income families; almost all assistance for low-income groups has been channelled through state housing agencies. Herein lies the major criticism of the BNH since government housing policy in Brazil has been firmly oriented towards eradicating squatter settlements 'and other sub-human dwellings'. The inclination of the Brazilian government has always been towards *favela* clearance, particularly after the 1964 military coup removed the political power of the squatters. Many critics thus regard the BNH as the main instrument of government policy towards squatters and assert that relocation into public housing estates has not brought about improvement in their living conditions (see Perlman 1974).

The defects of the government housing programme which the BNH supports have led to the not unjustified criticism that the financial system as it stands is of more benefit to middle-income groups than to the urban poor from whom it draws 80 per cent of its working capital — a situation similar to that in the Philippines. On the surface it would appear that the original goals of the BNH still exist but, as Batley (1977) has clearly shown, there are a variety of operational devices used by the agencies to ensure that most assistance is channelled to low-risk groups, many of whom could compete in the private market. Carpenter (in Perlman 1974:55) has acidly remarked that the BNH obviously views the urban poor as an excellent source of funds but not as a particularly desirable outlet for them. As far as the urban poor are concerned, 'the solution is the problem' (Batley 1977:5), and although Brazil has established a financial system within which it is possible to channel more savings into housing investment, it also illustrates the way that the system can be manipulated to exploit the poor rather than help them.

Private and Public Sector Co-operation

National policy commitments to co-operation between the public and private sectors are rare, but at lower levels of the administrative hierarchy pragmatic ventures occasionally take place — with mixed success. Two major characteristics have coloured the projects which have occurred so far. The first is the size of the private organisation involved in co-operation; this can range from a large, national development firm down to an individual household. The second is the extent of public contribution to a particular project; this could encompass heavy subsidies through land alienation and preparation, or may simply be a tied loan on favourable terms. In theory, these two variables produce a wide range of co-operative possibilities, but in fact very few schemes of this nature have occurred. The remainder of this section and the following country study will discuss a sample of the projects which have taken place and offer brief comments on their achievements.

One of the most common forms of co-operation is that which results from what might be called corporate philanthropy, or the commercial conscience. Often in such schemes the government contribution is limited to the provision of financial guarantees or occasional direct loans. In the Philippines there are two organisations which have been formed by local capitalists specifically to provide housing for the urban poor – the Land and Housing Development Corporation (LHDC) and the Philippine Business for Social Progress (PBSP) (Filio 1974/5). The former was instituted in 1968 as a consortium of all elements involved in housebuilding in order to effect economies through large and regular programmes and through minimal profit margins. In a country characterised by the absence of large housing developers, the LHDC was essentially attempting to create a situation leading to economies of scale. The principal link between the LHDC and the government was an arrangement with the Social Security System for favourable mortgage loans. The monthly amortisation was initially P105 (US$13) and the minimum monthly income required was P500 (US$63). However, the anticipated project scale did not materialise so that the cost of the finished houses gradually rose to around P38,000 (US$4,810) with the average household income of the present occupants being P1,200 (US$152) per month. Whilst rising land prices affected the overall costs, the acceptable 'minimum' profit margins seemed also to suffer a similar inflation.

The PBSP differs from the LHDC in that it comprises business interests from many fields other than that of housing and also involves itself in a similarly wide range of investment projects (Ylanan 1974/5). Its main housing development is the Sambahayan Condominium at Mandaluyong in metropolitan Manila (Ocampo 1974/5). The housing units cost between P17,000 (US$2,152) and P22,000 (US$2,785) and are meant for individuals with a monthly income of between P300 (US$38) and P700 (US$89). Intending purchasers can borrow up to 90 per cent of the cost through the Social Security System with repayment spread over thirty years at 6 per cent interest. In addition to these amortisation costs, there is also a monthly charge for management and maintenance of P20 (US$3).

Total monthly payments in the order of P90-120 (US$12-16) put the Sambahayan units well beyond the reach of low-income families unless there is another member of the household in regular employment. To this end the PBSP has integrated an 'industrial component' into the project which is designed to provide part-time employment and training facilities for the residents. The location at Mandaluyong was chosen because of the large concentration of existing industrial plants in the area. The necessity for having more than one income-earner in the resident households has long been recognised by the PBSP and it has always been mandatory for successful applicants to submit to this criterion. With a regular and reasonably high household income as a prerequisite for admission, the target population for this small project has obviously been carefully selected and it is clear that it lies more in the lower-middle-income groups.

The condominium is to be built in an old quarry of less than one hectare and yet economic feasibility has dictated a population of some 350 households. This means that densities will be relatively high and has posed serious technical and design problems. Fortunately, the resources of such a large organisation as the PBSP have enabled most of these difficulties to be overcome and in addition have brought about sensible modifications to some of the more costly building regulations. On the whole, however, the government contribution has been small and its approach disappointingly inflexible. The Social Security System, for instance, has refused to accept rental payments in lieu of amortisation in order to allow tenants to build up the 10 per cent equity which must be deposited prior to purchase.

The Private Sector in West Malaysia

By Asian standards the urban proportion of total population in Malaysia is considerable (see Table 1.1) — a feature not unrelated to its relatively substantial economic growth over recent decades. The present urban system in Malaysia is almost entirely the creation of the last 200 years, following the colonial exploitation of the peninsula and associated immigration from China and India (Lim 1978). The principal towns were either ports, such as Georgetown, or mining centres, such as Ipoh. However, few of the latter developed related processing and manufacturing industries within the colonial system and the major cities were largely coastal. During this phase of development the Malays remained outside the urban economy and in 1947 comprised only 7.3 per cent of the population of settlements of 10,000 persons or more.

Since 1947 urban growth has continued even more rapidly than before, with this process being fairly widespread throughout the settlement hierarchy. During the 1950s the communist emergency was a major factor in urban growth but in the post-war period rural-urban migration in general has become much more significant than overseas immigration. High natural growth rates have supplemented this movement so that all towns have experienced fairly rapid population expansion, but in general, urban growth in West Malaysia has been allometric with the largest cities experiencing the greatest increase in population. This does not imply that the country is characterised by excessive primacy; the relatively broad spatial framework of urban development within the federal system has acted against this and Kuala Lumpur only became the largest urban centre in the years immediately prior to independence. Since independence in 1957 the creation of a national administrative system has concentrated a substantial amount of urban growth in the capital.

The post-war urbanisation process has affected Malays more than any other ethnic group in West Malaysia. Rural-urban migration has brought many Malays into the towns in search of the job opportunities which the rise of national consciousness promised. This trend has been strengthened during the present decade by the government's determination to involve the Malays more directly in commerce and industry in order to reduce the hegemony of the Chinese and Indians. As a result, the Malays are the fastest growing ethnic group in most urban centres, although they tend to favour some cities more than others (Rimmer and Cho 1978).

The scale of urbanisation in Malaysia has resulted in a serious housing shortage, although it is difficult to estimate its full extent due to the primocentric bias in statistics. In general, the main characteristics of the problem are similar to those of other Asian countries. First, there has been an intensification of slum formation. Second, squatting seems to have increased markedly over the last decade. The precise extent and growth of squatter settlements is very difficult to assess because the official definition is confined strictly to the illegal occupation of land. There are, however, many types of housing built outside the formal public and private construction markets which contravene existing legislation other than that related to land occupation. One of the effects of this situation is to underemphasise the extent of illegal, semi-legal and temporary housing in the smaller urban centres. Johnstone (1978) has investigated this problem in some detail and has produced convincing evidence to show that non-conventional and hybrid housing is very prominent throughout the hierarchy of Malaysian settlements (Figure 6.3).

Figure 6.3: West Malaysia: Housing Types and Housing Construction, 1976

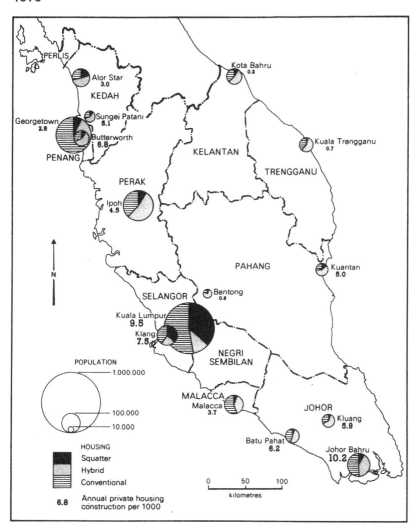

As discussion in earlier chapters has shown, the response of the Malaysian government to the housing needs of the urban poor has been neither generous nor realistic. At current credit rates, and with a 20 per cent equity, over three-quarters of the population were unable to afford the cheapest government units available in 1975. Mehmet (1978) has argued that this is partly a result of the traditional orientation of economic benefits towards the local elites and claims that such tendencies have been encouraged since independence because they fit in with Malay concepts of social relations. However, the government was undoubtedly dismayed by the revelation that there was greater income inequality in 1975 than in 1957, and in the Third Malaysia Plan housing received much more attention. Although the eradication of poverty, irrespective of race, was retained as the major goal in the current plan, the government realised that one effective way of reducing inequality is to assist directly in the improvement of the life of the urban poor. Overall government investment in housing has increased to 3.8 per cent of the total development expenditure and its share of the units constructed is expected to rise to 54 per cent. The plan puts particular emphasis on meeting the housing needs of the lowest-income groups and almost 60 per cent of the investment will be spent on this objective through such measures as squatter improvement schemes and site and service programmes. Commendable as these objectives are, many of the improvements are still on paper and eventual success depends on a thorough reorganisation of the present administrative framework. The Third Malaysian Plan also emphasises the need for increased involvement by the private sector in housing the urban poor, in both the direct construction of workers' housing and greater participation in low-cost housing programmes. Such involvement already exists in various joint venture schemes but to date few can claim to have produced really low-cost housing. However, in view of the uncertainty over the government's ability to meet its own objectives in housing the urban poor, the task of inducing the private sector to direct some of its vast resources towards this goal has become increasingly important. At present, the full potential of the private sector in this respect is unknown, largely because its structure and capacity are so little understood.

The Structure of the Private Sector and the Potential Target Population

The open housing market in Malaysia is dominated by developers rather than specialist construction firms. Not all registered housing developers are actively engaged in building programmes at any one time. In 1976, for example, only about two-thirds were engaged in any housebuilding activity. The construction firms outnumber the developers by about two to one but despite their numbers most of the work is undertaken by relatively few large firms. In 1972 a survey of the industry revealed that 90 per cent of the building activity, by value, was completed by only 30 per cent of the 1,147 registered firms. This allometric relationship between firm size and degree of activity is also characteristic of the developers themselves, with the larger private companies, by virtue of their extensive paid-up capital and diversified connections with other types of activity, dominating the private housing market. However, there are indications that the smaller developers can successfully engage in more modest programmes.

Johnstone (1977) has shown clearly that as the larger firms are usually part of companies of diverse interests, their activities are closely tied to those of the highly capitalised formal sector. As a result, the bulk of the housebuilding activity is disproportionately concentrated in the largest cities (Figure 6.3). The corollary is that the smaller towns, together with those cities located outside the main growth areas, receive a low priority in private development projects. To a certain extent this is the consequence of high costs for materials and labour; with increasingly sophisticated building techniques more of these have to be transported from the federal capital. But the major cause is the lower income in provincial centres, which affects the profits that can be made. It is perhaps axiomatic to state that private developers build for profit, but in Malaysia this motive strongly affects the patterns of construction activity. With the multiple interests of the larger Malaysian housing developers, investment tends to flow into whichever section of the company offers the most promising returns. This means that housing supply does not necessarily relate to demand.There may be relatively limited programmes when world prices for tin, rubber or oil palm are high, but a great deal of speculative building during recessions.

Whatever the relationship between supply and demand, house prices on the open market are very high in relation to incomes, particularly in view of the cost of credit to propsective buyers. Virtually all homes built by the private sector cost in excess of M$20,000 (US$8065). Using these criteria, together with data on the cost and eligibility for public housing, three separate consumer populations can be identified (it must be noted that although inflation has dated the absolute value of these statistics, the relative positions are still valid). Households with monthly incomes below M$300 (US$121), which in 1971 comprised 57 per cent of the urban population, must remain the responsibility of the government even though most families cannot afford the present cost of public housing. Extended and extensive investment in self-help schemes is urgently needed to reduce the cost of housing to reasonable levels. Households with monthly incomes above M$500 (US$202), some 23 per cent of the urban population, are in theory housed by the private sector. However, at current commercial credit rates even the cheaper units at M$15,000 to M$17,000 (US$6,855) are beyond the lower-income ranges. These families must obtain some form of subsidised credit, usually through employers, or reduce their expenditure on other elements of the household budget. Households with monthly incomes of between M$300 and M$500 would therefore seem to comprise Filio's 'grey zone' of families who cannot afford homes on the open market and yet are ineligible for public housing. At 1971 income levels, realistic selling prices which give a controlled profit to the builder and yet fall within the repayment capacity of the families concerned, would seem to lie between M$7,000 (US$2,823) and M$10,000 (US$4,032). These assume credit terms of 6 to 7 per cent per annum spread over twenty-five years. Although the identification of a target population gives an indication of the price range and size of the potential market, it is also necessary to discuss how these cost savings can be effected in Malaysia and how to ensure that they are passed on to the consumer.

Reducing Costs

Land. Land purchase and preparation in Malaysia amount to about 25 per cent of total costs per unit, fairly reasonable in comparison to other countries in the region. However, land prices are rising in Malaysia, particularly in and around the larger cities, and to date the rather weak speculation tax has not had any appreciable effect in preventing this escalation (Yeh and Laquian 1979). Land prices themselves are primarily the result of land availability and the degree of speculative activity. Whilst land for building is not scarce in and around most Malaysian cities, much of it is held in large blocks related to tin-mining or rubber plantations. Its release for housing development is closely tied to relative profitabilities within the interests of the development firms and their parent companies. The actual process involved has never been adequately investigated. Certainly much of the land is sold and developed on a large scale and it is doubtful whether the present system is conducive to a reduction of costs. On *a priori* grounds there would seem to be a good case for increased activity by state governments in alienation of non-productive primary lands. However, most states already hold a good deal of land around the urban areas and appear to be caught up themselves in some form of reluctant speculative activity. Another major problem in Malaysia which affects land costs is the administrative delay involved in conversion, subdivision and distribution of legal titles. On average the land is held for about six years whilst these are sorted out and during this time is subject to a holding charge which is in turn passed on to the consumer. Such delays also provide an additional excuse for speculative holding.

One of the main ways in which national, state or municipal governments could assist the private sector and reduce costs would be to acquire and assemble land for low-cost housing projects. However, the effectiveness of this measure would also depend on streamlined administrative procedures. Costs could be further reduced through government use of alienation powers and, if possible, by subsidised selling or leasing prices. Such reductions could be substantial if accompanied by subsidised land preparation and infrastructure provision. This would lead to additional savings through reduced labour costs and will be discussed later in the chapter.

Materials. The materials used in the construction process comprise the largest cost component, usually amounting to between 60 and 70 per cent of the total. After 1973 costs rose markedly due to world inflation and the building boom within Southeast Asia. By 1976 the effects of both elements had considerably slackened so that costs have generally stabilised and for some commodities, such as steel and bricks, even declined. However, for certain scarce materials, such as cement, prices have continued to rise and a black market flourishes. As noted above, this has allowed increased profits to be made by incorporating into house prices a risk factor which does not always materialise.

Given the overall cost of building materials, their regular supply is a prerequisite for the production of cheap housing units by either the public or private sectors. Unfortunately, its importance and significance does not yet seem to have been recognised so that related considerations, such as the elimination of monopoly holdings or increased development of indigenous resources, are not pursued as vigorously as they might be. In Malaysia, as in most Asian countries, timber is one of the most abundant building resources but to date this cheap, abundant material has been only marginally utilised in the urban construction industry. This is partly due to the previously noted psychological association between timber and low-quality housing, but its use is also affected by world market prices for timber and related export earnings. When these are high, the domestic market experiences significant shortages. Other inhibiting factors relate more to technological considerations such as the durability and fire-resistance of timber used in the urban environment. These in turn give rise to insurance problems which restrict the household's ability to raise mortgage credits. Whatever the reasons for the present underuse of timber, there is a growing need for co-ordinated research on this valuable building material if substantial reductions in construction costs are to be achieved. Fortunately, the Third Malaysian Plan has proposed a much needed Housing and Building Research Institute to investigate matters of this nature.

Labour. During the last few years labour costs have virtually doubled in Malaysia and now account for about a third of total construction costs. To a large extent this rise is the result of the higher wage rates which are being offered in order to overcome the shortages that exist in certain areas of the labour force. The shortages are felt particularly amongst skilled manual workers and in the highly specialised professional and managerial fields. In all these instances the root cause is the shortage of adequate training facilities within Malaysia. As a result, young people are forced to go overseas to receive professional or vocational instruction. Many stay abroad and those who return are proselytes for Western values. In addition, the competition from Singapore for skilled labour has attracted many trained Malaysians to the higher wages offered in the republic.

The shortages of skilled labour and escalating costs have forced many developers, both public and private, to consider semi-industrialised building techniques as an alternative to the labour-intensive methods favoured at present. The introduction of such techniques has ramifications far beyond the immediate area of the building industry itself and the political role of labour-intensive development would seem to make any future reduction in labour costs unlikely in Malaysia, particularly as improved efficiency still depends on advances in intermediate or on-site technologies which will themselves demand training programmes and increased wages. Whilst overall labour costs are unlikely to be reduced in the near future, there could be a shift in the burden of some costs from the shoulders of the private developer to the public sector. The most suitable form for such a subsidy would again be site preparation and servicing, the importance of which has already been noted within general land costs.

Standards. In spite of the importance of the cost components discussed above, reform of the building and planning regulations is seen by the Malaysian government as the principal area in which cost reductions can be made. Most standards and regulations date from the 1930s and reflect the middle-class values of the British colonial administrators rather than the realities of the present situation. Although the revision of such legislation is undoubtedly overdue, the current critical zeal seems more a function of the relative ease with which changes might be made *vis-à-vis* other improvements within the building industry. Among the many inadequacies of the regulatory framework, several items emerge as being particularly noteworthy; the demands of road and drainage reserves are a case in point. At present these requirements, together with recreational and educational spaces, take up 50 to 60 per cent of prepared building land, leaving a reduced number of house plots from which the developer is to derive his profits. Various suggestions have been made to improve this situation, such as halving the minimum acceptable road width, thereby lowering costs and creating higher ground densities. However, initial moves on this matter have been halted by the regulations of the state and federal transport departments which prohibit servicing of any roads that are less than the stipulated minimum widths.

In addition to proposals for improvements in area regulations, there have been many suggestions for more realistic approaches to standards in individual housing units. Minimum room sizes could be reduced, cheaper materials could be used, and communal plumbing or sanitary facilities could be installed. Obviously these proposals will need to be considered carefully as some will be more acceptable than others. Most local authorities are reluctant to lower construction standards because they fear this will increase subsequent maintenance costs, but one experimental project in Kuala Lumpur, at Cheras, has shown that even with a limited suspension of standards, construction costs for conventional housing can be substantially reduced (Amato 1975, 1976).

Closely connected to the problem of building standards for low-cost housing is that of overall design. Government housing programmes in developed countries, as well as in Singapore and Hong Kong, have been characterised by high-rise mass housing and industrialised technology. The apparently impressive results have commended such approaches to both private and public sectors throughout the Third World, irrespective of local economic and cultural conditions, and in Malaysia both private developers and local governments are constantly subjected to pressures from overseas construction companies specialising in such techniques. However, the whole question of labour- versus capital-intensive development opens up very wide issues which must be considered when decisions of this nature are being made. In this context it is very important that the high-rise projects in Georgetown and Kuala

Lumpur are comprehensively evaluated in terms of their successes and failures.

Consumer Finance. The Malaysian government does not consider the housing finance system now operating to be a major constraint in denying the urban poor access to improved accommodation. Whilst it is true that the most urgent savings are needed on construction costs, the present credit system is extremely restrictive. Not only are there few loan outlets but borrowing is also expensive, with interest rates of about 11 per cent and a short repayment period of ten years. There are, however, exceptions to this and many employers, notably the government, offer much more favourable credit terms. For example, the Housing Loans Division of the Treasury charges only 4 per cent over fifteen years.

In general terms, the urban poor have only limited access to housing credit; this is caused by two important deficiencies in the present system. First, the present lending institutions invest only a small proportion of their resources in housing loans, despite the directives of Bank Negara (National Bank). Specified minimum percentages could substantially increase the flow of credit from such institutions, particularly from the Employers Provident Fund which in many countries is a major source of housing finance. In Malaysia the accumulated funds tend to be directed towards more profitable investment projects so that less than 4 per cent of the Employers Provident Fund is invested in the Malaysian Building Society for release as housing loans.

A second area for improvement in Malaysia is the need to reduce interest rates and lengthen repayment periods to correspond more with the 30- to 40-year working life of the prospective borrower. To a large extent these improvements depend on greater competition among lending institutions, particularly from specialist mortgage and housing credit outlets. However, such changes are unlikely to materialise without the Bank Negara taking a more positive role as a second-line guarantor of reserves in order to provide front-line agencies with greater liquidity and flexibility. Closely connected with the problem of financial reforms is the question of acceptable profit margins. If the benefits are not passed on to the consumer then the purpose of these measures is lost. The risk-inflated profits which have characterised Malaysia during the 1970s are excessive and some form of profit tax needs to be introduced. On the other hand, given the multiple interests of the larger developers, there is little room for manoeuvre in this field since profit controls on housing will simply cause a flow of capital into other projects.

Private and Public Sector Co-operative Schemes

In Malaysia the concept of joint venture projects between the public and private sectors is being given increased support at the national level. However, the responsibility for housing rests with the individual state governments and not all have reacted favourably to this move. At present there are several examples of hybrid construction organisations which have emerged in response to federal encouragement of co-operative ventures. They vary tremendously in the degree of government 'assistance', but almost all involve the larger private developers or construction firms and follow conventional building techniques. Most of the practical instances of co-operation occur in the so-called 'joint venture' projects between the private sector and some of the state governments, usually State Economic Development Corporations (SEDC). However, the great majority of such schemes have only minimal SEDC participation, usually in the form of land alienation, assembly and preparation. Whilst this is useful, it has not resulted in land being sold to the private developer at any substantially reduced cost. House prices are consequently not really low. In Malacca, for example, virtually all of the joint enterprise units built in 1976 cost more than M$20,000 (US$8,065). One of the main reasons for these high prices is the meagre participation by the public sector in land preparation, an area in which substantial savings could be effected in both land and labour costs. The joint venture projects have also been affected by an adherence to existing standards and regulations; not only has this kept costs disproportionately high but it has also resulted in large estates of tiny terraced houses surrounded by vast tracts of road and pavement space (Plate 11).

The most fruitful joint venture projects in Malaysia are still essentially in the experimental stage. One of the most important of these is at Cheras in Kuala Lumpur, where Dewan Bandaraya (City Hall) and a special consortium of the Housing Developers Association (HDA) are constructing 700 high-density 'double storey cluster link' units. The city has provided prepared land at the subsidised price of M$1 per square foot and in addition has reduced the required standards on densities, road widths, infrastructure and quality of finish. The resultant houses are built at 58 per acre with a narrow 14-foot frontage and cover about 90 per cent of the 550 square foot lot. The total cost of each unit, including land, is M$7,500 (US$3,024) which makes them by far the cheapest type of conventional accommodation available in Malaysia.

Only the experimental housing projects, such as Salak South, are likely to undercut this figure. Although the Cheras scheme illustrates the cost savings which can be made through well-organised joint venture projects, it does rely for much of its effectiveness on the scale of the private sector contribution since the HDA consortium has large resources at its disposal. Thus, whilst this type of co-operation might have an important role in large cities, it is doubtful whether small- or medium-sized settlements would offer the same opportunities. It is consequently very important to examine the potential of the small private builder in this field.

It is quite likely that at present a substantial amount of construction activity by small builders goes unrecorded or unregistered. To a certain extent the administrative delays involved in such formalities are to blame. Undoubtedly this activity overlaps into squatter settlements where impressive feats of construction are occasionally recorded. For example, over the 1976 Hari Raya holiday in Ipoh more than 100 *rumah kilat* were erected which sold for M$700 (US$282) to M$1,300 (US$524). Obviously the builders were experienced and had good connections with the suppliers of basic materials. The activities of such builders have been condemned by the authorities as syndicate exploitation of the people and yet they are obviously meeting a demand (far more cheaply than the conventional private developer). Thus, whilst squatting itself has been accepted, squatter enterprise has not.

As so little is known about small builders, whether legal or illegal, it is difficult to suggest ways in which their contribution may be increased. A great deal of information is needed on their operations and the general constraints which affect any residential construction outside the large cities, Kuala Lumpur in particular. To date, most research has been undertaken in the more accessible and favoured urban areas. One notable exception has been the work of Johnstone (1978) in Kuantan and Alor Star which has revealed the extensive amount of pragmatic housing construction which takes place outside the conventional guidelines of the federal government. In Kuantan, for example, the municipality offers three separate house plans for sale, each of which permits the erection of a dwelling to lower standards than is officially allowed. The purchaser, who must have his own land, pays only M$5 (US$2) to obtain his house plan and makes his own arrangements for its construction. The dwelling can therefore be built by the owner, a hired artisan or a small construction firm on contract. In a country where the private sector is dominated by large developers, this scheme would seem to offer some scope for increased participation by the small builder in cheap housing programmes.

Conclusion

This brief examination of the urban housing situation in West Malaysia indicates that the private sector has an important role to play in alleviating current shortages. Realisation of this potential, however, will depend upon policy and programme changes at several distinct levels. The present attempts to reduce costs in the conventional sector through changes in building and planning regulations or the introduction of more sophisticated design techniques are unlikely to be very effective. Attention must be transferred to the supply of land, material and credit, if costs to the consumer are to be substantially reduced. It is clear that to reach even the rising poor, the private sector will need some form of government subsidy and the indications are that such support will be most effective through the provision of cheap, prepared sites ready for construction.

The role of the private sector in other developing countries is unlikely to be the same as in Malaysia. Even in the nearby Philippines, for example, there is no comparable group of large-scale developers and most residential construction is undertaken by small, informal groups organised by a foreman employed directly by the builder or architect. These foremen play a crucial role in the Filipino construction industry, operating at the interface between the conventional and non-conventional sectors and offering an important opportunity for government subsidy to small-scale builders. Perhaps such groups exist in Malaysia too, but before any detailed policies can be formulated, much more extensive and intensive research is necessary on the characteristics of the private sector in all developing countries.

Of course some radical analysts of the Third World may dismiss the role of the private sector in constructing low-cost homes as unimportant because profit motives make it limited in scale and restricted in its assistance to the poorest families. However, the goal of this book has been to examine all possible ways of improving the housing of the urban poor and within the context of the present system, with all its faults, there is undoubtedly some unrecognised and untapped potential in the private sector. Obviously, longer-term and larger-scale assistance for the poor will depend on broader changes in society and on other sources of housing supply. But there is no single solution or best combination of modes of production, and all possible avenues must be explored. The final chapter will discuss this variation in relation to the development process as a whole.

7 CONCLUSION: HOUSING AND THE DEVELOPMENT PROCESS

Introduction

The previous chapters have examined at some length the evolution of urban housing problems, investment in low-cost housing provision, and some of the alternatives which exist for the allocation of these funds. The question which has not yet been answered is whether it is possible to devise a suitable framework for housing investment which relates alternative strategies to specific stages in the development process. The final chapter will address itself to this problem. In this discussion it is essential to establish at the outset that there are two clearly different types of 'housing policy'. The first encompasses policies towards housing and primarily involves what might be termed macro-level decisions. As Figure 7.1 indicates, there are several stages in this decision-making process, each with its own set of alternatives. At the most general level there is the broad political philosophy governing the development process as a whole, from communist to capitalist with all of the shades between. In addition to influencing areas of investment which indirectly but substantially affect construction, this also has more direct repercussions in determining the role of the state *vis-à-vis* that of the private sector in housing provision.

Figure 7.1: Influences on Policies towards Housing

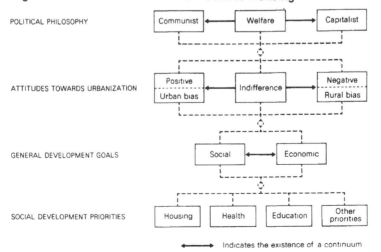

Below this general level of development philosophy, macropolicies are also affected by attitudes towards, and the nature of, urbanisation *per se*. These attitudes may vary from negative to positive and affect a whole range of investment strategies related to the balance between urban and rural development. Within this framework, investment in urban growth can further be subdivided into that favouring economic or social objectives, and in the latter field a wide variety of considerations, such as education, health, or birth control programmes, compete for finance along with low-cost housing.

Policies at each of these levels determine the overall dimensions of investment in conventional housing, particularly by the public sector. The ways in which this amount is spent constitutes policies *for* housing, or micropolicies, the crucial elements of which are the identification of specific goals and the methods by which these are to be achieved. Most discussion of Third World housing tends to examine only the latter component of this second group of policies, usually analysing a restricted set of programmes in a limited spatial frame. One of the main objectives of this book has been to illustrate not only the wide variety of options which exist, but also the need to evaluate policy goals themselves if real benefits are to be obtained from programme changes. Any attempt to relate housing strategies to development must therefore begin by examining some of the more pertinent macropolicies which affect overall investment.

Development Philosophy and Housing Provision

One of the most interesting attempts to relate housing investment to overall growth patterns was that of William and Mary Wheaton (1972) who put forward a model which attempted to illustrate how the allocation of housing resources changed at various stages of economic development (Figure 7.2). Their purpose was to discover which stage was likely to produce the best returns, in terms of capital formation, for the lowest cost. Almost inevitably, self-help housing was identified as the best investment value, although the rationale for this was not clear. One of the main limitations of this, like many other economic models, was that it was conceived in a political and social vacuum. The realities of established power structures, whether capitalist, socialist or totalitarian, were conveniently ignored. As a result, there is an oversimplification of the various alternatives for economic development into a continuum of three stages. This condensation results in an unconvincing grouping of 'typical' countries. It is suggested, for example, that Japan, Hong Kong and Singapore are representative of the intermediate stage, a very wide category encompassing average per capita incomes which range from US$300-1,000. Empirical analysis of statistics relating to the distribution of housing resources in each of these states shows that the assumed proportional allocation for high, middle and low income groups cannot be confirmed for any of the three 'representatives'. Similar criticisms can be made of other stages in the model, with stage one being more indicative of a pre-urbanisation situation than a pre-takeoff stage. There is often a considerable lag between urbanisation and industrialisation, and most Third World cities are currently in this position, yet the Wheatons' model fails to distinguish this important difference.

Figure 7.2: Housing Resource Distribution and Economic Development

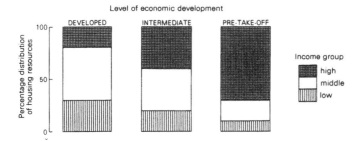

Although the model presented by the Wheatons can be severely criticised from many points of view, the overall concept of illustrating the relationship between housing investment and economic growth through housing resource distribution is an extremely useful methodological technique. The Wheatons' model suffers from excessive simplification of the real world into a situation in which only one evolutionary path for housing provision is suggested. Admittedly their construct is primarily aimed at analysis of the early stage of economic/housing investment, but even at this level distortion exists. Figure 7.3 attempts to amplify the model in two ways: first, by incorporating an extended range of economic situations, and second, by introducing the additional consideration of development philosophy. Due to the lack of reliable data on housing resource allocation, the model remains somewhat tentative, being exploratory and illustrative rather than definitive. As it provides the basis for much of the remainder of this chapter, some aspects of its construction need to be discussed.

Housing 'resources' correspond neither to a socio-economic classification of population nor to a proportional distribution of housing.

Figure 7.3: Housing Resource Distribution and Development Philosophy

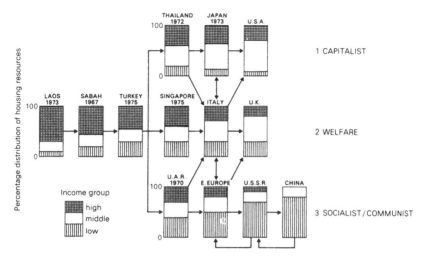

They represent a combination of the two and comprise the proportional distribution of housing units multiplied by an average value per unit per socio-economic group – either construction cost or selling price will suffice as long as a single criterion is used for the entire country. If private, public and popular housing are incorporated this produces an estimate of the total housing resources invested in each socio-economic sector. Figure 7.3 is the result of analysing the housing resource allocations for as many countries as possible and relating them to three broad development paths. The model also incorporates a loose indication of economic growth which can be assumed to increase from left to right. However, this assumption is not valid for the socialist/ communist countries since their resource allocation is often influenced more by political rather than social or economic goals.

The specific countries named in the model are suggested as representative of certain stages of development. In most instances these have been verified from existing statistics and have been dated because subsequent changes in resource distribution may have occurred. Some annotations, on the other hand, may be regarded as symbolic rather than proven because of the absence of sufficient or reliable data. Finally, it must be noted that the positions of the boxes or stages within the diagram do not correspond to any fixed points of economic growth. Thus Singapore, Thailand and Egypt are not intended to represent equivalent stages of development along their respective paths. The model is compressed in this way for clarity of presentation since it is not so much the individual details that are important as the overall progression of resource allocation.

For the early stages of economic development and urbanisation, prior to any large government commitment to housing programmes, the model puts forward a gradual, common distributional deployment of resources. Throughout this phase the resource share of low-cost housing is commensurate with the growth of urban migration and the resultant appearance of squatter communities. The limited public housing constructed during these early stages is mainly for government or quasi-government employees, thus expanding slightly the middle level of resource allocation. A close statistical correlation with the earliest stage could be found in Laos in 1973 before the communist takeover. At that time urbanisation was not extensive and the capital Vientiane had few squatters even with the wartime refugee movement into the city (Chounlamountri 1974). The only government housing was a handful of units for prominent civil servants so that housing provision was dominated by private firms operating on a profit-making basis. The second stage of resource allocation is more difficult to relate to a particular country and the example of Sabah, in East Malaysia, in the late 1960s is somewhat tentative. During that period the annual rate of population growth in the capital Kota Kinabalu was near to 9 per cent but the total population was still relatively small (33,365 in 1967), so that the private sector was able to cope with most of the housing demand, aided by a limited amount of government building. Thus, despite the rapid population growth, the proportion of temporary structures in the town fell from 37 per cent in 1960 to 9 per cent by 1967. The situation had changed considerably by the mid-1970s with a greatly extended resource allocation for the lower-income groups. This was partly due to increased government construction but was primarily the result of a largely undocumented refugee influx of Muslim separatists from the nearby South Philippines who set up their own squatter camps.

Stage three represents the point at which population growth becomes overwhelming in absolute terms and cities are flooded with migrant families for whom neither the public nor the private sector constructs much low-cost accommodation. In such circumstances the migrants build their own shelter in the form of squatter huts, thus by their own efforts raising the proportion of housing resources deployed in the low-cost category. Most developing countries are at this broad stage in the model —Turkey is simply a well-documented example. Although political or economic circumstances may vary considerably in these countries, the urban housing situation remains largely one in which the contribution of the non-conventional sector heavily outweighs the conventional, despite recent sporadic attempts to exploit the possibilities of aided self-help. Stage three, therefore, comprises a rather volatile group of countries and cities in which changes are constantly occurring.

Beyond this stage the model assumes some national commitment to improving the housing situation so that the influence of the various developmental paths on the relative importance of public, private and popular housing becomes more discernible and, in theory, predictable. One feature common to all three paths is a reduction in resource allocation to the upper-income echelon, but the reasons for this differ substantially as do both the rate of reduction and the related beneficiaries. Path one indicates housing resource distribution in capitalist systems in which public commitments to low-cost housing are limited and heavy reliance is placed upon stimulating the private building sector through increased incomes in the middle and upper groups. Housing 'filtration' is then assumed to take place in which the poor move into old homes vacated by those with increased incomes. In practice this does not occur on a large scale because of family splitting within middle-income households or because of landlord exploitation. The major beneficiaries are therefore the middle-income group and this is shown in path one. The urban poor suffer because eradication of slums or squatter areas is usually for commercial expansion and is not necessarily accompanied by low-cost housing replacements. Within this system the poor are forced to pay increasingly high rents for the diminishing amount of slum accommodation available.

In the socialist/communist approach towards housing provision, the state takes almost complete responsibility for improving the living conditions, particularly of the proletariat, at the expense of a disappearing upper-income group. Under the socialist system of Eastern Europe, the middle class continues to exist as a consumer of housing resources, frequently supplemented by the more favoured Party members. Thus, the type of housing available to this sector does not necessarily diminish and is to some extent maintained by the state through a system of loans to enable private house purchases to continue. In Czechoslovakia since 1945, the amount of housing built by the state has fallen from 75 per cent to 20 per cent of the total, although this has not reduced the control of the central government on the overall pattern of construction. Similarly in the Soviet Union, whilst the amount of co-operative housing construction has been allowed to rise in recent years in order to absorb 'surplus' income, the proportion of housing built by the state has steadily increased since the end of the Second World War (Herman

1971).

Extension of these socialist principles in the more committed communist states has brought about further erosion of expenditure on luxury housing together with a gradual replacement of middle-income accommodation by more simple low-cost units. Two approaches which have proven useful in China to improve the housing conditions of the urban poor are the more even redistribution of existing resources and a renewed emphasis on factory housing. Towers (1973) has reported that in most Chinese cities the development of new residential areas has been closely tied to new industrial projects and that once the housing is completed it is handed over to the factory administration. In the largest cities, however, rehousing is the responsibility of the municipal authorities and Towers claims that two million have been rehoused since 1949 in Shanghai alone. This figure is higher than the total rehoused in Hong Kong and despite the larger size of Shanghai must be viewed somewhat sceptically. In most Chinese cities there has also been a redistribution of residential space to improve the living conditions of the workers, although some differentials do exist by employment category and Party status.

But despite the success of the reallocation programmes and the promotion of development in more remote regions, population growth has continued in the largest cities and considerable housing problems remain in China and the Soviet Union. Forced relocation in the rural areas has been attempted in both countries, as well as in Vietnam, but any success in terms of population reduction would seem to be short-lived. As Falkenheim (1973) has noted, the dynamics of hyperurbanisation defy simple solutions as much in the totalitarian states as elsewhere.

The remaining path is difficult to label but in general represents a compromise in housing development between the two extremes previously described. 'Welfare economics' constitute the main feature and produce a situation in which squatter and slum housing are gradually replaced in a programme of low-cost subsidised housing for the poor. The proportion of housing resources allocated to this sector remains constant but represents a continued improvement of a diminishing element. As economic growth continues, rising incomes push many households into the middle-income sector where government or commercial credit facilities encourage the development of the private building industry.

Although the model identifies three major approaches to development philosophy and thus to housing provision, it is not intended to suggest that these paths are rigidly separated. Changes in housing policy will undoubtedly follow in the wake of new economic or political circumstances, so that the position of any individual country within the model will vary over time. Complete interchangeability does not exist across the identified paths although the mellowing of extreme socialist patterns in Eastern Europe suggests a possible shift across to 'welfare' situations in which the middle-income/private housing market is given opportunities to expand. Change from extreme capitalist situations is likely to be even more difficult to achieve because the powerful commercial elements within those societies will undoubtedly resist any erosion of their privileged and profitable position. Redistribution of resources in these circumstances may therefore depend upon more radical structural changes to the society as a whole, probably by revolutionary means. One instance where such a transformation in housing policy has been achieved is in Cuba where the Castro government has successfully induced a major shift in housing resource allocation (see Bonilla 1964, Mesa-Lago 1969/70, 1971).

Urbanisation Policies and Housing Provision

Within the political and economic factors outlined in the previous section, there are many other aspects of national development policy which have considerable repercussions on residential construction. Population growth, regional planning and rural development are but three of the most important, all of which may be said to find their most direct expression within national urbanisation policies. The Third World has been divided into three broad groups with respect to attitudes on urbanisation as expressed in national development plans (United Nations 1976). The largest group is characterised by a predilection for neglecting urbanisation as a factor in development, with national planning targets being formulated along sectoral or regional lines irrespective of the distortions which rapid and erratic urban growth is likely to cause. This does not mean that the governments concerned are unaware of the urbanisation occurring in their own countries; indeed, in many instances sectoral policies have been deliberately adopted in order to permit the continuation of the unfettered urban economic development on which national prosperity is thought to be based. Urban bias is therefore a natural corollary of the development process in most countries. In some cases ruling elites often appear to be unaware of the problems which rapid growth creates for the urban poor, or else are more concerned with other issues. In Nigeria, for example, in 1963 a survey revealed that 60 per cent of the population thought that the housing shortage was the most serious problem facing the country. But when the same question was asked of the members of the national legislature, concern was expressed with the overseas image of Nigeria, the republican constitution and control of foreign businesses, but no mention was made of a housing problem (Umeh 1972). However, in most instances such ignorance is feigned rather than real and the poor are deliberately left to take care of their own needs so as not to impede resource allocation in what are considered to be more profitable areas. And yet, as many have pointed out, the prosperity of the formal sector is to a large extent based on the industry and industriousness of petty producers.

Whatever the motivation, the absence of co-ordinated policies directed towards or related to urbanisation means that little or no attention is paid to its associated problems, such as housing. South Korea illustrates this situation very well. For many years its national development plans have continued to place heavy emphasis on sectoral investment, particularly in agriculture and industry, without formulating a well-defined policy towards urbanisation. As a result, cities such as Seoul and Pushan have experienced a massive but virtually uncontrolled expansion, whilst at the national level there has been no co-ordinated effort to tackle the intumescent urban housing shortage. At least four major agencies are involved in overlapping and even conflicting attempts to meet this problem, but the capital itself has no formal link with the prime source of supply, the Korea Housing Corporation, and municipal authorities in Seoul pursue their own independent housing programmes (Rho 1976).

The second group of countries are those which attempt, in the face of apparently irreversible trends, to slow down the rate of urban growth by reducing the extent of what is often referred to vaguely as 'rural-urban imbalance'. This has been pursued in a variety of ways ranging from general birth control programmes to the deliberate favouring of rural areas in investment priorities. The latter approach has been particularly popular in African countries which have not yet experienced large-scale urbanisation and are anxious to prevent the materialisation of its attendant problems, particularly in employment and housing. One of the most intensive campaigns of this nature has occurred in socialist Tanzania which as long ago as 1968 instigated an ambitious programme of regional growth poles set within a network of *ujaáma* villages, rural co-operatives and domestic industries (Gould 1970, de Souza and

Porter 1974). Unfortunately, administrative shortcomings have produced disappointing results, although it is unlikely that even the most well-organised system could effectively restrain urban migration. In Israel, for example, where successful rural settlement programmes have been in operation for many years, decentralisation policies have only diverted the inevitable urban growth onto the medium-sized cities (Samuelson 1974, Soen *et al*, 1976). This phenomenon, together with its related problems, has tended to remain hidden because of the 'primocentric' nature of most urban research.

The third group comprises the relatively few developing countries which have accepted urbanisation as a positive factor in economic development – something to be encouraged rather than prevented. In most cases this enthusiasm is understandably tempered by a desire to restrict the excessive growth of one primate city so that development planning is often characterised by the selection of a series of regional growth centres acting as foci for development. One of the most enthusiastic examples of decentralised urbanisation has occurred in Turkey over the last ten years (Keles n.d.). Faced with the continued growth of Istanbul and the Marmara region, two successive Five Year Development Plans laid down a series of objectives aimed at balancing urban growth between the eastern and western halves of the country. Fortunately, the Turks have had a long commitment to decentralised urban growth, partly fostered by the restriction of the best agricultural land to narrow coastal strips, each of which has developed its own outlet port. Furthermore, Turkey was one of the first modern states to adopt a new capital city away from the existing urban concentration of political and economic power.

However, a commitment to urban growth does not necessarily ensure a commitment to welfare programmes in the cities. Both of the major development strategies associated with decentralised urbanisation, viz. redistribution with growth and export substitution, see spatial integration of the national urban economy as a major factor in the disbursement of the benefits of growth. However, many development strategists, such as Friedmann (1979) and Wu (1979), see this as an avenue for increased capitalist exploitation rather than improving the welfare of the urban poor. An analogous situation exists in the primate cities themselves where decentralisation is encouraged by the creation of satellite or overspill towns. Unfortunately as far as the urban poor are concerned, the type of housing construction generated in the Third World by these policies is primarily geared towards the middle- and upper-income groups. In Ankara, for example, the new town of Oran has simply become the latest fashionable residential district for the city's bourgeoisie (Figure 4.3). The amount of low-cost housing in the 'new towns' of Hong Kong and Singapore is very much an exception rather than the rule. Positive attitudes towards urbanisation and urban growth, therefore, do not necessarily lead to positive policies for low-cost housing provision.

Social Development and Housing Provision

Whilst earlier chapters have shown that increased housing investment is a function of political or economic rather than social considerations, it is the latter which is still used, no matter how cynically, to justify changes in funding. However, the provision of a better dwelling is only part of the daunting task of improving the life of the urban poor. Effective social development also requires expenditure on other essential elements of the alleviation of poverty and exploitation, such as the provision of education and health facilities, and the expansion of employment opportunities. In short, housing provision must be seen in perspective. It is only one of many worthwhile areas of investment for social development and must not be treated in isolation. Unfortunately, this is rarely the case and most administrators regard housing improvement as an end in itself rather than as one of the ways of achieving the broader goal of alleviating poverty. One illustration of the effects of the compartmentalised approach can be seen in Australia in relation to government attempts to improve the living conditions of Aborigines who have been moved from their traditional lands. In combining Third World problems in a First World setting, this encapsulates the core of the problem.

During the 1970s a great deal of money was set aside by the Labour Party government in Australia for the improvement of Aboriginal housing. Communities were encouraged to form housing associations and engage the services of professional architects and engineers to design houses which would meet the special needs of their particular customs and preferences. Few architects knew anything of the very different Aboriginal lifestyle and communication between the two groups was minimal, although the fees charged were not. The result was a frightening series of failures described in detail by Heppell (1979). Between 1972 and 1975, in the Northern Territory alone, A$831,257 (US$923,619) was paid in architects' fees but only 76 houses were constructed.

However, more serious than the structural and financial inadequacies of the building programme itself was the negligible consideration given to the place of housing provision in the general strategy of social development. Apart from the relentless pressure on the Aborigines to adopt 'civilised' Western standards of living, there was little attempt at integrated development. Housing was thus erected in areas where there were no employment prospects or few services; sites and layout took little account of the cultural traditions of the people themselves; and even infrastructure and maintenance facilities were frequently inadequate. The outcome was not difficult to foresee and the great majority of the new housing projects have been abandoned. Unfortunately, it seems that few lessons will be learned from these mistakes as research assessment and monitoring have been sadly neglected for many years.

Although improved social welfare, including better housing, is not incompatible with economic development, there are few Third World or First World countries which have successfully managed to blend the two. This has recently led to a new wave of regional development theory which has as its principal objective the promotion of balanced growth aimed at bringing a fair share of benefits to those sectors, spatial and social, most neglected within the present systems. Whilst these equitable goals primarily revolve around rural development strategies, they also stress the need to orientate urban growth towards the lower-income groups. At present, all this is still so much theory, and disputed at that, but it does illustrate the broad developmental changes necessary at the macro-level before micro-level policies can even begin to become effective. As previous chapters have shown, any successful housing programmes which currently exist in the Third World — successful in terms of the benefits brought to the urban poor — usually occur in spite of overall development goals and investment priorities rather than because of them. The following section will briefly synthesise some of the more important elements which have made this possible.

Micropolicies

In the same way that macropolicies *towards* housing are affected by wide-ranging considerations, so too are micropolicies *for* housing; this has formed the basis of the discussion in previous chapters. It is from this myriad of often quite contradictory influences that housing programmes are formulated. The aggregation of factors and their evaluation is likely to be unique to each government, even if levels of investment appear to be quite similar. Thus, notwithstanding the trends indicated in Figure 7.3, there are both capitalist and socialist countries in the Third World committed to extensive public housing programmes; of course there are many more of various political persuasions which are hardly committed at all. A corollary of this is that although the degree of involvement in some countries may ostensibly be similar, the rationale behind such commitments and the housing programmes themselves may be very different. Given such variations in both policy rationale and housing programmes, it is obvious that standardised housing strategies would not only be difficult to formulate but also of dubious value. Thus, although this book has emphasised the need for maximum possible investment in low-cost housing, it has concentrated its attention on the more realistic goal of reviewing the range of ways in which the funds themselves may be more usefully allocated. Successes in individual countries and cities are closely tied to local circumstances and it would serve no useful purpose to itemise them at this point. However, several major factors have emerged in this review and deserve brief reiteration.

First, there is a need for flexibility in both housing programmes and investment policy in order to cope successfully with changes in social, political and economic circumstances. The individual family makes regular adjustments in its resource allocation to match its own changing priorities. Government policies should be similarly dynamic. Second, the limited nature of most housing investment means that implemented programmes must be as comprehensive as possible and draw on all potential sources of low-cost housing, whether conventional or non-conventional. The adopted mix should retain the flexibility stressed above and be open to change when necessary. This leads on to the third point. Housing policies ought to be appropriate to the task and circumstances at hand — scaled to meet the requirements of specific groups of people, within their technical and financial capabilities and employing as many local resources as possible. Unquestioning attempts to emulate the apparent successes of other wealthier countries should be particularly avoided. Such schemes need careful evaluation in terms of local needs and resources before being incorporated into the planning process and yet it is only in the last few years that there has been any debate on the important question of the suitability of high-rise housing in the Third World (see Lim 1975, Angel and Benjamin 1976, Yeung 1976).

All three points raised here seem straightforward but they have seldom received full implementation or even consideration to date.

Such criticism raises the basic question of the structure of decision-making processes in developing countries and whether these also need to be changed, a problem which was discussed in Chapter 5. At present, there is an undoubtedly elitist nature to the planning process in most Third World cities with very little contact between the authorities and the theoretical beneficiaries of low-cost housing schemes — the urban poor. Full representation from, rather than of, this group is essential if flexible, comprehensive and appropriate programmes are to be drawn up.

Postscript

The principal goal of this book has been to examine the current provision of low-cost housing for the urban poor and to identify ways in which the situation can be improved. In each of the chapters on the components of the low-cost housing system, suggestions have been made both for widening the range of options open for housing investment and for increasing overall production. It is important to emphasise, however, that these individual recommendations do not produce a total, comprehensive housing policy from which strategies for individual countries may be identified. They simply present a range of alternatives which become feasible or not according to the various characteristics of national development outlined above.

The emphasis throughout has been on improvements which, as far as possible, bring real benefits to the poor rather than serving the interests of a privileged few. Most Marxists would argue that peripheral capitalism ultimately channels the benefits from incremental improvements into the pockets of the capitalist elite. Whilst admitting the basic truth of this claim, there seems to be no feasible alternative in most societies to piecemeal change. Certainly there are neither instant solutions nor universal strategies for the housing problems of the urban poor, and any transformation which occurs will be strongly linked to wider political, social and economic forces. Even without Marxist upheaval, any improvement will require societal change and this will always involve struggle and sacrifice, as the following incidents from Manila illustrate only too well (*Ugnayan ng mga Samahan ng mga Mamamayan ng* Tondo Foreshore 1976:17, Pinches 1977:8).

> . . . since the declaration of Martial Law in September 1972 . . . the government ordered stepped-up demolition of squatter shanties. In

1973 and 1975, accelerated demolitions were also ordered by the President, but most recently by Metro-Manila Governor Imelda Marcos. In every instance, squatter organizations reacted by either marching to the presidential palace or by sending representatives to talk with the President or the First Lady and succeeded in limiting the demolition. The most recent meeting brought together a dozen leaders of the Alyansa [the liaison body of all squatter organisations throughout greater Manila] in a dialogue with Mrs Marcos in her office. Two days after the meeting, the Palace ordered the arrest of all the community leaders who took part.

. . . when the World Bank, which is the projected source of funds for the Tondo Foreshore Development scheme, sent a mission to Manila to discuss the plan with government and community leaders in 1975, one of those leaders, Mrs Trinidad Herrera, was arrested temporarily and locked in a military stockade until the World Bank group had left. Mrs Herrera was also scheduled to attend the United Nations Human Settlements design competition held in Vancouver . . . since the design was meant for housing in Tondo. But again, an order went out for her arrest and she went into hiding thus negating the possibility of attending the Vancouver meeting.

In June 1976 five squatter representatives from Tondo were invited by the World Council of Churches, at its expense, to attend the Vancouver Habitat Conference, where the Tondo redevelopment project was to be a major topic of discussion. The five squatters were refused permission to leave the country. On the day of Mrs Marcos's speech at Habitat massive demonstrations were staged in both Vancouver and Manila . . . Today a number of the most active members of Tondo's squatter groups are in jail for 'subversion' whilst those still working in the Tondo are under constant surveillance.

REFERENCE BIBLIOGRAPHY

Abraham, C.E.R., 1975, 'The impact of low cost housing on the employment and social structure of urban communities: Penang' in S.H. Tan and S.H.S. Tan, 381-484

Abu-Lughod, J., 1971, *Cairo: 1001 Years of the City Victorious*, Princeton University Press, Princeton

——, 1973a, 'Problems and policy implications of Middle Eastern urbanization', *Studies on Development Problems in Selected Countries of the Middle East, 1972*, UNESOB, Beirut, 42-62

——, 1973b, 'The legitimacy of comparisons in comparative urban studies: a theoretical position and an application to North African cities', mimeograph, School of Architecture and Urban Planning, UCLA

——, 1975, 'A comparative analysis: Cairo, Tunis and Rabat-Sale', *Ekistics*, Vol. 39, No. 233, 236-45

Ahluwalia, M.T., 1974, 'Income inequality: some dimensions of the problem', *Finance and Development*, Vol. 11, No. 3, 3-8

Alithambi, M.T., 1975, 'Administration of public housing' in S.H. Tan and S.H.S. Tan, 82-116

Amato, P.W., 1975, *Housing Needs and Programmes in the Federal Territory 1975 to 1990*, United Nations Advisory Project, MAL/72/015, Urban Development Authority, Kuala Lumpur

——, 1976, *Project Findings and Preliminary Recommendations*, United Nations Advisory Project MAL/72/015, Urban Development Authority, Kuala Lumpur

Amin, S., 1965, *Maghreb in the Modern World*, Penguin, Harmondsworth

——, 1974, *Accumulation on a World Scale: A Critique of the Theory of Underdevelopment*, 2 Vols., New Monthly Review Press, New York and London

Anderson, S.A.N., 1972, 'Slums of hope', *Ekistics*, Vol. 34, No. 201, 114-15

Andrews, F. and Phillips, G., 1971, 'Squatters of Lima: who they are and what they want', *Ekistics*, Vol. 31, No. 183, 132-6

Andrzejewski, A., 1967, 'Housing policy and housing system models in some socialist countries' in A.A. Nevitt, 149-61

Angel, S. and Benjamin, S., 1976, 'Seventeen reasons why the squatter problem can't be solved', *Ekistics*, Vol. 41, No. 242, 20-6

Angel, S., Benjamin, S. and de Goede, K.H., 1977, 'The low-income housing system in Bangkok', *Ekistics*, Vol. 44, No. 261, 79-85

Ashton, G.T., 1976, 'Slum housing attrition: a positive twist from Cali, Colombia', *Human Organization*, Vol. 35, No. 1, 47-53

Atman, R., 1975, 'Kampong improvements in Indonesia', *Ekistics*, Vol. 40, No. 238, 216-20

Awotona, A.A., 1977, 'Financing appropriate housing in Nigeria', *Ekistics*, Vol. 44, No. 261, 101-4

Bairoch, P., 1973, *Urban Unemployment in Developing Countries*, International Labour Office, Geneva

Balandier, P., 1966, 'The colonial situation: a theoretical approach' in I. Wallerstein, 34-61

Banerji, S., 1972, 'Innovative techniques in low-cost housing; the North Bengal experience' in D.J. Dwyer, 231-9

Batley, R., 1977, 'Expulsion and exclusion in São Paulo – an overview', mimeograph, Institute of Development Studies, Conference on Access to Housing, University of Sussex, Brighton

Batt, M. and Chawda, V.K., 1976, 'Housing the poor in Ahmedabad', *Bombay*, Vol. 11, No. 19, 706-11

Beck, D., 1971, 'Seattle: labour and politics, 1918-1960' in M. Morgan (ed.), *Skid Road: Seattle, the First 100 Years*, Ballantine Books, New York

Bell, G., 1974, 'Banking on human communities in Brazil', *Ekistics*, Vol. 38, No. 224, 27-34

Berry, B.J.L., 1973, *The Human Consequences of Urbanization*, Macmillan, London

Bettelheim, C., 1972, 'Appendix 1: theoretical comments' in A. Emmanuel, *Unequal Exchange: A Study of the Imperialism of Trade*, Monthly Review Press, New York, 271-322

Blake, G.H. and Lawless, R.I., 1974, 'Continuity or change: the example of Tlemcen, a pre-colonial town in Western Algeria', mimeograph, Seminaire 'Espace Maghrebin', Institut des Techniques de Planification et d'Economie Appliquée, Algiers

—— (eds.), 1980, *The Changing Middle Eastern City: Processes and Problems*, Croom Helm, London

Bonilla, F., 1964, 'The urban worker' in J.L. Johnson (ed.), *Continuity and Change in Latin America*, Stanford University Press, California, 186-205

Brigg, P., 1973, 'Some economic interpretations of case studies of urban migration in developing countries', *IBRD Staff Working Paper*, No. 151, Urban and Regional Economics Division, Development

Economics Department, Washington D.C.

Bromley, R.J., 1977, 'Organization, regulation and exploitation in the so-called "urban informal sector": the street traders of Cali, Colombia', Proceedings of the Institute of British Geographers Symposium on *The Urban Informal Sector in the Third World*, School of Oriental and African Studies, University of London

Bruner, E.M., 1961, 'Urbanization and ethnic identity in North Sumatra', *American Anthropologist*, Vol. 63, 508-21

Bryant, J.J., 1977, 'Urbanization in Papua New Guinea: problems of access to housing and services', *Pacific Viewpoint*, Vol. 18, No. 1, 43-57

Buchanan, I., 1972, *Singapore in Southeast Asia*, Bell and Sons, London

Buchanan, K.M., 1963, 'The Third World – its emergence and contours', *New Left Review*, Vol. 18, 5-23

Burgess, R., 1977, 'Informal sector housing? A critique of the Turner school', Proceedings of The Institute of British Geographers Symposium on *The Urban Informal Sector in the Third World*, School of Oriental and African Studies, University of London

Burns, L.S. and Mittelbach, F.G., 1972, 'A house is a house is a house', *Industrial Relations*, Vol. 11, 407-21

Cain, A., Afshar, F. and Norton, J., 1976, 'Indigenous building and the Third World', *Ekistics*, Vol. 41, No. 242, 29-32

Cantacuzino, S., Browne, K. and Faghih, N., 1976, 'Isfahan: special issue', *Architectural Review*, Vol. 159, No. 951

Carlson, E., 1960, 'Evaluation of housing projects and programmes: a case report from Venezuela', *Town Planning Review*, Vol. 31, 187-209

Casanova, R.N., 1974/5, 'Evolving a Philippine land policy for low-cost housing', *NEDA Journal of Development*, 349-69

Castells, M., 1977, *The Urban Question*, Edward Arnold, London

Chounlamountri, S., 1974, 'Basic housing data' in The National Task Force on Low Cost Housing (ed.), *Low Cost Housing in Laos*, International Development Research Centre, Southeast Asian Low-Cost Housing Study, Vientiane

Cockburn, C., 1971, 'Construction in overseas development', *Ekistics*, Vol. 31, No. 186, 347-52

Correa, C.M., 1976, 'Third World housing: space as a resource', *Ekistics*, Vol. 41, No. 242, 33-8

Costello, V.F., 1977, *Urbanization in the Middle East*, Cambridge University Press, Cambridge

Cullingworth, J.B., 1967, 'Housing or the state: the responsibilities of government' in A.A. Nevitt, 27-36

Davies, S. and Blood, R.W., 1974, 'Residential site selection of urban migrants in Latin America', *Antipode*, Vol. 6, No. 1, 74-80

Davis, K., 1969, *World Urbanization 1950-1970 Vol. 1*, Population Monograph Series 4, University of California, Berkeley

Dick, H.W. and Rimmer, P.J., n.d., 'Beyond the formal/informal sector dichotomy: towards an integrated approach', unpublished manuscript, Department of Geography, University of Newcastle, New South Wales

Drakakis-Smith, D.W., 1973, *Housing Provision in Metropolitan Hong Kong*, Monograph No. 16, Centre of Asian Studies, Hong Kong University

——, 1975, 'Perspectives on urban housing problems in developing countries', mimeograph, Department of Human Geography, Research School of Pacific Studies, Australian National University, Canberra

——, 1976a, 'Urban renewal in an Asian context', *Urban Studies*, Vol. 13, No. 3, 295-306

——, 1976b, 'Slums and squatters in Ankara: case studies in four areas of the city', *Town Planning Review*, Vol. 47, No. 3, 225-40

——, 1976c, 'The role of the private sector in housing the urban poor', mimeograph, Department of Human Geography, Research School of Pacific Studies, Australian National University, Canberra

——, 1977, *Yau Ma Tei, Hong Kong: An Inner City Tenement District*, Report to the Centre for Housing, Building and Planning, United Nations, New York

——, 1978, 'The role of the private sector in low cost housing provision' in R.D. Hill and J.M. Bray (eds.), *Geography and Environment in Southeast Asia*, Hong Kong University Press, Hong Kong, 297-322

——, 1979a, 'The role of the private sector in housing the urban poor in West Malaysia' in M. Rudner and J.C. Jackson (eds.), *Issues in Malaysian Development*, Southeast Asian Publications Series No. 3, Heinemann (Asia), Hong Kong, 305-38

——, 1979b, *High Society: Housing Provision in Metropolitan Hong Kong*, Monograph no. 40, Centre of Asian Studies, University of Hong Kong, Hong Kong

——, 1980, 'Socio-economic problems in Middle-Eastern cities: the role of the informal sector' in G.H. Blake and R.I. Lawless, 92-119

—— and Fisher, W.B., 1975, *Housing in Ankara, Turkey*, Occasional Paper (New Series), No. 7, Department of Geography, University of Durham

—— and Johnstone, M.A., 1977, *Kampong Maxwell: Kuala Lumpur, Malaysia*, Report to the Centre for Housing, Building and Planning, United Nations, New York

—— and Yeung, Y.M., 1977, 'Public housing in the city-states of Hong Kong and Singapore', *Occasional Paper* No. 8, Development Studies Centre, Australian National University, Canberra

Dwyer, D.J., 1975, *People and Housing in Third World Cities: Perspectives on the Problems of Spontaneous Settlements*, Longmans, London

—— (ed.), 1972, *The City as a Centre of Change in Asia*, Hong Kong University Press, Hong Kong

Engels, F., 1892, *The Condition of the Working Class in England*, Panther, London, 1969 edition

Ewing, J.R., 1969, 'Town planning in Delhi, a critique', *Economic and Political Weekly*, Vol. 4, No. 40, 1591-600

Falkenheim, V.C., 1973, 'Urbanization in China', *Problems of Communism*, Vol. 22, 77-80

Fanon, F., 1963, *The Damned*, Prescense Africaine, Paris

Feldman, K.D., 1975, 'Squatter migration dynamics in Davao City, Philippines', *Urban Anthropology*, Vol. 4, No. 2, 123-44

Filio, C.P., 1974/5, 'Rationalizing the land and housing package', *NEDA Journal of Development*, 438-48

Forbes, D., 1978, 'Urban-rural interdependence: the trishaw riders of Ujung Pandang' in P.J. Rimmer *et al.*, 219-36

Frank, A.G., 1971, *Capitalism and Underdevelopment in Latin America*, Pelican, Harmondsworth

Fraser, T.M., 1969, 'Relative habitability of dwellings: a conceptual view', *Ekistics*, Vol 27, No. 158, 15-18

Friedmann, J., 1979, 'The crisis of transition: a critique of strategies of crisis management', *Development and Change*, Vol. 10, No. 1, 125-53

Gans, H., 1969, 'Culture and class in the study of poverty' in D.C. Moynihan (ed.), *On Understanding Poverty*, Basic Books, New York, 201-28

——, 1972, 'The positive functions of poverty', *American Journal of Sociology*, Vol. 78, No. 2, 275-89

Garmondsway, G.N., 1965, *The Penguin English Dictionary*, Penguin, Harmondsworth

Geertz, C., 1963, *Peddlers and Princes: Social Development and Change in Two Indonesian Towns*, University of Chicago Press, Chicago

Gerry, C., 1977, 'Shanty-town production and shanty-town producers: some reflections on macro- and micro-linkages', mimeograph, Burg

Wartenstein Symposium, No. 73, *Shanty-towns in Developing Nations*, Wenner-Gren Foundation, New York

Gorynski, J., 1971, 'Modern and traditional design techniques in construction and housing', *Ekistics*, Vol. 31, No. 186, 353-9

Gould, P., 1970, 'Tanzania 1920-1963: the spatial impress of the modernization process', *World Politics*, Vol. 2, 149-70

Grebler, L., 1955, 'Possibilities of international financing of housing' in B. Kelly (ed.), *Housing and Economic Development*, Massachusetts Institute of Technology, Boston, 30-1

——, 1963, 'The role of housing and community facilities in economic development', *United Nations Conference on the Application of Science and Technology for the Benefit of Less Developed Areas*, Geneva

——, 1973, 'The role of housing in economic development', mimeograph, Third World Congress of Engineers and Architects, Tel Aviv

Grimes, O.F., 1976, *Housing for Low-Income Urban Families: Economics and Policy of the Developing World*, World Bank Research Publication, Johns Hopkins Press, Baltimore

Grindal, B.T., 1973, 'Islamic affiliations and urban adaptation: the Sisala migrant in Accra, Ghana', *Africa*, Vol. 43, No. 4, 333-46

Gutkind, P.C.W., 1972, 'The socio-political and economic foundations of social problems in African urban areas: an exploratory conceptual overview', *Civilisations*, Vol. 22, No. 1, 18-33

Hambro, E., 1955, *The Problem of Chinese Refugees in Hong Kong*, A.W. Sijthoff, Leyden

Hance, W.A., 1970, *Population, Migration and Urbanization in Africa*, Columbia University Press, New York

Harris, C.D., 1972, *Cities of the Soviet Union*, Association of American Geographers Monograph Series, No. 5, Washington DC

Hart, K., 1973, 'Informal income opportunities and urban employment in Ghana', *Journal of Modern African Studies*, Vol. 2, 61-89

Harvey, D., 1973, *Social Justice and the City*, Edward Arnold, London

Hasan, P., 1978, 'Growth and equity in East Asia', *Finance and Development*, Vol. 15, No. 2, 28-32

Hasnath, S.A., 1977, 'Consequences of squatter removal', *Ekistics*, Vol. 44, No. 263, 198-201

Hassan, R., 1975, 'Social and psychological implications of high density in Hong Kong and Singapore', *Ekistics*, Vol. 39, No. 235, 382-6

——, 1976, 'Public housing' in R. Hassan (ed.), *Singapore: Society in Transition*, Oxford University Press, Kuala Lumpur

——, 1977, *Families in Flats*, Singapore University Press, Singapore

Havens, A.E. and Flinn, W.L. (eds.), 1970, *Internal Colonialism and Structural Change in Colombia*, Praeger, New York

Hayes, J., 1978, 'The impact of the city on the environment: before and after development' in R.D. Hill and J.M. Bray (eds.), *Geography and Environment in Southeast Asia*, Hong Kong University Press, Hong Kong, 69-78

Heppell, M., 1979, 'Introduction: past and present approaches and future trends in aboriginal housing', in M. Heppell (ed.), *A Black Reality: Aboriginal Camps and Housing in Remote Australia*, Australian Institute of Aboriginal Studies, Canberra

Herman, L.H., 1971, 'Urbanization and new housing construction in the Soviet Union', *American Journal of Economics and Sociology*, Vol. 30, 203-19

Hollnsteiner, M.R., 1972, 'Becoming an urbanite: the neighbourhood as a learning environment' in D.J. Dwyer, 29-40

——, 1977, 'Think small: a strategy of access for the urban poor', mimeograph, Institute of Development Studies, Conference on Access to Housing, University of Sussex, Brighton

Honjo, M., 1967, 'Urban Planning Administration in Japan', fugitive manuscript, University of Tokyo, Tokyo

Hopkins, M. and Scolnik, H.J., 1976, 'Basic needs, growth and redistribution', *World Conference on Employment, Income Distribution and Social Progress and the International Division of Labour, Background Papers*, Vol. 1, 'Basic Needs and National Employment Strategies', International Labour Office, Geneva, 9-50

Horvath, R.V., 1969, 'In search of a theory of urbanization: notes on the colonial city', *East Lakes Geographer*, Vol. 5, 69-82

——, 1972, 'A definition of colonialism', *Current Anthropology*, Vol. 13, No. 1, 45-57

Jackson, J.C., 1975, 'The chinatowns of Southeast Asia: traditional components of the city's central area', *Pacific Viewpoint*, Vol. 16, No. 1, 45-77

Jackson, R., 1978, 'Housing trends and policy implications in Papua New Guinea: flaunting the flag of abstracted empiricism' in P.J. Rimmer *et al.*, 171-88

Jellinek, L., 1976, 'The life of a Jakarta street trader, part 1', Working Paper No. 9, Centre for Southeast Asian Studies, Monash University, Melbourne,

——, 1977, 'The life of a Jakarta street trader, part 2', Working Paper No. 10, Centre for Southeast Asian Studies, Monash University, Melbourne

——, 1978, 'Circular migration and the *pondok* dwelling system: a case study of ice-cream traders in Jakarta' in P.J. Rimmer *et al.*, 135-54

Johnstone, M.A., 1977, 'Urban housing development in Peninsular Malaysia: a problem of provision', mimeograph, Department of Human Geography, Research School of Pacific Studies, Australian University, Canberra

——, 1978, 'Unconventional housing in West Malaysian cities: a preliminary inquiry' in P.J. Rimmer *et al.*, 111-34

——, 1979, 'Problems of Access to Urban Housing in Peninsular Malaysia', unpublished doctoral thesis, Department of Human Geography, Research School of Pacific Studies, Australian National University, Canberra

Jongkind, F., 1974, 'A reappraisal of the role of the regional associations of Lima, Peru', *Comparative Studies in Society and History*, Vol. 16, 471-82

Juppenlatz, M., 1970, *Cities in Transformation*, University of Queensland Press, St Lucia, Brisbane

Kapferer, B., 1977, 'Marginality, processes of urban integration and the urban poor', mimeograph, Burg Wartenstein Symposium, No. 73, *Shanty-towns in Developing Nations*, Wenner-Gren Foundation, New York

Kaye, B., 1960, *Upper Nankin Street, Singapore*, University of Malaya Press, Singapore

Keles, R., 1971, *Eski Ankara'da Bir Şehir Tipolojisi*, Ankara Universitesi, Siyasal Bigilar Fakultesi, Yayinlari 314, Ankara

——, n.d., *Urbanization in Turkey*, International Urbanization Survey, Ford Foundation

Kendall, S.H., 1976, 'The *barangay* as community in the Philippines', *Ekistics*, Vol. 41, No. 242, 15-19

Kessler, E., 1977, 'Institutional support for community-based housing', *Ekistics*, Vol. 44, No. 263, 203-7

Keyes, W.J. and Burcoff, M.C.R., 1976, *Housing the Urban Poor: Nonconventional Approaches to a National Problem*, Institute of Philippine Culture, Poverty Research Series, No. 4, Quezon City

Khoo, S.H., Voon, P.K. and Cho, G., 1974, 'The Teluk Bahang fishermen's settlement scheme, Pulau Pinang: a comment on the modular concept of housing', *Royal Australian Planning Institute Journal*, Vol. 12, No. 2, 63-9

King, A.D., 1976, *Colonial Urban Development*, Routledge and Kegan Paul, London

Kingsford, C.L., 1908, *A Survey of London by John Stow: Reprinted from the Text of 1603*, Clarendon Press, Oxford

Koenigsberger, H. and Mosse, G.L., 1968, *Europe in the Sixteenth Century*, Longmans, London

Lakha, S. and Pinches, M., 1977, 'Poverty and the "new society" in Manila', *Australian Outlook*, Vol. 31, No. 3, 371-8

Lamb, G., 1976, 'Hierarchy and access in the Trinidad National Housing Authority', mimeograph, Institute of Development Studies, University of Sussex, Brighton

Laquian, A., 1969, *Slums are for People*, D.M. Press, Manila

Lea, J.P., 1979, 'Self-help and autonomy in housing: new approaches to old problems' in H. Murison and J.P. Lea (eds.) *Housing in Third World Countries: Perspectives on Policy and Practice*, 1-21, Macmillan, London

Lean, W., 1971, 'Housing, rehabilitation, or redevelopment: an economic assessment', *Journal of the Royal Town Planning Institute*, Vol. 57, No. 6, 226-8

Leeming, F., 1977, *Street Studies in Hong Kong: Localities in a Chinese City*, East Asian Social Science Monographs, Oxford University Press, Hong Kong

——, 1958, *The Passing of Traditional Society: Modernizing the Middle East*, Free Press, Glencoe, Illinois

Lerner, D., 1967, 'Comparative analysis of processes of modernization' in H. Miner (ed.), *The City in Modern Africa*, Pall Mall, London, 21-38

Lewis, O., 1966, 'Culture of poverty', *Scientific American*, Vol. 215, No. 4, 19-25

Lim, H.K., 1978, *The Evolution of the Urban System in Malaya*, Penerbit Universiti Malaya, Kuala Lumpur

Lim, W.S.W., 1975, 'Tall buildings for urban centres in Third World countries', *Ekistics*, Vol. 40, No. 238, 196-8

Linsky, A.S., 1969, 'Some generalisations concerning primate cities' in G. Breese (ed.), *The City in Newly Developing Countries*, Prentice-Hall, Englewood Cliffs, 288-94

Lo, H.M., 1972, 'Living Conditions and the Utilization of Space in a Mark II Resettlement Block', unpublished BA dissertation, Geography Department, Hong Kong University

Logan, M.I., 1972, 'The development process in the less developed countries', *The Australian Geographer*, Vol. 12, No. 2, 146-53

Lomnitz, L., 1977, 'Mechanisms of articulation between shanty-town settlers and the urban system', mimeograph, Burg Wartenstein Symposium, No. 73, *Shanty-towns in Developing Nations*, Wenner-Gren Foundation, New York

Mabogunje, A.L., 1968, *Urbanization in Nigeria*, University of London Press, London

MacEwan, A., 1972, 'Stability and change in a shantytown', *Sociology*, Vol. 6, No. 1, 41-56

Ben Mahmoud, W. and Santelli, S., 1974, 'What to do with Medina?', *Ekistics*, Vol. 35, No. 227, 259-63

Makanas, E.D., 1974/5, 'Interindustry analysis of the housing construction industry', *NEDA Journal of Development*, 150-73

Mangin, W., 1963, 'Urbanisation case history in Peru' *Architectural Design*, Vol. 33, 366-74

——, 1967, 'Latin American squatter settlements: a problem and a solution', *Latin American Research Review*, Vol. 2, No. 3, 65-98

Marga Institute, 1976, *Housing in Sri Lanka*, Marga Research Studies No. 6, Marga Publications, Colombo

Mathey, K., 1978, 'The rehabilitation program of Alagados squatter settlement, Brazil', *Ekistics*, Vol. 45, No. 270, 257-61

Matos Mar, J., 1961, 'Migration and urbanization: the *barriados* of Lima' in P. Hauser (ed.), *Urbanization in Latin America*, Columbia University Press, New York, 170-90

Maunder, W.F., 1969, *Hong Kong: Urban Rents and Housing*, Hong Kong University Press, Hong Kong

Mazumdar, D., 1976, 'The urban informal sector', *World Development*, Vol. 4, No. 8, 655-79

McGee, T.G., 1967, *The Southeast Asian City*, Bell and Sons, London

——, 1971, *The Urbanization Process in the Third World*, Bell and Sons, London

——, 1973, *Hawkers in Hong Kong*, Centre of Asian Studies, University of Hong Kong

——, 1976a, 'Hookers and hawkers: making out in the Third World city', *Manpower and Unemployment Research*, April, 3-16

——, 1976b, 'The persistence of the proto-proletariat: occupational structures and planning for the future of Third World Cities', *Progress in Geography*, Vol. 9, 3-38

——, 1976c, 'Rural urban mobility in south and southeast Asia: different formulations . . . different answers', mimeograph, Department of Human Geography, Research School of Pacific Studies, Australian National University, Canberra

——, 1977, 'Conservation and dissolution in the Third World city', mimeograph, Burg Wartenstein Symposium, No. 73, *Shanty-towns in Developing Nations*, Wenner-Gren Foundation, New York

—— and McTaggart, W.D., 1967, *Petaling Jaya: A Socio-Economic Survey of a New Town in Selangor, Malaysia*, Pacific Viewpoint Monograph No. 2, Department of Geography, Victoria University of Wellington

—— and Yeung, Y.M., 1977, *Hawkers in Southeast Asian Cities*, International Development Research Centre, Ottawa

McNamara, R.S., 1977, *Address to the Massachusetts Institute of Technology*, World Bank, Washington DC

Mehmet, O., 1978, *Economic Planning and Social Justice in Developing Countries*, Croom Helm, London

Meillassoux, C., 1972, 'From reproduction to production: a Marxist approach to economic anthropology', *Economy and Society*, Vol. 1, 93-105

Mesa-Lago, C., 1969/70, 'Ideological radicalization and economic activity in Cuba', *Studies in Comparative International Development*, Vol. 5, No. 10, 203-16

—— (ed.), 1971, *Revolutionary Change in Cuba*, University of Pittsburgh Press, Pittsburgh

Missen, G.I. and Logan, M.I., 1977, 'National and local distribution systems and regional development: the case of Kelantan in West Malaysia', *Antipode*, Vol. 9, No. 3, 60-73

Mitchell, R.E., 1971, 'Some sociological implications of high density housing', *American Sociological Review*, Vol. 36, 18-23

——, 1972, *Housing, Urban Growth and Economic Development*, Asian Folklore and Social Life Monograph, Taipei

Modavo, C.E. and Haldane, D., 1974, 'The serviced site approach to urban shelter', *Ekistics*, Vol. 38, No. 227, 287-90

Moorhouse, G., 1972, *Calcutta*, Weidenfeld and Nicolson, London

Morell, S. and Morell, D., 1972, *Six Slums in Bangkok: Problems of Life and Options for Action*, UNICEF, Bangkok

Mukherji, S., 1975, 'The mobility field theory of human spatial behaviour: foundation to the movement dynamics', mimeograph, Department of Human Geography, Research School of Pacific Studies, Australian National University, Canberra

Mumford, L., 1961, *The City in History*, Pelican, Harmondsworth

Muth, R.F., 1969, *Cities and Housing*, University of Chicago Press, Chicago

Nathalang, W. (ed.), 1978, *Housing in Thailand*, International Development Research Centre, Southeast Asian Low-Cost Housing Study, Applied Scientific Research Corporation of Thailand, Bangkok

National Economic and Development Authority (NEDA), 1974/5,

'Housing in the Philippines', *National Economic and Development Authority (NEDA) Journal of Development*, Vols. 1 and 2, Nos. 2-4

Nelson, J.M., 1969, *Migrants, Urban Poverty and Instability in Developing Nations*, Occasional Paper No. 22, Centre for International Affairs, Harvard University, Cambridge

Nevitt, A.A. (ed.), 1967, *The Economic Problems of Housing*, Macmillan, London

Newcombe, K. and Millar, S., 1977, 'Some biological costs of urbanisation' in G.S. Sneddon (ed.), *Urbanization*, Centre for Environmental Studies, Melbourne, 55-67

Noranitipadungkarn, C., 1975, 'Social policy analysis: two public housing projects, Bangkok, Thailand', *Ekistics*, Vol. 40, No. 235, 387-9

Norwood, H.C., 1972, 'Ndirande: a squatter colony in Malawi', *Town Planning Review*, Vol. 43, No. 2, 135-50

Oberschall, A.R., 1969, 'Rising expectations and political turmoil', *Journal of Developmental Studies*, Vol. 6, 5-22

Obregon, A.Q., 1974, 'The marginal pole of the economy and marginalised labour force', *Economy and Society*, Vol. 3, 393-428

Ocampo, L.V., 1974/5, 'Sambahayan: the Philippine Business for Social Progress (PBSP) Mandaluyong social condominium project', *NEDA Journal of Development*, 241-8

Onibokun, G.A., 1973, 'A system for evaluating the relative habitability of housing', *Ekistics*, Vol. 36, No. 216, 313-17

Oram, N.D., 1976, *Colonial Town to Melanesian City: Port Moresby 1884-1974*, Australian National University Press, Canberra

Osborne, J., 1974, *Area, Development and the Middle City in Malaysia*, Department of Georgraphy, University of Chicago Monograph No. 153, Chicago

Oxall, I., Barnett, T. and Booth, D. (eds.), 1975, *Beyond the Sociology of Development: Economy and Society in Latin America and Africa*, Routledge and Kegan Paul, London

Papagiourgiou, G., 1968, 'Athens in its historical setting', *Ekistics*, Vol. 26, No. 152, 101-15

Papanek, G.F., 1975, 'The poor of Jakarta', *Economic Development and Cultural Change*, Vol. 24, No. 1, 1-27

Papua New Guinea Housing Commission, 1975, *National Housing Plan* (Part One), Ministry of the Interior, Port Moresby

Peet, R., 1977, 'The development of radical geography in the United States', *Progress in Human Geography*, Vol. 10, No. 2, 240-63

Perlman, J.E., 1974, *Government Policy towards Brazilian Favela Dwellers*, Working Paper No. 243, Institute of Urban and Regional Development, University of California, Berkeley

Phillips, D.G., 1958/9, 'Rural to urban migration in Iraq', *Economic Development and Cultural Change*, Vol. 7, 405-21

Pinches, M., 1977, 'Squatters, planning and politics in Tondo, Manila', Asian Bureau Australia, *Newsletter* No. 32

Planhol, X. de, 1973, 'Ankara: aspects de la croissance d'une metropole', *Revue Geographie de L'Est*, Vol. 1-2, 155-88

Poethig, R., 1972, 'Life style of the urban poor and people's organizations', *Ekistics*, Vol. 34, No. 201, 104-7

Portes, A., 1971, 'The urban slum in Chile – types and correlates', *Land Economics*, Vol. 47, No. 4, 235-48

Power, J., 1972, *The New Proletarians*, Community and Race Relations Unit of the British Council of Churches, London

——, 1973, 'The Third World in Paris', *New Internationalist*, No. 5, 24

——, 1976, *Western Europe's Migrant Workers*, The Minority Rights Group, Report No. 28, London

Pryor, E.G., 1971, 'An Assessment of the Need and Scope for Urban Renewal in Hong Kong', unpublished doctoral thesis, Department of Geography, Hong Kong University

——, 1975, 'Environmental quality and housing policy in Hong Kong', *Pacific Viewpoint*, Vol. 16, No. 2, 195-206

Pryor, R.J. (ed.), 1979, *Migration and Development in Southeast Asia*, Oxford University Press, Kuala Lumpur

Rahim, A., 1976, 'An overview of housing in Malaysia', Technical Paper No. 3, *Proceedings of the Conference on Human Settlements for the Rakyat in the Lower Income Groups*, EAROPH, Kuala Lumpur

Rapoport, A., 1973, 'The ecology of housing', *Ecologist*, Vol. 3, No. 1, 10-17

Ray, T., 1969, *The Politics of the Barrios of Venezuela*, University of California Press, Berkeley

Reissman, L., 1964, *The Urban Process: Cities in Industrial Society*, Free Press, Glencoe, Illinois

Rew, A.W., 1977a, 'Access and implementation in low-income housing in Metro Manila', mimeograph, International Conference on Low Income Housing – Technology and Policy, Bangkok

——, 1977b, 'Accumulating applicants: the state and shanty-town property', mimeograph, Burg Wartenstein Symposium, No. 73, *Shanty-towns in Developing Nations*, Wenner-Gren Foundation, New York

Rho, Y.H., 1976, 'Green belt and urban land use control in the case of Korea' in J. Wong, 81-105

Rimmer, P.J. and Cho, G., 1978, 'Urbanization of the Malays since independence: evidence from West Malaysia, 1957-1970', mimeograph, Asian Studies Association of Australia, University of New South Wales, Sydney

Rimmer, P.J., Drakakis-Smith, D.W. and McGee, T.G. (eds.), 1978, *Food, Shelter and Transport in Southeast Asia and the Pacific*, Publication HG/12, Research School of Pacific Studies, Australian National University, Canberra

Ross, M.H., 1973, 'Community formation in an urban squatter settlement', *Comparative Political Studies*, Vol. 6, 296

Rosser, C., 1972, 'Housing and planned urban change: the Calcutta experience' in D.J. Dwyer, 29-40

Rostow, W.W., 1966, *Stages of Economic Growth: A Non-Communist Manifesto*, Cambridge University Press, Cambridge

Rothenberg, J., 1967, *Economic Evaluation of Urban Renewal*, Brookings Institute, Washington DC

Rudé, G.F., 1971, *Paris and London in the Eighteenth Century: Studies in Popular Protest*, Viking Press, New York

Russell, J.C., 1972, *Medieval Regions and Their Cities*, David and Charles, Newton Abbot

Saini, B.S., 1973, 'Slum improvement and squatter rehabilitation: the Calcutta and Bombay experience', *Design* (incorporating *Indian Builder*), Vol. 17, No. 9, 27-31

Sakornpan, C., 1971, *Klong Toey: A Social Work Survey of a Squatter Slum*, Thammasat University, Bangkok

Samuelson, M., 1974, 'Immigration and absorption', *Built Environment*, Vol. 3, No. 12, 621-2

Santiago, A.M., 1976, 'Urban land policy in land reform areas in the Philippines' in J. Wong, 137-51

Santos, M., 1972, 'Economic development and urbanization in underdeveloped countries: the two flow systems of the urban economy and their spatial implications', mimeograph, Department of Geography, University of Toronto

——, 1972/3, 'Underdevelopment and poverty, a geographer's view', *Latin American in Residence Lecture*, No. 3, University of Toronto

——, 1977a, 'Studies on the diffusion of innovations; a critical restatement', mimeograph, Columbia University, New York

——, 1977b, 'Spatial dialectics: two circuits of urban economy in underdeveloped countries', *Antipode*, Vol. 9, No. 3, 49-59

Seltz, M., 1970, 'Saigon 1969: urbanization and response', *Journal of the American Institute of Planners*, Vol. 9, No. 9, 310-13

Sewell, G.H., 1964, 'Squatter Settlements in Turkey: Analysis of a Political and Economic Problem', unpublished doctoral thesis, Massachusetts Institute of Technology, Boston

Simic, A., 1973, *The Peasant Urbanites, a Study of Rural-urban Mobility in Serbia*, Seminar Press, New York

Sjoberg, G., 1960, *The Pre-Industrial City: Past and Present*, Free Press, Glencoe, Illinois

Slater, D., 1976, 'Anglo-Saxon geography and the study of under-development', *Antipode*, Vol. 8, No. 3, 88-93

——, 1977, 'Geography and underdevelopment Part II', *Antipode*, Vol. 9, No. 3, 1-31

Smith, C.T., 1967, *An Historical Geography of Western Europe before 1800*, Longmans, London

Soedjatmoko, 1971, 'Traditional values and the development process', *Development Digest*, Vol. 9, No. 1, 45-54

Soen, D., Honig, M. and Tamir, M., 1976, 'Social distress in settlements in Israel', *Ekistics*, Vol. 41, No. 242, 50-4

Solow, A.A., 1967, 'Housing in Latin America: the problems of urban low income families', *Town Planning Review*, Vol. 38, No. 2, 83-102

Souza, A.R. de and Porter, P.W., 1974, *The Underdevelopment and Modernization of the Third World*, Association of American Geographers, Resource Paper No. 28, Washington DC

Srikantan, K.S., 1973, 'Regional and rural-urban socio-demographic differences in Turkey', *Middle East Journal*, Vol. 3, 275-300

Sternstein, L., 1976, 'Migration and development in Thailand', *Geographical Review*, Vol. 66, No. 4, 401-18

Stokes, C.J., 1962, 'A theory of slums', *Land Economics*, Vol. 38, No. 3, 187-97

Stone, C., 1972, 'Social class and partisan attitudes in urban Jamaica', *Social and Economic Studies*, Vol. 21, No. 4, 1-29

Strassman, W.P., 1970, 'Construction, productivity and employment in developing countries', *International Labour Review*, Vol. 101, No. 5, 503-18

——, 1976, 'Measuring the employment effects of housing policies in developing countries', *Economic Development and Cultural Change*, Vol. 24, No. 3, 623-32

Stretton, A., 1976, 'The building industry and urban employment generation in the Philippines', mimeograph, Department of Economics, Research School of Pacific Studies, Australian National

University, Canberra

——, 1978, 'Independent foremen and the construction of formal sector housing in the Greater Manila Area' in P.J. Rimmer *et al.*, 155-70

——, 1979, *Urban Housing Policy in Papua New Guinea*, Monograph no. 8, Institute for Applied Economic and Social Research, Port Moresby

Suparlan, P., 1974, 'The *gelandangan* of Jakarta: politics among the poorest people in the capital of Indonesia', *Indonesia*, Vol. 18, 41-52

Suzuki, P., 1964, 'Encounters with Istanbul: urban peasants and village peasants', *International Journal of Comparative Sociology*, Vol. 5, 208-16

——, 1966, 'Peasants without plows: some Anatolians in Istanbul', *Rural Sociology*, Vol. 31, 41-52

Tan, S.H. and Tan, S.H.S. (eds.), 1975, *Aspects of Housing in Malaysia*, Southeast Asia Low Cost Housing Monograph 1, International Development Research Centre, Ottawa

Thai University Research Associates, 1976, *Urbanization in the Bangkok Central Region*, Social Science Association of Thailand, Kurusapha Press, Bangkok

Todaro, M.P., 1971, *Development Planning: Models and Methods*, Oxford University Press, Nairobi

Towers, G., 1973, 'City planning in China', *Journal of the Royal Town Planning Institute*, Vol. 59, No. 3, 120-7

Trevelyan, G.M., 1966, *Illustrated English Social History*, Vol. 1, Pelican, Harmondsworth

Turner, J.C., 1967, 'Barriers and channels for housing development in modernizing countries', *Journal of the American Institute of Planners*, Vol. 33, 167-81

——, 1968, 'Housing priorities, settlement patterns and urban development in modernizing countries', *Journal of the American Institute of Planners*, Vol. 34, 354-63

——, 1969a, 'Architecture that works', *Ekistics*, Vol. 27, No. 158, 40-4

——, 1969b, 'Uncontrolled urban settlement: problems and policies' in G. Breese (ed.), *The City in Newly Developing Countries*, Prentice-Hall, Englewood Cliffs, 507-34

——, 1972, 'Housing issues and the standards problem', *Ekistics*, Vol. 33, No. 196, 152-8

Ugnayan ng mga Samahan ng mga Mamamayan ng Tondo Foreshore, 1976, *Whatever Happened to the Human in Philippine Human*

Settlements?, Navotas, Malaban, Manila

Umeh, J., 1972, 'Economics and politics of African slums and shanty-towns', *Journal of the Royal Town Planning Institute*, Vol. 58, No. 3, 215-18

Umezawa, T. and Honjo, M., 1968, *'Company Housing in Japan'*, fugitive manuscript

United Nations, 1974, *World Housing Survey 1973*, Geneva
——, 1976, *World Housing Survey 1974*, New York

Vaughan, D.R. and Feindt, W., 1973, 'Initial settlement and intracity movement of migrants in Monterrey, Mexico', *Journal of the American Institute of Planners*, Vol. 39, No. 6, 388-401

Vera, J.S. de, 1974/5, 'Housing needs up to the year 2000 and its financing implications', *NEDA Journal of Development*, 41-65

Wallerstein, I. (ed.), 1966, *Social Change: The Colonial Situation*, John Wiley, New York

Walter, M.A., 1978, 'The territorial and the social: perspectives on the lack of community in high-rise/high-density living in Singapore', *Ekistics*, Vol. 45, No. 270, 236-42

Ward, D., 1971, *Cities and Immigrants*, Oxford University Press, London
——, 1976, 'The Victorian slum: an enduring myth?', *Annals of the Association of American Geographers*, Vol. 66, 323-36

Ward, P., 1976, 'The squatter settelement as slum or housing solution: evidence from Mexico City', *Land Economics*, Vol. 52, No. 3, 330-46

Waterbury, J., 1973, 'Cairo: Third World metropolis', *American University Field Staff Reports*, Vol. 18, No. 5

Weiner, M., 1967, 'Urbanization and political protest', *Civilisations*, Vol. 17, 44-52

Wheaton, W.L.C. and Wheaton, M.F., 1972, 'Urban housing and economic development' in D.J. Dwyer, 141-51

Whiteford, M.B., 1976, 'A comparison of migrant satisfaction in two low-income housing settlements of Popayan, Colombia', *Urban Anthropology*, Vol. 5, No. 3, 271-83

Williams, B.V. and Mok, Y.K., 1978, 'Redevelopment of public housing estates' in S.K. Wong (ed.), *Housing in Hong Kong*, Heinemann, Hong Kong, 309-24

Wong, A.W.F., 1976, 'Hong Kong: the implementation of the resettlement program' in G.V. Iglesias (ed.), *Implementation: the Problem of Achieving Results*, Eastern Regional Organization for Public Administration, Manila, 268-308

Wong, J. (ed.), 1976, *The Cities of Asia: A Study of Urban Solutions and Urban Finance*, Singapore University Press, Singapore

Wong, K.Y., 1972, 'The effects of renewal on relocated families', postgraduate research seminar paper, Geography Department, Hong Kong University

World Bank, 1972a, *Urbanization*, Sector Working Paper, Washington DC

——, 1972b, *Population*, Sector Working Paper, Washington DC

——, 1975, *Housing*, Sector Policy Paper, Washington DC

——, 1979, *World Development Indicators*, Washington DC

Worsley, P., 1964, *The Third World*, Weidenfeld and Nicolson, London

——, 1972, 'Frantz Fanon and the lumpen proletariat' in R. Miliband and J. Saville (eds.), *The Socialist Register*, London, 193-230

Wu, C.T., 1979, 'Economics or politics: the new regional planning', *Proceedings of the Eighth Waigani Seminar*, University of Papua New Guinea, Port Moresby

Yeh, S.H.K. (ed.), 1975, *Public Housing in Singapore*, Singapore University Press, Singapore

——, and Laquian, A.A., 1979, *Housing Asia's Millions: Problems, Policies and Prospects for Low-Cost Housing in Southeast Asia*, International Development and Research Centre, Ottawa

—— and Lee, Y.S., 1968, 'Household size and housing conditions in Singapore', *Malayan Economic Review*, Vol. 13, No. 1, 11-29

Yeung, Y.M., 1976, 'Location of housing in urban development plans in Southeast Asia', mimeograph, Low-Cost Housing Workshop, Habitat Forum, Vancouver

——, 1976, 'High-rise, high-density housing. myths and reality', mimeograph, Workshop on the Role of Tall Buildings in Human Settlement, Habitat Forum, Vancouver

—— and Yeh, S.H.K., 1975, 'A review of neighbourhoods and neighbouring practices' in S.H.K. Yeh, 302-34

Ylanan, M., 1974/5, 'The PBSP: private participation in housing', *NEDA Journal of Development*, 430-7

Zelinsky, W.S., 1971, 'The hypothesis of the mobility transition', *Geographical Review*, Vol. 61, 219-49

Zielinski, Z.A., 1969, *Low-Cost Housing: Designs for North Bengal*, Siliguri Planning Organization, Siliguri

INDEX

For Product Safety Concerns and Information please contact our EU
representative GPSR@taylorandfrancis.com Taylor & Francis Verlag GmbH,
Kaufingerstraße 24, 80331 München, Germany

Printed and bound by CPI Group (UK) Ltd, Croydon, CR0 4YY

08/05/2025

01864363-0001